The Book of
BUCKLAND MONACHORUM & YELVERTON

A Portrait of the Parish

PAULINE HAMILTON-LEGGETT

HALSGROVE

First published in Great Britain in 2002

To my darling husband Peter, for his patience, hours of research and archives, without whom this book could not have been written.

Frontispiece photograph: *Pony rides at a fête held at the Abbey in 1963.*

British Library Cataloguing-in-Publication Data
A CIP record for this title is available from the British Library

ISBN 1 84114 151 8

HALSGROVE

Halsgrove House
Lower Moor Way
Tiverton, Devon EX16 6SS
Tel: 01884 243242
Fax: 01884 243325
email: sales@halsgrove.com
website: www.halsgrove.com

Printed and bound by
Bookcraft Ltd, Midsomer Norton

Whilst every care has been taken to ensure the accuracy of the information contained in this book, the author disclaims responsibility for any mistakes which may have inadvertently been included.

FOREWORD

That the past fashions the future is a true saying. This excellent book portrays it well. Buckland Monachorum is a very old parish and Yelverton a rather new one. In coupling the two together the author has produced an interesting history of both and of the outlying villages.

Continuity and the linking of many families are illustrated in the schools chapter. This demonstrates that it is the working and living together of communities to provide each other with mutual support that ensures the survival of the chosen way of life.

Ever changing circumstances are described in accounts dealing with local industries, the copper mines, the coming and going of the railway, the war and the aerodrome. The author also describes the chequer board of farming, building and the development of gardens which have provided employment and influenced living conditions throughout the changing years, in good times and in bad.

Pauline has portrayed all of this from the perspective of a historian as well as of a long term inhabitant. In doing so she has produced a book that is not only very informative but which also gives a fascinating insight into a way of life. It is illustrated by excellent photographs.

Lady Kitson DL

Volunteers, including Carole Fry, work in the Elizabethan Garden, 2002.

River Tavy at Denham Bridge.

Above: *Bertha Bridge over the Tavy, 1936.*

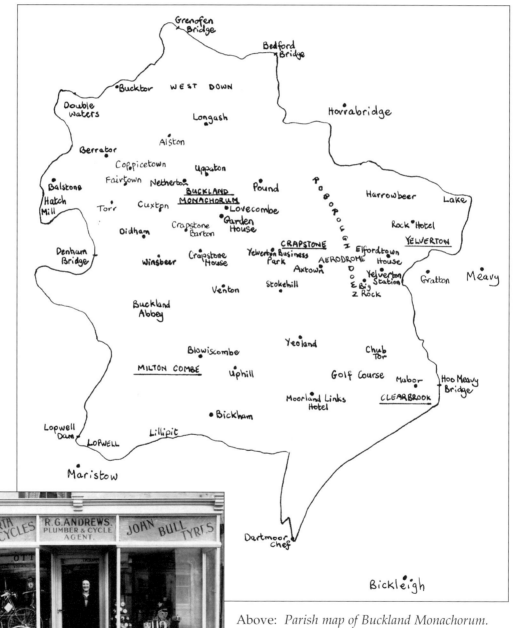

Above: *Parish map of Buckland Monachorum.*

Left: *George Andrews's shop at Leg o' Mutton.*

CONTENTS

ACKNOWLEDGEMENTS

Marilyn Allen, John Alway, Les Andrews, Peter Argles, Robin Armstrong, Mary Baker, Dorothy Ball, Elizabeth and William Ball, Sybil Ball, Hilary Banks, Nicky Bannon, Michelle Barley, Doreen Barons, Peter and Anne Barons, Victor Barton, Richard Bayly, Eric Bellan, Ian Bellan, Barbara Beyer, Tamsyn Blaikie, Margaret Blowey, John Brindle, Thomas Bromidge, Pauline Brown, Peter Brown, Philip Brown, Mark and Jenny Bruton, Frances Buckingham, David and Helen Butland, Mary Callen, Sue Callow, Sally Challiss, Joan Charleston, Christine and Graham Cotter, Michael Coxson, Rene Creber, Ivy Cross, Mary and Geoff Davey, Alice Daw, John Dawe, Muriel and Derek Diggins, Brenda Dilnot, Linda Downing, Kerry Elson, John Emerson, Tim Emerson, Norman and Pam Fendall, Sara Ferry, Pat Finnigan, Sue Frappell, Anne Garcia, Margaret Garton, Philip Gasche, John Gelsthorpe, David German, Gill Graham, Minnie Grainger, Michael Green, Sarah Greenway, Peter Hamilton-Leggett, Phyllis Harris, Patricia Harwood, Marian Hicks, Ann and Richard Hillson, Mary Horn, Charles Horn, Bill Houldsworth, Stephen Hughes, Cathie Hunt, Paula Hunter, Tom Huxham, Annie Inman, Ronald Isherwood, Doreen Johnston, Hannah Jones, Sister Julian, Rita Kennedy, Jill Keys, Elizabeth and Frank Kitson, Joy Lakeman, George Langton, Muriel Lashbrook, Lilian Lethbridge, Pat Lillyman, Richard Mabey, Mary Maddison, Christine Maddock, Frank Mares, Basil Margrett, Jan Marks, Andrew 'Jock' Maxwell, Tim Miall, Betty Middleton, David and Jenny Miles, Celia Mills, John Morley, Joyce Neno, Kathleen Northam, Mary and John Northey, Pauline Northmore, Richard and Sue Northmore, Mary Osborn, Mavis Palmer, Nelson Palmer, Richard Palmer, Brenda Partridge, Joy Pike, Charles and Joy Piper, Daphne Piper, Peter and Mary Price, Ron Price, John Rawlings, Paul Rendle, David Richards, Robert Ricketts, Margaret Rogers, Derek Roper, Alan Rowe, Winnie Rowe, Elaine Simkins, Margaret Simms, June Smalley, Hazel Smith, Rachel Smith, Denie Snushall, Millicent Spencer, Betty Spry, Evelyn Stacey, Gordon Stansbury, Michael Stephens, Peter and Joyce Stephens, Celia Steven, Richard Tebbs, Penny Tendrill, Jean Thomas, Winnie Thomas, Stephen Thrall, Susan Totty, Stephen Trahair, Anne Tucker, Carol Tucker, Diana Wallace, Gerald Wasley, Kay Welch, Charles Westlake, Jo and Hugo White, Richard White, Keith Wiley, Amanda Willats, Peter Wing, Susan Woolacott.

The staff at Plymouth City Library, West Devon Local Studies Library, Plymouth and West Devon Record Office, Tavistock Library, The Sydney Taylor Collection.

'Walking is a sheer delight for the roads and pathways are springy and easy, the panorama ever changing and the atmosphere bracing and health giving. A fact which brings in its train a wholesome appetite, sound sleep and rest to face tomorrow with a smile.'
Come to Devon Guide (c.1925)

Right: *Peter Hamilton-Leggett with Sam at Hatch Mill, 2002.*

INTRODUCTION

The parish of Buckland Monachorum, in the south-west corner of Devon, boasts of no large town, manufacturing commodity or population growth at the beginning of the twenty-first century. In the twentieth century the parish boundary to the north was altered, giving some of the land to the parish of Horrabridge, which had formerly been the postal town of the parish. Parish lands extend from the River Tavy in the west to Meavy Parish in the east and from Horrabridge to Bickleigh Parish in the south. In past times it was a rural parish with fields and moorland farmed by landowners and tenants living in the many mansions and farmsteads within the boundary. The old village of Buckland Monachorum was the hub of the parish until the nineteenth century when large houses and cottages were built in the growing hamlets of Clearbrook, Crapstone and Yelverton on parish land.

The villagers, employed on the land, worshipped in the church of St Andrew and their children attended the separate boys' and girls' schools in the village centre. Children living in the distant parts of the parish boarded at the school, others walking or riding their ponies many miles each day. There was never a shortage of water despite it having to be carried, as many streams, or brooks, pass through little valleys between the many hills to the River Tavy. This river, reputed to be the fastest flowing water in England, flows from Tavy head on remote north Dartmoor, to the River Tamar beyond the western parish boundary.

In these valleys ore was mined, providing varying employment, and flour-mills were built on the banks of the river. Management of machinery, the grooming of horses, the welfare of stock and the year-round crop production gave employment to parishioners. Trees were planted for timber and fuel, and miles of hedgerows were maintained. The parish was self-reliant and the weekly round of six long working days and attending the village church on Sunday was taken for granted. Colourful characters live on in people's memories in this country parish where the life of a century ago is in contrast with living in the country today. Settlements in the parish are dormitories for Plymouth, unlike the close-knit communities of past years.

How changed parish life is in this year of 2002 compared with the unchanging centuries that have gone before us. Much employment for men and women is found outside this rural parish and older children are educated in towns and cities miles away. The small farms have amalgamated, hedgerows have been removed and only a few farmers remain to nurture the land for future generations. The last years of the twentieth century saw the ownership of a car for almost every parishioner and visitors from all over the world travelling to enjoy the beauty of the parish. What still remains are the network of narrow lanes and large magnificent houses.

We who have contributed to this book will not see how changed parish life will be in another 100 years' time. We who live within the parish have a duty to preserve what is good, plant trees for the future and hold on to that which is beautiful as those who have gone before us left for our inheritance. This book is a record of research, of my memories, and impressions of those listed in the acknowledgements with pictures that are worth thousands of words. Small snapshots from family albums are recorded before they are lost forever as well as treasured photographs never published before. Each chapter of this book is worthy of a book itself and I know much has been omitted. I plead therefore, in the words of Lord Byron, 'And what is writ is writ, Would it were worthier!'

Pauline Hamilton-Leggett
Summer 2002

Buckland Abbey, founded in the thirteenth century, attracts many tourists to the parish.

Below: *Double Waters, where the River Walkham meets the River Tavy north-west of the parish.*

Inset: *First Ordnance Map of 1809.*

Chapter 1

THE PARISH OF BUCKLAND MONACHORUM

The English parish evolved from a private institution in Saxon times endowed by the lord of the manor. In Norman times the manorial lord gave way to the Church under the guidance of the diocesan bishop. An Act was passed by Parliament in 1402 for a secular person 'to do divine service, to instruct the people and to keep hospitality there'. In seven centuries the English parish had become established and 600 years later it has evolved from this foundation. The first meeting of the Parish Council was held in the boys' schoolroom in the village on Monday 31 December 1894. The Parish Councillors were John Hamlyn, Charles Horn, Henry Dawe, F. Lewis, Robert Took, W. Crossman, C.H. Radford, W.H. Penny, R.C. Merson, W. Doidge, Henry Peter and James Dockett. Six weeks later it was resolved that the headmaster, Mr Baker, should provide fuel and lamp oil at 9d. for each meeting and that Sophie Hawkins be paid 1s. each meeting for lighting the fire, the lamps and sweeping the floor. The Parish Council meetings were often held on a Saturday.

Buckland Monachorum is an historical parish and a village in the south-west of Devonshire in the borderland of Dartmoor. Exposed undulating moorland, wooded valleys and fertile fields make up this romantic rural parish with distant views of Dartmoor tors to the north and east and Cornish hills to the west. The discovery of stone tools dating from the Stone Age is slight evidence that early man lived here. Inhabitants on Dartmoor may have travelled from the hills through the wooded country setting up home in the security of the River Tavy and moving on to the sea. In 1999 Dr Tom Greeves and Mr Alan Rowe studied Buckland Down and the north-west moorland of Roborough Down and discovered four deserted medieval settlements – see Greeves (*TDA* 131) and Rowe (1999) for detailed evidence and documentation.

They examined longhouses and buildings on the Down north of Pound House and westwards to north of Alston Farm. It is interesting that children walking from Buckland village for picnics at Double Waters run over ridges and furrows which had been the homes of former settlers centuries ago. It is suggested that these people grew corn on the hillside and lived here in the thirteenth century in the comparative shelter of the slopes on the left bank of the River

Walkham. Wildlife on the moor would have been plentiful supplying animals, plants and berries for food, and the rivers Tavy and Walkham have always been noted for fishing.

In Devon there are eight parishes of this name – Buckland Brewer, Buckland Filleigh, Buckland-in-the-Moor, Buckland Monachorum, Buckland Tout Saints, East Buckland, Egg Buckland and West Buckland. In the Domesday Survey of 1086 (ed. C. & F. Thorn) it is recorded that:

William holds Buckland [Monachorum] himself, Brictmer held it before 1066. It paid tax for 3 hides and 1½ virgates of land. Land for 15 ploughs. In lordship 3 ploughs, 12 slaves; 1½ hides. 24 villagers and 10 smallholders with 7 ploughs and 2 hides, less ½ virgate. A salt-house; a fishery which pays 10s.; meadow 8 acres; pasture 1 league long and as wide; woodland 4 leagues long and 2 furlongs wide. 20 cattle; 40 pigs; 130 sheep; Formerly 50s.; value now 100s.

(4 virgates = 1 hide = app. 120 acres; 1 league = app. 3 miles.) Baldwin de Redvers was created Earl of Devon at the age of 51. He gave the tithes of his fishery to Tavistock Abbey before 1130, although no amounts are recorded. Parishioners who were taxed in 1332 are listed, the average amount for each man being 8d. each year: John Rykeman, Walter Wal, Robert Baig, John Noble, Gilbert Aysa, John Roger, John Alewey, William Penne, John Renal, Gilbert Inthelegh, Henry de Bykelegh, John White, Roger Frensha, Walter Aunger, Philip Browning, Geoffrey Odimere, Richard Inthelegh, William Pleymede, Thomas de Bykelegh, Walter Cresa, John Aunger, Gilbert Aunger, Nicholas le Webbe and Richard le Coppere.

Our Buckland on early parish maps is spelt BOCHELAND and probably derived from 'bookland', a land held under a charter. The title Monachorum (of the monks) was added when Cistercian monks founded Buckland Abbey in the thirteenth century. Listed in the Devon Lay Subsidy of 1524 under MONKYN BOCKELOND parish, were family names found nearly 500 years later albeit with various spellings: Palmer, Taylor, Edgecombe, Stephens, Crossman, Rowe, Clarke, Walter, King, Schobell, Hancock, Hooper, Reep, Gloyne and Foot to name but a few. It was also recorded as MONKEN-BUCKLAND at this time. In the seventeenth century the abbey lands were known as Buckland Drake and the other parish lands as Buckland Crymes, named after two influential landowners. Arthur Mee wrote,

'We are in the world of Francis Drake. This is where he used to walk. These are the trees he loved. This is his old home.'

Buckland Monachorum Parish Registers are almost complete from the sixteenth century and these church records are informative on both secular and church matters. Diseases reported from this time affected the parish. The sixteenth century was a bad time for influenza, many people losing their lives in the early 1550s. In the next century bubonic plague was a scourge and there was a high number of burials in 1644. Smallpox caused a crisis in the mid-eighteenth century and the

The Drake family home for 400 years.

burial registers show a high mortality in children at this time. A Plymouth doctor, John Huxham, kept a diary of illnesses from 1728–52. Ronald Isherwood carefully recorded these illnesses in the parish for the Cambridge Group for the History and Population and Social Structure in 1978 from the Buckland Monachorum Parish Records for a statistical analysis.

Marriages in the parish mostly occurred after Easter and before Christmas in any year. As the parishioners were employed on the land harvest time was avoided, as were the solemn festivals of the Church, Lent and Advent. The churchwardens' accounts and Parish Registers contain more information than baptisms, marriages and burials. Valuable details of wildlife may be gleaned from the accounts, as up to 1830 amounts are listed for the payments of vermin caught in the parish. Until recent times country folk spoke of little varmints, meaning pests. In the eighteenth century any person who presented to the churchwardens any wildlife creature causing damage to crops or to livestock, received payments from church funds – fox 5s., stoat, weasel, buzzard and jay 4d., badger, marten and otter 1s., and hedgehog 2d. Hedgehogs were thought to suck milk from cows as they lay down on the grass.

The manor and vicarage of Buckland Monachorum was given to Richard Crymes, haberdasher of London, and his wife, Elizabeth, on 21 April 1546. The manor included property at Netherton, Cuxton, Milton Combe, Harrowbeer and South Wood. 300 acres of Buckland Abbey land had been surrendered to the King's commissioners in

1537 and sold to Richard Grenville four years later. After 40 years he sold it to Francis Drake. Another London merchant who bought abbey lands was John Slanning. Crymes and Slanning became involved in court proceedings over the boundaries of their land on Roborough Down; Slanning owning Bickleigh and Crymes owning Buckland. Their sons, Nicholas Slanning and Ellis Crymes, continued this feud after their fathers' deaths and in 1579 they threatened each other, accompanied by their tenants, 'armed with swords, staves and daggers' on the Down. Court proceedings lasted four years until the death of Nicholas Slanning. Ellis built and lived in Crapstone Barton in the late 1560s. William Crymes, son of Ellis, became involved in a dispute with Thomas Drake when he took water from the Plymouth Leat to work his tin mines. Again there were riots on Roborough Down. Elize Crymes, grandson, married Mary Drake in 1636 who bore him 15 children before she died in childbirth. He married a second time and had 11 more children and married again after her death. Not surprisingly he had to sell off most of the estate to support his large family although many of the children did not survive. In 1708 Amos Crymes became the vicar of Buckland for one year inheriting what was left of the estate. Another Amos Crymes appointed himself the vicar from 1752–83 and had 15 children before his wife died in childbirth. Such was the plight of many mothers. His son, Amos, became the Vicar of Walkhampton and another Amos Crymes (grandson) became a clergyman. He sold his right of recommending a man of the clergy to the vacant position of the parish to Sir T.T.F.E. Drake of the abbey in 1827 and so ended the Crymes association with Buckland Monachorum.

Rivers flowing from Dartmoor, the Walkham and Tavy on the north and west, and the River Meavy on the east, border this delightful rural parish. There is a 25-inch parish map hanging on the wall in Buckland Abbey that may be seen by parishioners. This was donated by Charles Radford in 1895, in the year following the beginning of the Parish Council, and repaired and hung in St Andrew's school in 1993. More damage was found as it was rolled up so this large map, 10-feet square, was hung in Buckland Abbey in 1996. Before the majority of people understood maps, a perambulation was undertaken in every parish when parishioners walked around the boundary. Boys would often be beaten at corners or ducked in rivers during these 'beating of the bounds' to enable them to remember the boundary in adult life. In 1717 the churchwardens recorded that it cost 9s. to view the bounds of the parish. Perhaps the adults were given drinks in the hostelries as they passed. The boundary stones were set up on Roborough Down in 1769, according to the church accounts, and cost 10s. This annual event was not only good for people to get to know their parish but a welcome get together as families met with their neighbours they rarely contacted, as they walked through the beautiful countryside.

John Leland, the famous antiquary of the sixteenth century, visited Buckland on his journeys through England and Wales and wrote:

Then is the uppermost wher Tave Water cummith onto Tamar. And on the est side of this creek is Bukland. Bukland is two miles from the creke mouthe.

As in many Devon parishes there were once many orchards providing apples for the making of cider. Traditionally the orchard at Buckland Abbey was one of the very first planted in Devonshire. The roads were mostly rough tracks, intended for packhorses but were widened for horse-drawn vehicles in the twentieth century. According to a diocesan document of the fourteenth century:

There are few chariots nor such horses in this part of the county, for all the transporting we do here we do on packhorses or in bullock carts because of the mountains and valleys and bad ways which are here.

Travelling through the parish would have been slow and difficult.

In an inventory of 6 February 1648 a yeoman of Buckland Monachorum, Christopher Edgcomb, left the following items in his will to Robert Foote, Richard Balhatchet and William Foote:

His wearing apparel £7; books £1.10s.; plate and silver spoons £7.3s.; a bedstead and bed £5.2s.; tooe chestes tooe boxes and one cheare 13s.; in chattle £24; in money billes and desperate debtes £629 and other things not mentioned or specyfied £2.
Total £676.

In the Militia Returns of 1715 Buckland Monachorum Parish is listed for giving money to the Militia for the upkeep of the Army. John Drake and John Crymes were responsible for collecting money to provide horses and foot soldiers.

The civil parish now includes the villages of Buckland Monachorum, Milton Combe, Yelverton, Crapstone and Clearbrook. Until 1949 Horrabridge was part of the parish but it became a separate parish, taking in parts of Walkhampton, Sampford Spiney and Whitchurch as well as Buckland Monachorum to form a new parish. The settlements of Yelverton,

Crapstone and Clearbrook as we know them today did not exist before the second half of the nineteenth century. Yelverton became a separate ecclesiastical parish in 1935 and Clearbrook was incorporated into Meavy Church Parish in 1985. Two stones with inscriptions, now in the vicarage garden in Tavistock, give the earliest information. The lord of the manor, Sir Ralph Lopes, gave permission for the vicar of Tavistock to remove these stones from the village, one found south of the church gate when the smithy was pulled down, the other used as a gatepost in the parish, in the nineteenth century. These Dark-Ages memorial stones were taken to the garden of Tavistock Vicarage on a cart drawn by a team of horses. The first reads *'Sabini Fili Maccodecheti'* and the second, written vertically, *'Dap.fili Nicin..sci'*. It could be that Irish missionaries converted the people in the south-west before St Augustine preached the Christian gospel in the south-east. Polwhele saw the first of these stones in 1797 and recorded, 'And there is an upright stone, by a smith's shop, near the churchyard of Buckland Monachorum.' Revd Edward A. Bray first saw this stone at the entrance to the churchyard in 1804. In 1831 he wrote:

... the blacksmith's shop has recently been taken down and the stone in question is lying with its inscription exposed towards the street, with the possibility of being worn if not obliterated by every passing wheel.

This stone was given to Revd Bray by Ralph Lopes and a wagon and three horses took it from Buckland Monachorum to Tavistock. Villagers refused to allow his servant to lift the stone with his lifting gear, until Ralph Lopes arrived. Bray recorded the stone as 7ft 2.5ins high with a breadth of 17ins at the bottom and 14ins at the top.

Erected before the Saxons came to the area these stones were probably the gravestones of two men. The first stone was removed by the vicar of Tavistock, Revd E.A. Bray, in 1831 and the second stone, discovered in 1836, was taken to Tavistock in 1868. The Parish Council decided that the stones should remain in Tavistock in 1985 but at a time when there was a proposed development of Tavistock Vicarage in 1990 Buckland Parish Council made an application for the stones to be returned. The Department of the Environment refused this. Should the vicarage garden be made into a car park it is hoped that the stones will be returned to the church at Buckland but at the time of writing they are safe in the lovely garden of Prebendary and Mrs John Rawlings. A third inscribed stone, dated between the sixth and eighth centuries by Elisabeth Okasha, stands in a field in the south of the parish, the owner of which is not willing to allow publication of the stone's whereabouts.

Archaeological studies made at Buckland Abbey between 1983 and 1995 reported 'a ploughed out

Left: *The River Tavy estuary at Lopwell.*

Below: *The village of Buckland Monachorum.*

Left: *The village of Milton Combe.*

Below: *Yelverton, c.1900.*

double-banked circular enclosure of Iron-Age date' (Devon Archaeological Society proceedings no.53, 1995). At Berrator in the north-west of the parish (SX479692) there is a scheduled ancient monument clearly visible to the north-east of the rocks. Known as Castle Field, the pound dates from the Iron Age. Many ancient tumuli on Roborough Down were destroyed in the last century. Tumuli at SX511681 and SX509682 were destroyed by airfield construction during the Second World War. The parish was inhabited therefore from about 600BC–AD200. An early Iron-Age camp in the southern tip of the parish (SX506641) was formed of concentric circular banks, the outer one being 100m in diameter, the keep, or centre, being 30m. On Spry's sixteenth-century map of the Plymouth Leat it is marked as Rowben Beacon and recorded by R. Hansford Worth in 1948. E. Masson Phillips noted a boundary stone between the parishes of Bickleigh and Buckland Monachorum with the letter B cut in relief, just east of the main road (SX507638).

Prebendary John Rawlings in the garden of Tavistock Vicarage with one of the Buckland stones in 2002.

The Prince of Wales reviewed 10,000 troops near to Pound Plantation on 21 August 1873. It was reported that these soldiers were badly behaved and that a roll-call was taken every hour. The officers, apparently, spent much of the day and night trying to keep order. The vicar of the parish, Richard Hayne, wrote to the War Office requesting them to instruct the troops to take care of the barrows on the Down. The reply from the War Office was that they knew nothing of any wheelbarrows left on Roborough Down! The ground was levelled for the purpose of the march-past and one of the three ancient barrows at the top of Pound Lane was destroyed and 'material and burnt clay carted to some distance across the road.' Mr Hayne noted that some old pottery and bones were found.

In the parish John Jetsome murdered his brother-in-law with a potato axe on 16 May 1812. He struck and beat Oliver Palmer on the back of the head causing rupture of the blood vessels of the brain. Oliver was the husband of John's sister, Prudence. They had a young baby, Grace Sophia, and it is not known why the 17-year-old young man delivered the fatal blow. Oliver died the next day and John was tried in Exeter Court the following July. The sentence was 'convicted of manslaughter John Jetsome is fined 1s. and imprisoned in the Common Gaol for one calendar month and further until the said fine be paid.' The

leniency of the sentence is surprising as a woman tried on the same day for stealing handkerchiefs was given two years' hard labour.

Listed in the *Plymouth, Stonehouse and Devonport Directory* of 1830 the parish is recorded as being 10 miles from Plymouth, diverging to the left of the Tavistock road. It describes the parish as delightful with orchards and meadows. In 1850 it was recorded that the parish of Buckland Monachorum was 6,838 acres (2,767 hectares) in area with 1,411 souls, the population being 918 in 1801. In 1676 there were 423 conformists and six non-conformists recorded as living in the parish. The area is now 6,472 acres (2,619 hectares) with a population of 3,494; the parish is in the West Devon district, the hundred of Roborough, the rural deanery of Tavistock, Archdeaconry of Plymouth and diocese of Exeter. In the fourteenth century a weekly market was held and an annual fair recorded as being held from this time on Trinity Monday. A June summer fair has been restored and is held on a Saturday in the village school.

Roborough Down lies within the parish and mineral mines on the banks of the River Tavy produced copper, mundic (iron pyrites), tin, silver and lead, none of which are now worked. Two leats carried fresh water through the parish to the coastal towns of Plymouth and Devonport. One of the leats, engineered by Sir Francis Drake in the sixteenth century, was taken from the River Meavy at Burrator while the other ran to the docks in the eighteenth century and was taken from the West Dart River near Wistman's Wood. These two channels are clearly visible in Yelverton and on Roborough Down. Alongside these waterways Sir Thomas Tyrwhitt constructed his horse-drawn railway from Princetown to Plymouth Wharf in the nineteenth century. The granite sleepers, some still with iron bolts, can clearly be seen on the footpath from Yelverton to Clearbrook on Roborough Down. This was built to carry granite from Dartmoor to ships that took the stone from Plymouth to London. The steam railway, the Tavistock and Launceston branch of the Great Western Railway, opened in 1859. The only station in the parish for passengers and goods was at Horrabridge. Nearly 30 years later the passenger station opened at Yelverton from where parishioners caught the train to Plymouth, Tavistock or Princetown or the many stations en route for work or leisure.

Left: *View towards Brent Tor from Yelverton.*

Below: *The parish boundary at Denham Bridge.*

Right: *Roborough Down.*

Above: *Berrator Rock above the Tavy valley.*

Left: *Plymouth and Dartmoor Railway (P & DR) crossing the green at Yelverton.*

The aerodrome at Yelverton, north of Roborough Down, opened during the Second World War and brought crews of many different nationalities to the area. A decoy aerodrome was built near Clearbrook to mislead enemy bomber pilots, changing Roborough Down moorland forever. The people of Plymouth were defenceless in the air raids and trekked to the moor for safety each evening in the spring of 1941. If the Village Hall at Roborough was full they walked as families or groups on to Clearbrook, Yelverton or even further to find shelter. Those with cars parked on the roadside, those that could afford the fares caught the train, and others walked, returning to work in the town the following morning. A canteen was opened at Yelverton for the many trekkers who were cold and wet from sleeping in the hedgerows or on the open moor. It is recorded that hundreds of people slept in the Rock Chapel, the golf clubhouse and in St Paul's Church Hall on one night at Yelverton. Others slept in churches and inns in Horrabridge and one night more than 5,000 trekkers arrived in Tavistock.

An early picture of Buckland School.

Today, water is piped underground and electricity and telephone cables link us to all parts of the world. The nearest airfield is at Roborough, the railway station and cross-channel ferry is at Plymouth and main bus routes run from Yelverton. In the parish there are seven pubs, as well as churches of different denominations and shops to serve the needs of the residents and visitors. Many residents, however, prefer to shop at supermarkets outside the parish.

The Parish Councillors work hard on behalf of the parish and twice yearly an update of events in the parish is published in their newsletter, *Monachorum Miscellany*. This publication, with a few breaks, has been produced for every household since 1976. In 1985 the Council set a competition for a design of the chairman's badge of office. The design of 16-year-old Paul Joyce of Laira Green Secondary School, where Betty Middleton was head of Religious Education, was chosen; the central motif is of a moorland cross.

The Parish was fortunate to be on the receiving end of many charities over the years, the first being given by Dame Elizabeth Modyford in 1702. Matthew Elford gave his in 1723 for 'the relief in sickness and in need and to the school at Buckland town'. Other gifts to the parish were from Catherine Ilbert, John Burrows, the Duke of Bedford and Sir Massey Lopes of Maristow. In 1858 Sir Massey granted a piece of land, called Thomas Austin's Garden near the church-yard, numbered 589 in the Tithe Apportionment map, upon trust for the girls' school that became Buckland School. In 1978 the charities amalgamated and money can still be granted to those in need.

Historical documents and objects continue to come to light after hundreds of years, which help to give a deeper insight into the life of a parish. In March 2002 a brass dog-collar inscribed 'Jonathan March Buckland Monachorum 1762' was sold by auction in Tavistock for £700.

The whole parish is designated as part of either the Dartmoor National Park (DNP) or the Tamar Valley Area of Outstanding Natural Beauty (AONB). Buckland is recognised as being of outstanding national significance as a land-scape of distinctive heritage. The landscape has been shaped by many years of settle-ment and local industry including farming, gardening, forestry and mining. Many of these activities have now largely ceased but their permanent marks add to the beauty and character of the land-scape of today. Tourism development can lead to jobs and income in the parish. Visitors are drawn to a few attractions such as Buckland Abbey, The Garden House and Lopwell as well as the beautiful moorland, rivers and public footpaths. Fencing was put up on Roborough Down in 1970 to prevent animals from straying on to the A386 road.

Denham Bridge (SX477679) is the lowest crossing point of the River Tavy. In 1661 and 1665 'Dinham or Didham Bridge' was in need of repair but this was not the present structure, which is of a later date. The bridge is probably eighteenth century and is unusual, having one pointed arch with projecting keystones over a ravine and another small semi-circular arch over a shallow stream. Double Waters, in the north-west corner of the parish where the rivers Tavy and Walkham meet, is a most beautiful, picturesque stretch of the Tavy, much loved by fishermen and walkers. This was the workplace of many copper miners. The Virtuous Lady Mine (SX474698), now disused, was probably named after Queen Elizabeth I and worked from 1588–1807. Opened again in 1830 it finally closed in the 1870s when it was worked to a depth of 37m with 43 people employed on site, far fewer than in former days. Considerable remains above the ground are visible and care must be taken when walking in the area. Hoo Meavy Bridge in the east of the parish, spanning the River Meavy below Clearbrook, was constructed in the eighteenth century.

Left: *Looking down on the aerodrome during the Second World War.*

Below: *276 Squadron, 29 January 1943.*

Rock Methodist Church.

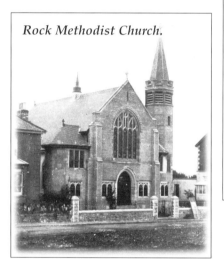

Right: *Huntsman, Stanley Roose, in 1946. Tom Kellaway is pictured with his daughter, Elizabeth, holding her son, Brian.*

Left: *Ponies, cattle and sheep roamed on the busy A386 before it was fenced in 1970.*

The single arch has a projecting keystone on the downstream side. Grenofen and Bedford Bridges span the River Walkham on the north parish boundary.

The parish is very much fox-hunting country and reports are published on the hounds following the scent across moorland and fields after each meet. Weather conditions, the sighting of a fox and alertness of the hounds featured in these hunt reports. There seem to be plenty of foxes to chase but hounds, huntsmen and huntswomen become frustrated when the smell is weak in adverse scenting conditions. The hunting of foxes in this way is very controversial throughout the UK at the time of writing. Field sports were once part of parish life and farming families followed the hunt. Villagers enjoyed the sight of horses, huntsmen and women and foxhounds, plus vets and farriers gained work from the activity. Hunting was revived after wartime restrictions for Mr Spooner's Harriers in 1948 and again after the foot-and-mouth restrictions in 2001.

Buckland School in 1920.

For many years legends have been passed down of numerous tunnels to the abbey from around the parish. Why monks should have wanted to escape or the secular society visit them is never explained. Supposedly there was a tunnel from St Andrew's Church and from farmhouses in the parish, particularly that of Axtown. A tunnel entrance was known here in the early-twentieth century under a flagstone of the kitchen floor as well as from the garden of Crossways where, it is remembered, there was a padlocked door a few feet along under the ground. A parish of natural beauty and historic secrets, Buckland Monachorum is home to those who have lived here for generations and those who have made it their home from countries all over the world.

The Parish Council put up five seats, one in each of the five settlements, on 1 January 2000 to mark the millennium. Walkers, beginning at Milton Combe on that day, visited each seat which was dedicated by a church minister. The most recent annual parish meeting at the time of writing was held at Yelverton on 8 May 2002 when seven members of the public joined the Parish Councillors. It was reported that 270 families were waiting to be housed in this parish, 30 of those already living in the parish. In the year of Queen Elizabeth's Golden Jubilee, the Parish Council presented all children under 12 years old with a commemorative medal. There have been many changes in the parish in the 50 years' reign of Queen Elizabeth II. In the villages in 1952 children were still collecting wood for fires, water for washday and earning pennies by running errands before and after school. In Yelverton and Crapstone children were taken by their nannies to play on the Big Rock, to visit friends for tea or were driven to their private schools in Yelverton.

There have been many caring people and colourful characters in the parish in each generation for whom no monuments were set up. Some full of their own importance driving vehicles in the middle of the road, others fearing them. Some firm and gentle, standing up for others, bringing improved living conditions to the poor. At a parish meeting in 1924, Jean Black enlisted the help of the WI to bring fresh piped water to homes in Buckland Monachorum, Crapstone and Milton Combe. A well-to-do bachelor farmer announced that it was good for village women to carry pails of water up the steep Buckland Hill from the brook. Mrs Black told him indignantly at the parish meeting that looking at him he would not be able to carry even half a pail of water up half the hill. She told him he had borne no war losses, had no family to provide for and had every comfort available with no regard for others in the village who had suffered. The motion was carried and water was piped to the villages in 1925. Jean Black lived in Willowby Park, Yelverton.

The millennium seat in Buckland Monachorum village.

Helicopters rescue both people and animals, 1963.

The village square in 1966, once the village green.

'Cruets' has replaced the old cottage on the right.

Bunting and flags decorate the wall (on the left) in Buckland village for the coronation of King George V and Queen Mary, 1910.

Below: *The church with the old school is shown on the right and the Baptist Chapel is on the left, 1960s.*

Above: *The tenth-century font in St Andrew's Church.*

Chapter 2

THE VILLAGE OF BUCKLAND MONACHORUM

Long ago the village had a different name to distinguish it from the parish. Now the village and surrounding farms and houses are known as Buckland and most of the people travel out of the parish to work away from the village each day. The village is designated as a 'medieval churchtown' in a conservation area. It was known as Buckland Crymes when the family of that name resided at Crapstone Barton to distinguish it from Buckland Drake and the lands held by Buckland Abbey. In the nineteenth and twentieth centuries it was Buckland Town or Churchtown, the name Churchtown recorded on tombstones in the churchyard. The village was the cluster of cottages around the village green outside the church with the school to the north-west of the church. Enclosed for the first time in 1864, the churchyard gates were provided by the church, walls built and the path made up to the old school, supervised by the churchwarden, Joseph Dawe. Listed in the churchwardens' accounts

One of the women from the Gift House.

are the men who undertook the work – Simmons, Spry, Toop, Coles, Langman, Hooper, Algar, Dawe, Seccombe, Foot, Hedge and Lethbridge. Mr Hedge sharpened the picks for picking stones in the churchyard, Mr Toop built the stile leading to the fields and 'half a thousand thorns' (trees) were used in the hedge, one presumes to keep the cattle out of the churchyard.

The village street led from the church, over the brook (called Buckland Brook or Vicarage Brook, which flowed from the vicarage, now The Garden House) and up the hill to the fields of Crapstone Barton and the abbey. The brook passing through the village once formed the water supply for the community. Before water was piped to the village there was a queue at the brook on Sunday nights when men and women collected water in buckets for washing the clothes in the coppers on Monday mornings. Several cottages were built with stone arches and doorways, perhaps taken from abbey buildings

and dating from late-medieval times. The *Western Morning News* called it the quaint village of Buckland Monachorum in 1928:

... which is now accessible by motor omnibus and attracts a good many visitors during the holiday months. There is a saying in the village, the best is good enough for us.

For centuries, Buckland Fair was an important event in the district. It was a large cattle fair and lasted three days, from Trinity Monday. Cattle lines, it is recorded, extended from Netherton to Bradford Cottages, filling the village. Stallholders were packed into corners, street sellers plied their wares and games and boxing matches were held in the fields. The cattle fair came to an end in 1867 and the last of these Buckland markets was held in 1883.

The discovery of a tenth-century font in the foundations of the church confirms the tradition that a much earlier church was built on the same site over 1,000 years ago with probably homes for families who worked in the large houses and on the farms constructed close by. Netherton, the near settlement, a short distance to the north had at least six cottages listed here in 1842. Netherton House, the cottage below and Whitehall on the corner have ancient foundations and in the fields above Whitehall the author remembers stone foundations and steps believed to be of Netherton cottages. Farmland surrounded Churchtown and the villagers walked for miles to work on the farms or in the mines, not many possessing any means of transport. The adjacent building to Whitehall, a seventeenth-century cottage, was the donkey house. Some folk had room to keep a donkey and all farmers had horses and carts on which they took their families to church. Very little is documented before Amicia, Countess of Devon, gave the land for the foundation of a monastery in the thirteenth century, located south of Churchtown.

An early-twentieth-century village outing in a charabanc. Roy Creber is at the front.

Above: *Jock Maxwell, a postman from Hill View, helps to rescue the poorly Mrs Lavers and her baby at Welltown near Walkhampton in January 1963. He walked there and home again after delivering the mail.*

Above: *Margrett and Gloyne, builders at Yelverton, building the Reading Room in 1919.*

Right: *Bridesmaids outside the WI Hall with the Reading Room behind in 1929. Pictured are,* left to right: *Elizabeth and Barbara Kellaway, Marjorie Searle.*

Far right: *The Allen family celebrating the coronation of Queen Elizabeth II in 1953 at 1 Hill View. Pictured are,* left to right: *Doris and Wilf with David, Peter, Brian, Graham, Christopher and Marilyn.*

In the Domesday Book, William held the manor but of the village nothing is documented. A chapel stood at the top of Hatch Mill Lane, used in ancient times by farmers and miners on the left bank of the River Tavy. Surrounding mansions would also have had private chapels for Christian worship.

Revd R.C. Streat in 1934 recorded that:

The village known as Buckland called Buckland Town on our signpost, was never called Buckland in the old days, but Churchtown; the name Buckland belongs to the whole manor.

Two important landowners, Drake at the abbey and Crymes at Crapstone Barton, were influential and provided much employment. Travel out of the village was via narrow lanes with high hedges leading to moorland. The roads were made for walking and for packhorses, which is only too evident when driving a car and one is met by gigantic farm machinery. Those who were born and bred in the village in the early part of the twentieth century remember the inhabitants as one big family, doors never locked and a welcome into every home. The village was self-sufficient; there was no need to leave as goods not provided by shopkeepers, farmers or householders were brought to the homes by travellers. The village outings to the seaside in the summer months were joyous occasions; men, women and children piling on to many charabancs parked by the church, leaving early in the morning and returning late in the evening, satisfied that there would be another outing the next year. Sand and sea, ice-cream and fish and chips, singing and laughter were all part of the day's fun. Six days were for working and Sundays were for going to church and family picnics on the moors.

Up to the late-twentieth century village folk rarely left the village except for the annual church outings. Visitors to the village found the dialect difficult to understand. There was a common bond amongst villagers, which has now disappeared but was a drawback for young people leaving the village searching for education and employment. Samuel Lewis wrote that the village was a market town picturesquely situated and that the parish contained 1,411 inhabitants in 1840. A 'foreigner' to the area must have written the following account of the village for a Plymouth newspaper in 1851 (*P. D. & S. Herald* 29 November) on a dismal day and when he was feeling 'out of sorts':

The reality of Buckland Monachorum village will not bear much note for anything about it to mark its ancient source or the peculiar supervision it received. It disappoints somewhat after the manner of the sight of a notorious or great person. It is after all but a common village! Its scenery is, even, second rate and its buildings, its people, its customs are all but as common, unromantic things.

The street through the village between cottages on each side of the road was always known as Buckland Hill and turning left at the top the next hill was understandably called Second Hill. At the top of Buckland Hill coming from the village and on the left was Buckland Abbey land which Lord and Lady Seaton gave for the building of a men's Reading Room in 1919. The men's club, as it became known, was pulled down and two bungalows built on the site. On the other side of the hill 12 council-houses were built between 1923 and 1929 called Hill View. Further along the road is Greenfield Cottage built as a home for the district nurse. Joyce Damerell lived here for many years and bought the house. It is now the home of her cousin, Anne Tucker. A plaque inside the porch reads:

This cottage was built in 1938 by the Buckland and Yelverton District Nursing Association for the use of the District Nurse. The land was given by Major A.F. Bundock who with many others generously subscribed to the cost of the building.

The nurses lived in Crapstone before this house was built.

Joyce Damerell died aged 72 years having lived in the house since 1954. She lived life to the full, whether delivering babies, hunting the fox, galloping across the moor or breeding puppies in her front garden. Christmas Day was like any other day in her work. The nurse's house had a surgery, now the kitchen, where Joyce dealt with minor ailments. In the 1950s she organised a ballet class in the WI Hall and little girls in the village, including the author, had to follow a strict regime. St Andrew's Church was filled to capacity at her funeral on 25 March 1997. The large congregation from all parts of the country represented all aspects of her life – nurse, midwife, hunt and horsewoman, dog breeder and trainer. Brenda Partridge, her friend and health visitor who worked with her, organised the placing of the seat on the moor to the north of Longash Garden Centre in her memory. It is simply inscribed, 'Rest, Relax, Rejoice'.

Houses were built between the two sets of council-houses and were numbered from 7 to 12 Hill View. In this field between the first sets of houses, Ian Bellan remembers there was an old fishery in his childhood. The numbers of the second group of old houses were renumbered 12A, 14 to 18. The first house on the corner at the top of the hill, 1 Hill View, was home to the Allen family (*pictured opposite*) from 1948. Marilyn was born in 1950, a daughter after five sons, and another daughter, Annette, was born ten years later. Marilyn lives in the house still. Her childhood memories are of deep snow in the winters making it impossible for the journey to Tavistock College. In 1964, despite the thick snow, the school bus arrived and those still at the bus stop unhappily went to school, thinking of the day they could have had

Above: *Freda Mayne in her fire-service uniform at Denham Bridge in the 1940s.*

Above: *Bill and Jessie Northam from Hill View celebrate their golden wedding anniversary with their grandchildren in 1977.*

Left: *Sunday-school children at Winsbeer with handbells in 1905.*

Left: *Hilda, Bertram and Alice Attwill at Quarry Park in 1900.*

Above: *Bertie Attwill could neither speak nor hear due to an infection of scarlet fever when he was six years old.*

Left: *Grace Tinkler outside Richmond Terrace in the village.*

sledging in the fields. After prolonged snowfalls that day the pupils in the country were sent home but the bus became stuck in a snowdrift at Pound Corner. As the children helped to dig the coach out of the drifts they sank in deep snow up to their waists. The author recalls walking to Yelverton to catch the bus in deep snow years before this on many days each winter and being delighted, along with other pupils at the grammar school, when no bus came and they could walk home and meet in Hilly Field later in the day. Trays and home-made sledges went so fast that many times the daring speed on the sledge ended by crashing through the brambles and into the brook. Always the journey to Tavistock had to be attempted – only in severe weather conditions was an absence from school excused.

Houses, bungalows and flats on the top of the hill down to the school are known as Modyford Walk. They were built by Tavistock Rural Council and were completed in 1977, next to Cuxton Lane down as far as the school's boundary hedge. A large estate of 41 houses was built at the top of Cuxton Lane and called Drake estate, but the residents opposed the name so in 1980 the estate was renamed Cuxton Meadow. At the top of the hill opposite is Fairfield, built by Thomas Waldron and lived in by Geoff and Hilda Waldron and their daughters for most of the twentieth century, now the home of John and Betty Spry formerly of Alston Farm. The road to Buckland Abbey leads from this corner, passing a turning on the right that leads to Denham Bridge. The cottages each side of the road form Winsbeer, a very old settlement. Ian and Jackie Bellan rebuilt the cottage on the right in 1970. It had been the home in the nineteenth century of Mrs Elizabeth Camp and her daughter, Emily Bertha, who worked in the church with Revd Richard Hayne. The land and cottage then belonged to the Lady Modyford Trust at Walkhampton. The owners and their families have lived in Quarry Park, Quarry Park Cottage and Bradford Cottages for many years. One inhabitant, Michelle Barley, has made ancient quarries into beautiful gardens, full of wildlife and 3D models she makes from willow, wire mesh and netting. Pat Harwood lives in the cottage next to her grandparents' home, Oliver and Elizabeth Gloyne. He was steward for Lady Drake at the abbey and their sixth child, Pat's father, was born in 1897 and was christened Stuart Alexander Diamond Jubilee Gloyne. Charlie and Joy Piper live in their home built by their ancestors, the Attwill family. Hilda Attwill dedicated her life to caring for her disabled younger brother at Quarry Park. Bertram, or Bertie, was unable to speak or hear due to the infection of scarlet fever when he was a young child, but he worked on the land and visited Winsbeer and played shove-ha'penny with a person of restricted growth who had been brought up by Miss Camp. She was Grace Tinkler, a well-known character in the village in the early-twentieth century.

Going down the village hill, past what was once a stone quarry where there are now detached houses on the right, is the Gift House, the home of Joan and Mike Charleston in 2002. They bought the Gift House from John Moore 'over the garden wall' when they lived next door at No. 1 The Village. Cecil Keast had moved here from Fredicott with John Moore who was then the postman. Sir Francis Drake, nephew of the famous Drake, gave £120 to build an almshouse in 1661 to accommodate six persons born and bred in the parish. Even in the last century free rooms at the Gift House were given to five women chosen by the owner of Buckland Abbey. In 1891 four elderly widows are listed living in the almshouse; Ann Wheaton with her grandson Ernest, Mary Honeywell, Ann Gill and Jane Brown. One room was listed as uninhabited and the women's occupations were formerly glovemaker, laundress and washerwoman, while Mrs Brown was a person 'living on her own means'. Marg Rogers who was born Pengelly in No. 5 The Village remembers Lizzie Jefferies, Mrs Stanley and Mrs Broad, all in their starched white aprons with bibs. The Northam family lived in No. 6. Windows and doorways of the cottages date from the sixteenth and seventeenth centuries.

Members of the WI, founded in Buckland in 1921, raised money for their own hall to be built opposite the old quarry. Land was purchased from the District Council for £25 and the local builders, Maben and Waldron, constructed the hall. Items were donated to the hall and the women were proud of their efforts, despite having to obtain water from a well, light paraffin lamps and clean two cast-iron coal stoves. Revd E.J. White, the curate, and his wife, Bertha, together conducted and accompanied the choral society to raise money for the WI and Johanna Kellaway was Queen Pippin in a play to raise funds in 1920. The official opening was in 1923 and a piano was purchased in 1926. The Southcotts ran the forge next door to the hall. Henry had a blacksmith's shop in the village below Richmond Terrace and built the bungalow next to the hall where his son, Alfie, took over the smithy. The hall was much used by all the villagers and Miss Alice Bere wrote the book *Buckland Monachorum*, compiled at the desire of the Buckland Monachorum WI in 1930. Lady Astor opened one of the bazaars here in 1931. Alice Bere died in 1936 and gave the rights of her book on Buckland Monachorum to the WI. Scotch fir trees were planted in the WI garden for the coronation of King George VI and Queen Elizabeth that have since been felled by the council. The WI members made a great contribution to the war effort during the Second World War. In 1941 the airmen were given free access to the hall until the buildings were constructed for them near the aerodrome. Each new year the women gave parties for the adults and for children; all the villagers arrived in party clothes and laden down with food for the teas. Among the 65 members of the

Right: *Villagers have always enjoyed drama productions. This picture shows the performance of* Pygmalion *in 1952, produced by Sadie Speight.*

Below: *Over-60s Club Christmas party in the WI hall, 1979.*

Thrift Shop ladies entertain villagers.

Joan Kellaway in 1923.

Drama group in the WI hall, 1950.

Marg Rogers in 2002.

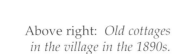

Above: *Richmond Terrace and Churchtown Villas.*

Above right: *Beatrice Greep, who was murdered in the village.*

Above: *Granny Rhoda Northey's old cottage in the village, 1935, which has since been demolished.*

Above right: *Old cottages in the village in the 1890s.*

Right: *Looking up the road in the early-twentieth century, with William Pike carrying a faggot of wood.*

A street party for the Queen's silver jubilee in 1977.

The Drake Manor Inn in the 1960s.

Below: *A group of villagers in the 1930s, with the Manor Inn on the left.*

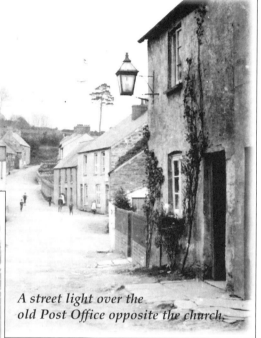

A street light over the old Post Office opposite the church.

Below: *Bertha Northey and Granny Ball sit with Mr Cole from the Post Office on the village bridge in the 1950s.*

Rene Creber.

WI in 1921 was the author's grandmother. In 1956 the author was the youngest member of the Buckland WI and her mother, Joan Bellan, wrote an exposé for the diamond jubilee in 1981.

The Reading Room became the Village Hall in 1981. In the following year plans were made to use the WI hall as the Village Hall as the members of the WI had dwindled to only a few. The site of the Reading Room was sold in 1986 and the membership of the WI closed in 1987. Much work has been carried out over the last few years to improve and enhance the Village Hall, applying for grants and organising charitable events.

Alfie Southcott worked in the forge, not only shoeing horses but also mending pots and pans brought to him by women and making iron hoops for the children. The Southcotts' bungalow had been built in an orchard belonging to Cuxton Farm. Marg and Les Rogers lived here with their children, Carol, Marjorie, Rita and Charles and their stepchildren, Fred and John Parker, for many years where Les and Marg created a lovely garden. Les, formerly the innkeeper at the Drake Manor Inn, was a keen and trained horticulturist. This bungalow, Hillside, has been pulled down and seven houses built in its place. Below this smithy were Rose Cottages, once owned by the farmer at Longash for his workmen. Opposite these and next to the Gift House is No. 1 The Village. This sixteenth-century cottage was reconstructed in the twentieth century but has the original stone stairs.

A terrible tragedy took place here on the afternoon of Saturday 26 July 1913. The cottage was then the home of the Greep family. Mr Greep had died on Dartmoor and Mrs Greep was ill in hospital. Her eldest son, William John Coombs, had recently come to live with his mother, his stepbrother and five stepsisters when he left the Navy. On this summer's afternoon this 31-year-old man shot one of his sisters, aged 18 years, and then himself. He had borrowed the gun from Arthur Rogers, the farmer at Didham, promising to return the weapon after he had shot some rabbits in Mr Hillson's cornfield. Mrs Julia Beer, wife of the local butcher at Brook Cottage, supplied Coombs with five cartridges. She told the reporter of the *Western Weekly Mercury* that he had been cheerful and went away whistling. Mrs Elizabeth Vanstone who lived opposite the Greeps rushed into the cottage when she heard three shots and found the two bodies. PC Kingdom, passing through the village, heard her screams and described the scene he found in the kitchen:

The girl was lying on her back near the door. Coombs was stretched out by the fireplace with the gun at his feet. Both were dead. Two spent cartridges were on the table, another was in the gun and two undischarged shots were in the deceased's pocket.

The Curno family lived next door and John Coombs had talked to little Jack Curno minutes before he shot

Beatie. John called Beatie downstairs before he shot her and attempted to call another sister, Annie, known as Nance, to the kitchen but she ran out of the back door on hearing a shot. The villagers believed that John had fallen in love with Beatie who wanted nothing to do with him. She was a girl adored by the children in the village who sat in the porch of her cottage knitting, sewing and talking to everyone who passed by. The inquest took place in the Manor Inn not far from the cottage, two days after the murder, while the bodies lay in the family home. The newspaper, under the heading 'A Double Dartmoor Tragedy', described the murder and suicide as one of the most terrible tragedies ever to take place on the borders of the moorland.

John Coombs was buried in the cemetery the following Tuesday morning after a service in the Baptist Chapel and Beatrice in the afternoon after a service in St Andrew's. The sisters and brother, Maud, Emily, Annie, Libby and Will Greep, attended both funerals and all the villagers walked to the cemetery to witness the burials. Their mother Mrs Greep was ill in the South Devon and East Cornwall Hospital which some of the witnesses told the jury depressed John greatly. Beatie's gravestone can still be seen, nearly 90 years later, in the cemetery on the south side and that of John Coombs is nearby under the hedge.

Richmond Terrace on the opposite side of the street was built on land where there were barracks for soldiers in 1791 when Militia regiments were stationed in the village. In the last century Joe Rowe ran the Post Office from 7 Richmond Terrace, and further up the terrace at No. 4 Mrs Sargent had a draper's shop where she sold pins, elastic, ribbons and dresses, etc. She was a large lady who seemed to fill her front room but she was a superb dancer at all the village gatherings. Her husband was a little man who travelled around all the nearby villages selling wrap-over aprons, calling at houses every two weeks. He was known as Johnny Fortnight. Opposite, through a gap in the terrace of cottages, was an entrance to the glebe fields and the back of the dairy run by William Crossman. His second wife had been the nanny to Rachel Chamberlin, daughter of the vicar. He kept five cows, two pigs, sheep, ducks and hens. He milked the cows behind the houses in his shippon and the residents of the upper part of the village collected their milk from the front of No. 2. The cottages below the Gift House once belonged to the Pound estate. Janny Dawe ran another dairy down the road at Brook Cottage and he served the customers in the lower part of the village. Mr Dawe drove his cows back up the hill after milking was finished to the Quarry Fields near the top of the hill. If he was short of milk he collected some from farmer Hillson at Crapstone Barton in a galvanised bucket. These dairies were open until the Second World War. Brook Cottage had formerly been the butcher's shop.

Further down the street on the right-hand side is a cottage that at one time was an inn; maybe this was The Rising Sun recorded in documents. In this same house a Dame school may have been held until the mid-nineteenth century. This was the home of Jim and Nellie Northam who both worked in the church, churchyard and cemetery and had the most beautiful cottage garden at the rear of their house in the village. Nellie had never slept away from her home until she was elderly and Jim had only been to Plymouth about three times in his life. Inside the entrance porch there were two doors, left and right, leading to separate homes; originally it was one house with a sixteenth-century granite doorway. The Northams lived to the left and at first Miss Chowen lived on the right followed by Mrs Millman. In the fields behind these houses Eric Bellan remembers when blasting took place to erect poles bringing electricity to the village in the 1930s. The little old cottage below this row of cottages seen on all the old postcards of the village was home to Mrs Northey. In her long dress and apron she stood in her porch watching life in the village passing by or sat on the stone seat doing some work. She was grandmother to the large Northey family. The little cottage was taken down and replaced by 'Cruets', home of Mr and Mrs Brian Salt.

Nellie Northam in the granite doorway
of her cottage in the village.

Buckland had its own poorhouses before the nineteenth century when the aged inhabitants were taken to the workhouse in Tavistock to end their days. The poorhouses may have been the cottages in a row at right angles to the street on the left bank of the brook. The churchwardens were obliged to find work for the able-bodied poor of the parish and house them in the village. Cottages were owned by nearby manors or lived in by tenants working for its owner. These tied cottages were fine when the landlord was a good employer but some families had to move out at short notice if the tenant was not servilely obedient or attentive. Tenants listed in the Maristow estate survey of 1765 in the village were Agnes Yealand,

Charles Bishop, John Wingate, Christopher Bishop, Nicholas Blanchard, Edmund Drake, Joan Cake, Joseph Dawe, John Doidge, John Edgcombe, John Bemball, Joseph Gill, Henry Hallett, William Light, Richard Oyns, Ambrose Staderton and Thomas Whidbourn. Curno Cottage, now April Cottage, is a seventeenth-century house which was altered in the nineteenth century.

The Drake Manor Inn, formerly the Manor Inn, is now one of the popular eating-places in the district. The parish owned this when it was the church house in 1660 and in 1670 it was taken over by the manor. It was probably extended in the nineteenth century. Mandy Fogwell, the present landlady, came to the inn in 1989. The Drake Manor is a typical old English hostelry and is popular with locals and visitors. The historic building still maintains its charm and character. It won the Ushers 'Pub in Bloom' competition in 1994 and was a finalist in the 'Pubs Food Competition' for several years, becoming a gourmet restaurant in the 1990s. Opposite are the cottages called Butt Park, the first one by the brook being the Post Office. Around 100 years ago this was a field where the children of the village played. At the side of this building was the access lane to Cuxton Farm. Mrs Rene Creber lives next door to the present Post Office but has lived in many houses in the parish, including Fairtown and Balstone Farms. Bertha and Sam Northey lived in this cottage where they brought up their daughters. Some of their grandchildren and great-grandchildren live in the village. Bertha and her family were 'chapel' but she attended the Parish Church and was a member of the Mothers' Union. Steve and Judy Parton took over the Post Office and stores in November 2001. Brook Cottage is by the village brook that rises beyond The Garden House. The cottage further along and opposite the church is owned and lived in by the licensee of the inn. Nellie and Jim Northam with their son, Percy, had lived here in the 1930s. The row of cottages was built on the village green in about 1830 and it was here that the steps of the old village cross were found – now the base of the cross in the churchyard. The first of these cottages was the Post Office before the one in Richmond Terrace and the present one in Butt Park. William Upcraft, helped by his daughter, Ethel, ran it here in the mid-twentieth century. The first stocks in the village arrived in about 1800. The first year's cost of putting out the stocks was 5s. but ten years later this had doubled.

On the corner of the road leading to St Andrew's School is Rose Cottage, 18 Buckland village, and home of the author's grandparents from 1910, followed by her parents from 1965 until 1985. Until the mid-twentieth century flood water poured down the hill from the moors into the village, flowing over the step and into Rose Cottage. The author recalls times when her grandmother's furniture including the harmonium floated in the front room. Sandbags were placed at the front door with little effect from the deep running water. This and the cottage next door were traditionally built for the monks from the abbey to live in whilst they constructed the Parish Church. The cottage next door was for many years the village shop where the Conybeares sold groceries and much else. Up to the 1950s everything was weighed out on brass scales and poured into grease-proof paper cones, made by twisting the paper around the fingers of the shopkeeper. Joshua and Isobel Conybeare were always able to obtain items their customers required. The biscuits were the most fascinating. Arrayed along a low sloping shelf behind the wooden counter the varieties were displayed for customers to choose and broken biscuits were sold at half price. The children eagerly sought and collected the empty tins for making ovens for their picnics on the moors. A purchase from the shop before school was four Oxo cubes for 1d. that children sucked behind their desks at school in the 1940s. Next to this was a tiny cottage with one bedroom where the cobbler lived, 'one-up one-down'.

The old house on the corner, which has ancient fireplaces, was the home of the village school's headmaster, the back door leading to the old school gate up the lane by the church wall. This lane led past the village allotments and the church gate in the northeast corner of the churchyard. Passing over the stile, that was cleaned regularly by young girls for the vicar to climb over, one way led up through the fields to Pound Corner and the other to Lovecombe, The Garden House and on to Crapstone. The former path was walked by villagers catching the train at Horrabridge Station for Tavistock and the other to Yelverton Station for the train to Plymouth or for picnics along the railway line to Princetown. A wide range of goods were sold door to door from horse-drawn carts before the coming of the tradesmen's vans.

Opposite Rose Cottage was the home and workshop of Jim Fox. He was the village carpenter and made all the coffins for burials. The sound of him sawing and hammering wood brought villagers to his shop to find out who had died in the parish. His house, Bedford Cottage, was down a short lane with a large orchard. A story is told of how Jim Fox's father, also an undertaker, was called to measure up somebody for a coffin when another villager called out to him, 'You just as well as come up an' run the rule over faither, cos he id'n long for this world.' James senr and his wife, Selina, lived in the detached cottage opposite the church. Next to the Fox's workshop was the Baptist Chapel built in 1850, now a hostel, which was run by the leaders of the church on Mutley Plain in Plymouth. Every Sunday afternoon the sound of singing from the worshippers, and the playing of the harmonium, carried right through the village. The ministers came from a distance but the congregation was made up of one family, the Northeys. Sam and

Bertha Northey, their children and grandchildren practised for these services and kept the little chapel bright and clean for so many years. At harvest time and on special occasions many people would have to stand outside when the little chapel was over-crowded, with the church people joining in the celebrations. Mrs Stone was the first organist then Bertha played the harmonium and on a few occasions the author played in her place. Two preachers were well loved; Mr Hurrell from Wrangaton and Mr Lang from Tickey Wood in Crapstone.

The field next to the chapel was Chapel Meadow and was part of Cuxton Farm. There always used to be cows in this field who seemed to be looking at their reflections in the water that collected in this watery meadow. The author remembers receiving food long past its sell-by date from her grandmother, to throw to the cattle on her walk home to Arranmore. In the meadow at the time of writing is St Andrew's C of E Primary School with footpaths to housing estates on each side of the village.

Chapel Meadow housing development next to the school was first outlined to the Parish Council in 1973 and planning permission was given the following year. Messrs Farnhams submitted a planning application for 64 houses in 1977 and details of the estate layout were displayed. The planning committee held 15 meetings in seven months discussing the mixed community and mixed housing of 52 dwellings. The Parish Council was concerned at the density of the development and the effect it would have on the roads through both Buckland village and Crapstone. The building of the estate began in 1978 although the residents opposed the development. It extends to the S bend in the road to Fairtown where there were once orchards and is a most pleasing housing development. Celia Steven, a descendant of Henry Merryweather who first cultivated the Bramley apple, lives here in Bramley Lodge. She promotes this variety of cooking apple for its versatility and flavour. Celia helped to set up a community orchard for the school in part of a field near Berrator with permission from David Northmore.

The cemetery, originally one and a half acres, was opened in 1882 at a cost of £400 and the churchyard around the church closed for burials except for those previously purchased. Joseph Symons was the overseer of the cemetery as well as being the village bootmaker and sub-postmaster. The avenue was lined with fir trees until the end of the twentieth century. Airmen who died in the war were buried on the left-hand side. Jim Northam was sexton here and for many years from 1930 so was the author's grandfather. She remembers being sent up to the cemetery as a small girl from Rose Cottage next door by her grandmother, with a jug of tea in which was placed a cup that contained a fruit bun. Looking for her grandfather down a six-foot-deep grave was not easy but he was always glad of the refreshment.

Left: *An early car in the village.*

Below: *The village shop, 1920s.*

Above: *Mr and Mrs Conybeare at their shop, 1926.*

Above: *May dancing through the village in 1951, led by Cynthia Northey and Joyce Northam.*

May dancing in 1946, led by Bertha and Sam Northey.

Floral dancing in the village square in 1972.

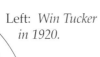

Left: *Win Tucker in 1920.*

Right: *Village folk on an outing, with Arthur Medland on the right.*

Below: *A group on the village green outside the shop, 1890.*

Right: *William (Tom) Kellaway in the early-twentieth century.*

Em Ball, Lilly Kellaway, Mrs Medland and Mrs Stansbury, 1930s.

31

Mrs Kellaway and Mrs Searle with dog, Peter, 1930s.

Joan Bellan, 1983.

Left: *The Kellaways' golden wedding day in 1949.*

Left: *Ladies' tea team in the village, 1920s.*

Below: *James Fox senr in 1903.*

The Fox family, with Jim and Dora on the right.

The cemetery in the early 1900s.

Tom Kellaway, who dug the graves in the cemetery, is pictured here with his wife in 1945.

Above: *Tug-o-war at the Flower Show in 1910.*

Left: *Buckland Monachorum tug-o-war team, 1971.*

Right: *Joan and Paul Bellan in their Whitehall garden.*

The cemetery has been extended and it is the burial-ground for the parish. Further along the road was the playing-field and two housing estates were built here. George Reeves built Netherton estate in 1937, the initials GER, George and Elizabeth Reeves, and date are on the front of a house; Cross Park was built in the 1950s. Elizabeth Reeves had been the daughter of William Pike, the man seen carrying a faggot of wood in many old Buckland picture postcards (*see page 25*). Before the building of Cross Park an old lane with high hedges topped with trees, known as Darky Lane, led from the playing-field along the back of the cemetery to the pathfields that led to Crapstone or to Horrabridge. Not a lane to be walked at night. There is now no public access to Churchtown Meadow from Cross Park, the only way to the footpaths being past the church. The Parish Council bought the field in 1995 and sold it for animal grazing in 2002.

Sunny Glen on the corner was built by Maben and Waldron for Thomas Waldron and his family and lived in by George Warne when he left Coppicetown Farm. The Waldron family moved to Fairfield, the house which Mr Waldron built at the top of the hill opposite Cuxton Farm. Ingledene was the home of Louie Butland for many years in the twentieth century and the house opposite, Ivy Cottage, the home of Nigel Rendal and his family in 2002, was owned by Mr and Mrs Gill. Their orchard extended as far as Whitehall where a house has been built. The cluster of houses at Netherton was part of a hamlet and on the border of the village.

The author's teenage years were spent at Whitehall, which had electricity and running water but no mains sewerage or drains. The long tin bath hung on a nail outside the back door and was brought indoors by the range every Saturday night for baths. Being the youngest in the family she had the first bath. All other personal washing was done by using the jug and basin in the bedroom set into the washstand. This ancient cottage had not been much altered since the seventeenth century and the linhay and donkey house with loft over were used to house ferrets and to store animal foodstuffs. The arched granite doorways, granite mullion windows, granite arch to the left of the entrance and projecting chimney stack with an oven, all added to the atmosphere of this old cottage.

Paul Bellan's garden here was unblemished – row upon row of vegetables and flowers with not a weed in sight. Rare apple trees in the orchard, ones the family called Blenheim Orange, Please Lady, Queenie and Pig's Nose, laying hens running free, a pig in the shed to provide meat, all surrounded by Devon hedges, neatly trimmed and bursting with wild flowers. Entering the 'Best Kept Garden' competition at the village Flower Show each year he always won the cup and took many of the show prizes in the vegetable sections. Working away from home every day he devoted his evenings to his garden. A few tips had to be kept secret by the family. When five potatoes had been selected, same size and shape, they were wiped with egg white; carrots were planted into holes filled with sand bored by a brace and bit into firmly-packed hard ground, only allowing one seed to grow into the perfect shape; beetroot roots were placed in a saucer filled with a salt solution to make them redder; onions, which were his speciality, grew to enormous weight and size by saving his own seed from the previous year's plants; runner beans grew long and straight with weights tied on the ends and all watered with liquid from water collected in a large tub of pigs' manure. Tomato plants were collected from seeds that had germinated on the edge of the sewer! When not in his garden in the evening he was in the church tower leading the ringers. The fun was that men in the village made every effort to beat him and visited his garden throughout the year. It may be imagined that his family was not allowed to take vegetables for eating until after the Flower Show! This show was a special event in the village every August, held in Dick Barons' field at the top of the hill. Women displayed their cooking skills and children collected grasses, ferns and wildflowers from the hedgerows. Sports and races were held in the afternoons with fancy dress and best baby competitions. All of this was very good-humoured at the time but highly competitive. Paul Bellan won the Netherton Challenge Cup in 1946 and the next three years it was won by Bill Kite from Churchtown Villas in the village. In 2001 his daughter, Margaret, presented the cup to the Flower Show committee in memory of her father and the show has been reinstated.

Netherton House on the opposite corner of Whitehall was home to Lt Col Godfrey and Dorothy Clarke from the 1930s. Probably a former seventeenth-century farmhouse this building suffered a severe fire in the 1950s. Their many horses were stabled in the courtyard and foxhound puppies were kennelled nearby, all rescued with no casualties. Godfrey Clarke set up a pig farm here in the 1950s. There were many alterations to the buildings at the end of the twentieth century. Netherton Lodge was built in the 1930s. Leaving Whitehall and passing up Fredicott Hill two houses were built on opposite sides of the road. On the left Fredicott, now Hope Cottage and on the right, Middlecroft, now Skelbrook House. Brother and sister, Major Alec Bundock and Miss Frances Penelope Bundock, moved here from Uppaton House. Margrett and Gloyne built Fredicott in 1926 for Major Bundock, a benefactor to the parish. The house is set in gardens of about an acre with old rhododendrons. The hill was always known as Fredicott Hill and leads to Alston Farm, Down Lane and the moors beyond, down to Bucktor and the rivers Walkham and Tavy. The road from Netherton behind the Chapel Meadow houses leads to Netherton Cottage and a footpath leads from here to the Alston and Coppicetown road. This old lane passes at the rear of West Park, lived in for many years by Jim Palmer, and Arranmore and was always known as Cuckoo's Nest Lane and led to Hele Cottages where there was once a farm. Traditionally this is part of the Monks' Way, a path from Buckland Abbey to Tavistock Abbey. Passing down the road to West Park and Arranmore there is a footpath that leads to Cuxton Farm and the sewer is on the left. This road leads on to Orchard Hill and Fairtown with roads branching off to farms and houses in the Tavy valley. The church and school have always been in the centre of the village and all paths and lanes seem to lead there.

The villagers raise funds all through the year in aid of a hospice for sick children in North Devon. Linda Downing from the village, the driving force behind this remarkable charitable effort, encourages others to use their talents and arranges events in the parish to raise money. The Children's Hospice South West appeal was launched in 1991 for terminally ill children in the West Country. Money for the hospice only comes from charitable sources and the village has donated thousands of pounds.

Buckland Monachorum darts team, 1980.

Buckland Football Club in their blue and white shirts, 1949. Left to right,
back row: *E. Bellan, B. Bennett, ?, P. Webber, O. Faulkner, T. Hooper,*
J. Savory, W. Turner, T. Northey, S. Gloyne, B. Northey, P. Northam;
front row: *G. Walters, D. Miller, R. Cook, ?, C. Northey.*

Right: *A print of the church by Charles Spreat, 1842.*

Above: *St Andrew's from the south-east.*

Above: **The interior of St Andrew's Church.**

Right: **The entrance porch at Venton.**

Below: **The building on the right of the church is the old Buckland School.**

Chapter 3

ST ANDREW'S CHURCH

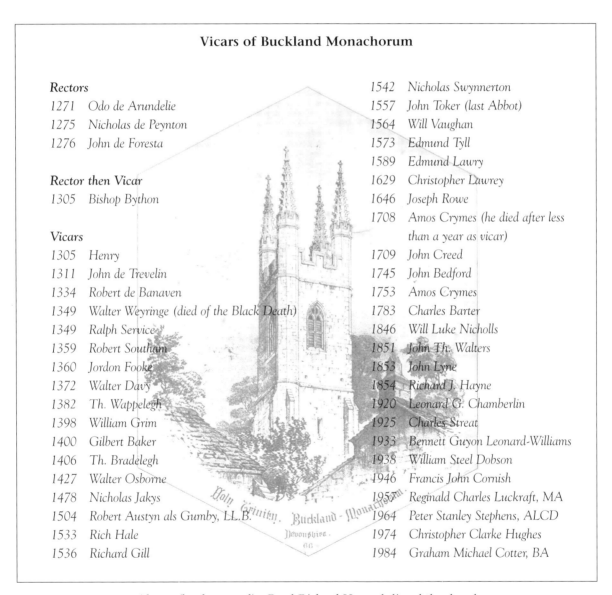

Vicars of Buckland Monachorum

Rectors

1271	Odo de Arundelie
1275	Nicholas de Peynton
1276	John de Foresta

Rector then Vicar

1305	Bishop Bython

Vicars

1305	Henry
1311	John de Trevelin
1334	Robert de Banaven
1349	Walter Weyringe (died of the Black Death)
1349	Ralph Service
1359	Robert Southam
1360	Jordon Fooke
1372	Walter Davy
1382	Th. Wappelegh
1398	William Grim
1400	Gilbert Baker
1406	Th. Bradelegh
1427	Walter Osborne
1478	Nicholas Jakys
1504	Robert Austyn als Gumby, LL.B.
1533	Rich Hale
1536	Richard Gill

1542	Nicholas Swynnerton
1557	John Toker (last Abbot)
1564	Will Vaughan
1573	Edmund Tyll
1589	Edmund Lawry
1629	Christopher Lawrey
1646	Joseph Rowe
1708	Amos Crymes (he died after less than a year as vicar)
1709	John Creed
1745	John Bedford
1753	Amos Crymes
1783	Charles Barter
1846	Will Luke Nicholls
1851	John Th. Walters
1853	John Lyne
1854	Richard J. Hayne
1920	Leonard G. Chamberlin
1925	Charles Streat
1933	Bennett Guyon Leonard-Williams
1938	William Steel Dobson
1946	Francis John Cornish
1953	Reginald Charles Luckraft, MA
1964	Peter Stanley Stephens, ALCD
1974	Christopher Clarke Hughes
1984	Graham Michael Cotter, BA

Above (background): Revd Richard Hayne believed the church may have been dedicated to the Holy Trinity in 1857.

The Parish Church in the centre of the village was built on the site of a much older church of Saxon origin in about 1490 in the reign of Henry VII. Built of wood, the first church would have been replaced by a stone church and some of the stones in the tower are probably from this earlier building. Patron of the church was the Abbot of Buckland. In 1342 when the Archdeacon made his visitation to the church it was recorded that:

The chancel is too dark. Its repair is the care of the rectors, the Abbot and Convent who can do it for 5 marks. The vicarage is adequate for the living. It has been put in order by Sir Robert, the new vicar, who had for the defects 40 shillings and 2 quarters of oats.

Payment in kind was rare in a visitation. In the time when monks lived at the abbey, ruled by the abbot, they were overseers of the village church and were

37

St Andrew's Church choir in 1972.

The screen by the west door was formerly at Sheepstor Church.

A Norman font was placed at the other side of the west door.

granted a charter to hold a midsummer fair in the village. The last abbot became vicar of Buckland Monachorum in 1557 and lived at the vicarage, then near the present Garden House. The abbot had ordered a vicarage and 40 acres of land to be given for use of the vicar in 1305, near to Lovecombe. Alice Bere wrote that the incumbent formerly lived at Sowton but Tamsyn Blaikie, translating a document of the time, believes the vicarage was at Venton, which would have been much nearer to the Parish Church for the priest. Nicholas Orme of Exeter University believes that the dedication of the church was that of St Andrew before the Reformation and then forgotten. Trinity was conjectured in 1742 from the date of the parish feast; Andrew was recovered in 1846 in the time of Revd William Nicholls.

Vicar Amos Crymes wrote on 23 November 1766:

We unanimously resolve and agree to prosecute at our joint expense, all and every person or persons who shall hereafter be discovered to have committed any felony or petty larceny whatsoever within the limits of this parish. A reward of two guineas to be paid by the church-wardens immediately on conviction of the offender.

The remains of the first vicarage at Lovecombe are the little turret with the spiral stone staircase, a fine and well-moulded late-fifteenth-century doorway in the garden wall and old granite window frames and doorways. Dr Creed enlarged this first vicarage at Lovecombe in 1710. It was of three storeys, built of stone and covered with slate. On the ground floor there was a parlour, hall, kitchen, dairy, beerhouse and cellar. On the floor above were four bedrooms, two closets and a study and the third floor consisted of three bedrooms and a closet. A later vicar, Revd Charles Barter, pulled down this house in 1826 and built a new one further up the hill. He did this without permission and to protect himself he obtained a faculty after the event. Charles Barter was vicar of Buckland Monachorum for 63 years. When the smaller vicarage was built along the top of the road in 1924, this old vicarage became known as Shiplake and is now The Garden House. This smaller vicarage is the home of the present incumbent and the views from the house and garden to the west and into Cornwall are magnificent. Rear Admiral and Mrs Richard Plowden named the house Shiplake in 1925 when they moved here from their ancestral home, Shiplake Court in the Thames Valley. The Plowden family is commemorated in the name of an inn on the Henley to Reading road – the Plowden Arms. Lionel Fortescue and family moved to the house in the 1940s. Revd Hayne added a sitting-room with bedrooms over in his time and a wooden room he used as a chapel. This is now called the annexe. There was a small organ here and at one time, when there was an orphanage at Lovecombe House, the Sisters and girls attended daily prayers.

Candlelight was the only form of lighting in the church until the mid 1930s. The font, used for baptisms of adults and babies through the centuries, is the most ancient object of the church. It was discovered in 1857 when repairs were being made on the church and was found buried beneath the ground. It is plain and roughly hewn from granite and perhaps was thought too crude in the church after the rebuild in 1490. The other font in the church dates from the fifteenth century and one shield on its side displays the letter T. The ancient font has been loaned to Horrabridge and Yelverton churches since its discovery, when they were first built, returning to St Andrew's in 1936 from St Paul's in Yelverton when the ecclesiastical parish of Buckland Monachorum insisted it was returned to the mother church. The author was baptised in this ancient font as a baby but in the tenth century it may have been sunk into the ground and used for the immersion of adults. A small building is shown in front of the church in paintings of about 1800. Probably built in the eighteenth century it gave an entrance to the churchyard with a room above, entered by a steep stone staircase. There was a fireplace and chimney and it was probably a vestry or home of the sexton. It was taken down in about 1832.

The church has a chancel and a nave with two transepts. Five high arches on each side support the roof of the nave and the special feature of this is the finely carved 16 wooden figures of angels playing musical instruments. The carved central boss shows Jesus Christ with his mother, Mary. Two chapels added after the Dissolution of the Monasteries in 1539 were named the Drake Chapel on the south side and Crapstone Chapel to the north. The Drake Chapel contains a very fine monument to General Elliot, later Lord Heathfield, the defender of Gibraltar during the Great Siege from 1779 to 1783. He was married to Anne Drake and their son, Francis August Elliot, inherited Buckland Abbey estate from Francis Henry Drake. Another monument here is one to Sir Francis Drake (1794). The number of burials in the last 50 years of the eighteenth century was 850. At that time Buckland was the only church in the parish. The Crapstone (or Crymes) Chapel contains the organ, built here in 1849 and given by Sir Trayton Drake of Buckland Abbey. This first organ was built to a design by the brother of Revd R. Hayne and rebuilt in 1876 by Heles of Plymouth. Dr L.G. Hayne wrote the hymn tune 'Buckland' set to the hymn 'Loving Shepherd of Thy Sheep', included in most hymn-books since Victorian times. Leighton George Hayne, born in 1836, only lived until he was 47 years old, his brother living to the age of 95 years. Parishioners before this time provided the music on instruments such as the violin, cello, flute and bassoon. The first mention of singers and a band was in 1753. From 1785 the church paid for a professional music teacher to instruct the singers and instrumentalists and a musicians' gallery was added at the west end in 1802. John Toop from the parish taught the music until 1810. The organ has been renovated and enlarged several times.

The unique Church Census, taken on 30 March 1851, provides numbers attending St Andrew's on that day. Matins had 150, with 50 in the Sunday school and in the afternoon, presumably to save on candles, 60 in the congregation with 44 in the Sunday school. In the Baptist chapel there were 75 in the morning, 125 in the afternoon and 100 in the evening. The Government conducted the Census throughout the country in an attempt to estimate church attendance. In one year, early in the nineteenth century, it was decided that poor persons were to be excused from paying their rates. Surprisingly, the lord of the manor, Sir Massey Lopes, only paid 3s.8d! In the 1830s it is recorded that the Church Council met in the vestry and afterwards adjourned to either the 'Horse and Jockey' or 'The Crown Inn'. Both these public houses were apparently in the village.

There are monuments to Dame Elinor Drake (1843) and Amos Crymes (1783) in the chancel. On the north wall of the church are those to Lancelot Elford (1782), George Leach (1823) and Jenny Leach (1829) who lived at Crapstone Barton, Mary Stopford (1816) and Georgina Hayne, wife of the vicar in 1912. Mrs Hayne died at the age of 92 years and was buried in 'a secluded corner of the churchyard, which had been reserved since the closing as a burial-ground, in a grave lined with moss and primroses.' The account of her funeral and the many parishioners who attended appeared in the newspaper. Others are memorials to the Lloyds of Pound, Thomas Wotton and to John Burrows, his wife and son.

The silver plate of St Andrew's was researched in about 1927 and found to be important chalices and patens. A pair of Queen Anne silver flagons and a silver paten were given by Jane Pollexfen in 1711 and made by Rowe of Plymouth. The Buckland Monachorum plate also includes a seventeenth-century continental porringer, a Victorian silver goblet, a Georgian chalice, a modern silver paten and an Edwardian silver inkwell. Two chalices and a small paten are inscribed with 'Buckland Monachorum 1685'. In 1970 the vicar, Revd Peter Stephens, suggested to the PCC that some of the church silver should be sold. It was to replace it with more simple silver, as the chalices are impractical, too large and awkward to drink from. Some members believed the value of the silver plate was so high that it was 'too hot to handle'. Others were outraged because of the historic association and wanted it kept in the parish. The votes cast were 9:7 not to sell the church silver.

The Revd Graham Cotter, vicar of the parish, has the care of Buckland Monachorum and Milton Combe in 2002. Almost 300 years ago, when the only means of transport was by horseback or carriage, the vicar, Revd John Creed, was also rector of Ashcombe in Somerset and a prebendary of Wells Cathedral.

Graham enjoys getting around the parish on his bicycle and outside the church gate while officiating at a wedding he leant his bicycle against the wall where a notice read 'reserved for vicar'. The press took the picture that appeared in the newspaper with the caption, 'Vicar rides on hard times'. He and his wife, Christine, have been known to walk with their three children to the school from behind the vicarage through the fields to the village.

Features of the church that attract attention are the chancel arch above the entrance to the choir that is lopsided with supporting pillars which do not correspond and the transepts of different widths. The undressed stone on the north side of the chancel may fill a former entrance to the rood loft. The south transept is remembered by the author as having an altar and being the area of the church where the vicar held Sunday school every Sunday afternoon, each pew packed with children of all ages. Here there is half a piscina (a holy-water basin where the priest washed his fingers) walled up and an aumbry (a place where vessels for the Eucharist were kept). Rachel Evans wrote of visiting the village in a rustic carriage in 1840. 'The great object of attraction was the church, a massive structure like a small cathedral that bears marks of the catholic rule.' She described the roads as being deeply rutted.

In May 1868 the vicar, Revd R.J. Hayne and the churchwardens, J. Pratt and E. Rabbidge, opened a restoration fund for the church to repair 'the dilapidated condition of this large and beautiful building so long a subject of regret to the Christian and to the Antiquarian'. They proposed to raise £1,200 to renew the decayed portions, removing the deal pews and gallery, carefully preserving the old carved oak roofs and seating, and restoring all the ancient features as far as possible. It seems £400 was received from the parish rates and £100 each from the Duke of Bedford, Sir Trayton F.E. Drake, Sir Massey Lopes, J.H. Gill and the vicar. St Andrew's is recorded by English Heritage as:

... late-fifteenth century restored in 1869 with notable vaulted roof in Drake Chapel, the other roofs are wood of the wagon type. A large range of eighteenth-and nineteenth-century wall memorials. Tower notable for the octagonal crocketted pinnacles. Impressive exterior and fine interior.

Mr Hayne preferred clear glass in the west window of the church:

He never would allow any donor to give stained glass for the west windows. None is needed. No effect can be more beautiful than the summer sunset light streaming in and glorifying the whole building.

The mosaic reredos below the east window, showing Andrew passing the loaves and fishes to Jesus in the miracle of the feeding of the 5,000, depicts the patron saint and was given by Mr Hayne. The plain-glass windows were restored in the 1920s. The missionary window in the north transept was given in memory of William and Mary White in 1874. The south chancel window is in memory of Sir Trayton Drake who died in 1870 and the south transept one is in memory of Joseph Godfrey of Plymouth who died in 1901. The south-west window is in memory of Philip Blowey who did much work in the building and died in 1907. The designs of these last two windows were left to Mr Hayne and at the funeral of Philip Blowey he spoke of Mr Blowey's work of restoring this church and many others in Devon and Cornwall. Born in the parish, Philip attended the village school and later employed men in the parish in his restoration work on churches, St Andrew's being his first enterprise.

The floor of the church before the restoration in Victorian times was covered in tombstones that were lifted and placed in and around the south porch. William Crymes of 1641 was moved to the floor of the porch and other members of the Crymes family were moved nearby. The encaustic tiles in the church replaced them. The entry to the church for many years was through the south porch until the ringers' gallery was raised. It is now by the west door and through the screen. The bells were formerly rung from ground level in the tower. A much-told story has passed down the generations of the ringers who practised until very late on Saturday nights so were forbidden the key one week. Knowing the carpenter was putting a lock on the church door they crept into the ringers' gallery with a barrel of beer and rang to their hearts' content through the night. These men were forbidden to ever ring again or even to sing in the choir. Churchwardens served for only one year in the eighteenth and nineteenth centuries and men such as John Dawe and Richard Corter kept the accounts and listed payments they made in that year. Much of the money was spent on the ringers and musicians, looking after the clock, cleaning the churchyard, the purchase of bread and wine for the sacraments, the minister's dinner, payment to workmen and for the killing of vermin.

The screen at the entrance from the west door was formerly part of the rood screen of St Leonard's at Sheepstor, which was removed in 1840. Alice Bere wrote that Mr Hayne rescued it from a yard in Horrabridge and placed it in its present position. 'The Sheepstor authorities asked to have the screen back, but this request was not acceded to.' Revd Hugh Breton, the vicar of Sheepstor, with the help of Revd Sabine Baring-Gould, replaced the screen in St Leonard's in 1914. The tombstone of Revd Joseph Rowe is set in the wall of the tower, one of the three long-serving incumbents of the parish. For 62 years as vicar he had to endure many religious changes in the worship of the church. The tower, 70 feet high, contains eight bells; six bells were erected in 1723 and two new treble bells were added in 1947. A new clock was added to the tower and set going on Easter Day in 1906 before the 11a.m. service. The clock was part of the celebrations to mark the golden jubilee of Prebendary Hayne as vicar of the parish.

Richard James Hayne was a small man and died in the vicarage in 1920, now The Garden House, in his 96th year after being vicar for nearly 65 years. His first curacy had been under his father at Pilton in Barnstaple and although he was offered the Bishopric of Natal and the Deanery of Jersey he preferred to remain at Buckland. During his time as vicar he supervised the restoration of St Andrew's, the building of the church and schoolroom at Milton Combe, the girls' school at Buckland, the room at Clearbrook for the Sunday school and the church at Yelverton. Revd Edward J. White was appointed his curate in 1904 and on the vicar's death he had to leave the parish on the orders of the bishop although the parishioners requested that he remained as their vicar. Edward and his wife, Bertha, did much for the parish and were both musicians, raising funds through concerts for the Parish Church and the churches in Milton Combe and Yelverton. They came to Buckland from St Andrew's in Plymouth as newly-weds and their three children were born in their home in Crapstone. It is interesting to read in the newspaper of that year (1920) that Miss Emily Camp of Winsbeer also died at the age of 84 years having been employed by the vicar for 60 years. These were long walks through the parish for an elderly woman. Emily Camp is remembered as the person who fostered orphans at Winsbeer.

In the summer of 1897 Mr Toop called a meeting of the Parish Council to discuss the proposal to place the village cross in the churchyard. He was against this but lost the vote by a large majority. The lord of the manor had given the council leave to erect the cross where they thought best. The remains of the old village cross had lain by the side of the road opposite the church from time immemorial. A happy idea was conceived of restoring the cross as a diamond jubilee memorial of Queen Victoria's reign. Mr Sedding of Plymouth prepared the design and Philip Blowey carried out the work at a cost of £140. In June 1898 the ceremony took place and the cross was erected in the churchyard. Prayers were said for the Queen and children waved flags. Mr Buller invited the entire parish to tea at Pound afterwards. 'A procession was formed and headed by the Buckland Brass Band, proceeded with flags and banners flying to Pound.'

Mr Hayne told the assembled people that the old cross had probably been a preaching as well as a market cross:

One time a market town, there had been a large space in front of the church here at Buckland Monachorum, now so enclosed and built upon, and the old cross was not found on its original site.

Right: *Revd E.J. White became the curate of Buckland Monachorum in 1904.*

Right below: *E.J. White (left) in the Army, aged 17 years, in 1892.*

Above: *The funeral of Revd Hayne in Buckland churchyard, 1920, with priests, F. Moore, B. Jones, C. Thorpe, E. Newman, F.W. Nutt, E.J. White, W. Champernowne and Archdeacon Sanders; bearers included W. Beer, S. Ward and J. Cooksley.*

Right: *Revd White visited parishioners on his bicycle.*

Below: *St Andrew's in 1896.*

Mr Hayne is reported to have said that he believed the original church might have been dedicated to the Holy Trinity. A fair usually followed the dedication of a church, and up to the nineteenth century it was the custom to have a fair in the village on Trinity Monday. This fine cross head was carved from soft stone, porphyry, found near Launceston. Two niches had figures of St Andrew and St Bernard of Clairvaux, the founder of the Cistercian order to which Buckland Abbey belonged. After 50 years this lantern cross had deteriorated so much it was decided to replace the head. The shaft was made from granite and the cross base was really old – it was not made on the date carved on it that commemorates Queen Victoria's jubilee. The plinth mounted on three steps is the remains of the ancient preaching or market cross. Carved into the granite, '1837 Victoria 1897' was added for the jubilee year when the base was moved into the churchyard. The surmounting cross was added in 1953, replacing the four-sided canopied head. To the south of the path is a sundial pedestal, 1.7m high. It is octagonal standing on a circular base and surmounted by a sculptured capital. A brass sundial plate is on the top.

The parish celebrated 500 years since the rebuilding in 1990 with a festival in the church of bell-ringing, floral displays and organ recitals. The churchyard was closed at the end of the nineteenth century except for the burial of the vicar, Revd R. Hayne and Mrs Hayne. It contains a fine collection of slate headstones with most interesting epitaphs. As the cemetery was opened in 1882 for burials, gravestones in the churchyard have been untouched for centuries. The churchyard has 16 chest tombs and nearly 400 memorials. Three and a half centuries of local history are recorded on these headstones, many of which are Grade II listed monuments. The deep trench around the church building exposes the bases of the outer walls, the actual surface having been raised by adding tons of earth to accommodate later interments. The raising of ground level caused dampness in the church, requiring this trench to be dug around the outside of the walls.

The Church of St Andrew is a Grade I listed building. Notable tombs listed as Grade II are to the Jacobson family 1786, a chest tomb by the south porch of 1647, the headstone of Richard Carter 1783, Elia Dunrich 1759, the Spry family 1734, Elizabeth Dawey 1743, the Carter family 1745 and 1759, Margaret Leane of Plymouth 1739, Richard Gent and his mother, Temperance 1736 and 1729, Richard Blanchard 1833, John Drake junr 1735, William Turner and his wife, Mary 1765 and William Drake of Netherton 1709.

A group by the sundial in the churchyard, 1905.

Above: *Joan and Paul Bellan with a Red Cross Guard of Honour, 1929.*

Below: *The Mothers' Union in 1953, with Mrs Cornish and Mrs Northmore at the rear. The children are,* left to right: *Sonia and Pam Boniface, Brian Ball, Carol and Diane Goff, Mervyn Williams (behind), Gillian and Judy Waldron, Brenda and Susan Ball.*

Above: *Emily and Cecil Reeves with little Pat Gloyne, 1934.*

Above: *The Sunday school at Lindisfarne in 1910.*

Right: *Bells at the foundry.*

On Wednesday 17 June 1870, when Revd Hayne was unwell, the funeral of Sir Trayton Drake (T.T.F.E. Drake) took place in St Andrew's. He died on 6 June aged 85 years at Nutwell Court near Exeter where he had lived for 30 years after the death of his wife. Buckland Abbey was, by all accounts, not fit for habitation. His body was taken by road through Tavistock where it lay in state in the Bedford Hotel. The hearse, taken from the abbey to church the next day, was drawn by six horses with all the tenants on the abbey estate in attendance. The Drake vault was opened in the church for his interment. The curate, Revd C. Comber, took the service and the coffin bearers were his tenants: Messrs Allett, Nix, Tremlett, Marshall, Salter, Atwater, Cowd and Chowen.

The tower is 70 feet high and six bells were set up here in 1723. From this time until 1947 the sound of the original peal of six bells was heard up and down the valley from the tower of this lovely Parish Church. A set of rules were printed and placed in the tower for the ringers by the vicar, Richard Hayne, on 16 January 1877. The churchwardens were J.D. Pratt and Robert Elliott. The rules stated that:

1 The Sexton for the time being shall be responsible for the chiming of the bells before Divine Service on Sundays and other days and that his salary in consequence be raised to £2.10s. per annum.

2 The bells are to be rung in peal early in the mornings of New Year's Day, Easter Day and Christmas Day. They may also be rung early in the mornings of Ascension Day and all Sundays: but the ringing must stop at ten minutes before 10 in the morning. The bells may also be rung on Monday and Thursday evenings and are to stop at 9 o'clock.

3 The bells are not to be rung on other occasions without the consent of the vicar and churchwardens.

4 On any vacancy occurring in the number of the ringers the Captain of the Belfry is to report it to the vicar, that a fresh appointment may be made.

5 The ringers and all other persons are strictly prohibited from entering the church during the hours for ringing; and any ringer conducting himself in a disorderly manner will be dismissed.

6 The Captain of the Belfry, or in his absence the treble ringer, is responsible that these rules are kept and good conduct maintained in the belfry as is suitable to the sacred character of the belfry which is part of the House of God.

7 That one sovereign per annum be paid to the Captain of the Belfry and 25 shillings be placed in his hands for distribution to the other ringers at his discretion.

For six months in 1947 there were no bells. At the bell foundry in Croydon the tenor was recast, two new trebles added and the five other bells carefully retuned. One of the old bells was repaired in memory of Major Bundock's brother and the two new bells in memory of Mrs Elizabeth Brown. At the morning

Bell-ringers in 1899.

Bell-ringers in 1929. Left to right: Beer, Warne, Hocking, Northam, Spry.

Bell-ringers and friends in 1949.

service on the Sunday before Christmas the bells were dedicated and Mr C.P. Brown read the lesson. As well as the Buckland Ringers teams from Tavistock, Whitchurch, Bickleigh, Meavy, Plympton, Emmanuel and St Andrew's Plymouth rang the bells all the afternoon. In recent years a bell simulator, worked by computer, was placed in the belfry. A plaque reads: 'To the Glory of God and in loving memory of Miss Dorothea Elizabeth Bellamy 1902–1995'.

Left: *The church choir in 1950.*

Right: *Revd Christopher Hughes in 1976.*

Below: *The Bishop of Plymouth meets parishioners at the south door in the 1950s.*

Background: *The hymn tune 'Buckland' was composed by the brother of the vicar in the nineteenth century, Dr L.G. Hayne.*

Revd Graham Cotter prefers to travel around the parish on his bicycle.

Revd and Mrs Graham Cotter, 2002.

*Bell-ringers in the 1970s with Joe Curno
on the village seat.*

*Bell-ringers in 2000 with Rosemary and Ken Farnham,
Christine and Revd Graham Cotter, Muriel and
Derek Diggins, captain.*

public were open that day and the distance walked was about 16 miles. After an open-air service at the Big Rock the boundary followed was to Bedford Bridge, Grenofen Bridge, Denham Bridge, Lopwell Dam, the café above Roborough and over the moor, returning to the Big Rock. Many trees and flowering shrubs in the churchyard had to be destroyed in September 1999 after the discovery of fireblight or *Erwinia amylovora*. Flowering almonds and ornamental prunus died rapidly and had to be burnt. Parish Council members keep an eye on the state of the churchyard.

Revd Graham Cotter cares for the ecclesiastical parish of Buckland Monachorum, which includes the churches of the Holy Spirit and St Andrew. The faithful congregation of Milton Combe enjoys the traditional service. They keep the church in beautiful condition and have recently recarpeted and repainted the building. The church at Buckland Monachorum holds family services, which are vibrant and well-attended and children of all ages are encouraged to take part in the life of the church and the community throughout the week. Over 100 of the congregation attend Buckland Parish Camp each year and a week's visit to Lee Abbey. The church has close links with the village school and the Baptist Church is pleased for St Andrew's to use the hostel in the village. Graham knows there are many challenges ahead for the Church as a whole and he is prepared to meet them with the people of Buckland Monachorum.

Prebendary Peter Stephens recalls parishioners such as Jim Northam and Bertha Northey who were content not to leave the village. Elderly villagers chose their own plots in the cemetery with care where they wished to be laid to rest. When the burial-ground was opened in 1882, members of the Church of England were interred on the right-hand side of the path and non-conformists on the left. Bertha Northey remembered that when Mrs Georgiana Hayne served soup to needy villagers she and her family weren't given any because they were chapel folk. Joyce Stephens entertained the Young Wives at the vicarage and was concerned when both the Buckland and Milton young women complained of her tea being frothy. It was years later when the family had moved to Plymouth that it was discovered that her two small sons at the time had put putting washing-up liquid in the teapots. The Mothers' Union has always played an important role for women in the parish and the Parish Church and the incumbents ruled the lives of the men and women for centuries.

In 1966 St Andrew's was the musical centre for choirs, choral festivals and organ recitals. The Buckland Festival Chorus and the Buckland Chamber Orchestra gave many performances of choral works to packed audiences. Michael Keck was organist and choirmaster and the Festival Chorus was officially constituted in March 1968. The patron was Gillian Weir, a world-famous organist. At the end of his first concert, young Michael Keck told the Buckland villagers, 'You may not have liked the music but it is good for you.' Musical concerts in Buckland Monachorum lasted for many years, attracting people to the Parish Church from a wide area.

St Andrew's Parish boundaries were 'beaten' or walked on 11 May 1985, the first time for many years on Rogationtide. Footpaths usually closed to the

An old print of St Andrew's in 1820.

Right: *The abbey, early-twentieth century.*

Below: *Cider House, 1981.*

Michael Coxson, property manager, in the doorway in 2002.

Another abbey doorway and porch.

BUCKLAND ABBEY

Chapter 4

Buckland Abbey (SX487667), built as a Cistercian monastery and later converted into a house and owned by two illustrious Elizabethan sailors, is at the time of writing open to the public. This National Trust property attracts many visitors to the south-west corner of the parish and contains a mix of period rooms and exhibitions. Situated in an area of outstanding natural beauty in the Tavy valley, Buckland Abbey estate was once one of the most important in England. It is one of the few medieval abbeys to undergo conversion into a house, incorporating much of the medieval fabric. Captain Arthur Rodd gave the abbey itself to the National Trust in 1948. Arthur Rodd, who lived in Willowby House in Yelverton, purchased the abbey estate after the Second World War when the abbey had been under requisition by the Admiralty, who paid £275 per annum, and Captain Richard O.T.G. Meyrick put the property up for sale in 1946. This ended ownership of the abbey by the Drake family for almost 400 years. Arthur Rodd died before he was able to live in the abbey. Comprising about 1,332 acres in 1981 the estate was sold off in 14 lots by Mrs Arthur Rodd. The house and grounds are scheduled ancient monuments.

The carved stone head of Amicia, Countess of Devon, on Walkhampton Church.

William the Conqueror gave the land to the husband of his niece, Baldwin de Brion, who was the great-grandson of the Duke of Normandy. The family were Earls of Devon and the Countess of Devon in 1273 was Amicia, who first decided to found the abbey as a Cistercian monastery in memory of her husband, Baldwin de Redvers. She founded Buckland Abbey in 1278 for the monks from the Isle of Wight.

We, Amicia, Countess of Devon and Lady of the Isle, trusting in the goodness of the Supreme maker of all good things, who disposes the wills of both men and women at his pleasure, and faithfully directs them though unseen, and sustains our hope by the revelation of His mind if we offer anything in perpetual memory to the honour of His name; we found the Abbey which we desire should be called or entitled St Benedict's of Buckland, which is in our manor of Buckland.

Amicia was a powerful lady. Legend supports the belief that a representation of her is in the form of a stone-carved head over a small outer doorway in the abbey. The land was a gift from her daughter, Isabella de Fortibus, who was a great lady in her own right and Countess of Abemarle and Devon, Lady of the Isle. On the wooded slopes of the left bank of the River Tavy, the abbey was dedicated to the Blessed Virgin Mary and St Benedict. Six years later Buckland Church was granted to the abbey on the Feast of St Peter, 29 June.

The first monks came from the Monastery of Quarr on the Isle of Wight. They were of the white Cistercian Order and wore habits of undyed sheep's wool. The men must have found the rich meadows and woodland of the Tavy valley ideal to farm and they became practical landowners. Not only was the land fertile, the river and ponds provided a plentiful supply of fish. Other priories and abbeys such as those of Tavistock, Buckfast and Plympton were within walking and riding distance for the monks. The Cistercians were renowned sheep farmers and they traded with other enclosed communities. At that time the river was tidal upriver from Lopwell and they may have also traded across the Channel. Most important to them, however, must have been the situation of tranquillity and peace where they were able to keep their rule, find joy in prayer and study and maintain contact with the outside world. On arrival at Buckland the small community was immediately placed under suspension by the Church authorities for two years, for failing to obtain permission to celebrate Mass and perform other religious duties from the Bishop of Exeter, Walter Bronescombe. It was two years later, however, on the day of the bishop's death in 1280, that he authorised the brothers to follow their rule. From this time up to the Reformation, the names of 16 abbots have been recorded. The last abbot, John Toker, was blessed on 7 January 1528 and it was he who after 11 years surrendered the house to King Henry VIII.

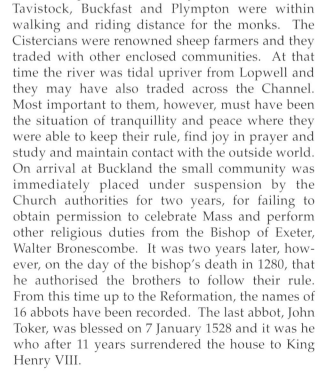

49

Right: *Buckland Abbey in the nineteenth century.*

Below: *The abbey in the late-nineteenth century, which was the ancestral home of the Drake family.*

Above: *Cider House in front of the abbey.*

Right: *View from the crenellated tower.*

Abbots of Buckland Abbey

(The dates of the abbots are vague and cannot be confirmed.)

1278	*Robert*	*1418*	*John*
1288	*William*	*1442*	*William Rolff*
1303	*Geoffrey (Galfridus)*	*1449*	*John Spore*
1311	*Thomas*	*1454*	*John Hylle*
1333	*William*	*1463*	*Thomas Olyver*
1356	*Thomas Walppelgh*	*1508*	*John Brundon*
1385	*John Bryton*	*1511*	*Thomas Whyte*
1392	*Walter*	*1528–39*	*John Toker*

A document of 1281 lists 37 monks living at the abbey with Abbot Robert in the new monastery. In 1291, after the death of Amicia, Isabella granted to Buckland Abbey the manors of Buckland, Bickleigh and Walkhampton with parts of Sheepstor and Shaugh. The manor of Cullompton in East Devon was also part of the abbey estate. Forty years ago John Somers Cocks translated the bounds of the estate from Latin text, and in my words, thus: ... from Lopwell in the west along the course of the Tavy northwards and the Walkham eastwards to just north of Greena Ball where Walkham crosses into the Forest of Dartmoor. Following the modern Walkhampton Parish boundary to Nuns Cross and Eylesbarrow and the small stream which joins the Plym at SX608682, the boundary is along the Plym to Legis Lake. Over Ringmoor Down to the modern Ringmoor Cot, down Smallacombe Lake to the Mewy and along the Sheepstor Parish boundary to the point under the reservoir where three parishes, Meavy, Walkhampton and Sheepstor, meet. Along the boundary to Yennadon Cross and to Lake Stream, following Buckland Parish boundary down the stream and the Mewy to Lower Elfordtown, down the River Mewy to the Plym to SX531623 and up the track to Beatland Corner; northward to the Cadover Bridge road at about SX552635 and turning east to the top of Saddlesborough. Somers Cocks then follows the reave [a boundary marker] to Hawks Tor and finds the next part of the bounds difficult to follow. To Fernhill, down the east side of the manor's land to Mainstone, up Pethill and to the modern Browney Cross and to the Plym for a short distance and up a stream to the old Woolwell Farm. Northwards along the A386 to Roborough Common and along Buckland Parish boundary to the Bickham Brook and down this stream and the parish boundary to the starting point at Lopwell. This vast area was granted in a charter of Isabella to the abbey and the boundary is that of different parish boundaries today.

Permission was granted in 1337 for Abbot William to crenelate his monastery. A royal licence was necessary before a house could be privately fortified. In 1522 Thomas Whyte appointed Robert Derkeham as organist of the abbey. He provided him with:

... a furnished room over the west gate, a gown every year, 5oz of bread and a quart of beer every night, a wax candle from November to February and 30 horse-loads of faggots for his fire.

The 12 monks living at the abbey with Abbot John in 1539 received pensions for the remainder of their lives and left the abbey. John Toker received £60 per annum and each monk received annual payments of between £3.6s.8d. and £5.6s.8d. More than 250 years of religious life in Buckland Monachorum were at an end.

Two years after the Dissolution of the Monasteries, on 28 February 1539, with the exile of the abbot and the 12 monks, Henry VIII sold the abbey to Sir Richard Grenville who built on it, as Risdon says, 'A fair new house'. John Slanning purchased the abbey lands in parishes other than those of Buckland in 1546. Grenville's grandson, Richard, inherited the house from his father, Roger, who was drowned whilst captain of the warship the *Mary Rose* off Portsmouth. This younger Richard completed the house adding the date 1576 in the plasterwork in the great hall.

In 1581 Sir Francis Drake purchased the abbey from the Grenville family with the help of two friends, Christopher Harris, whose descendants were to live in Yelverton 400 years later, and John Hele. Sir Francis returned to Plymouth a famous and wealthy man and found this ready-made home. He purchased it for £3,400 and lived there for the rest of his life when not on board ship. In this year he was knighted by Queen Elizabeth and became Mayor of Plymouth. Born in Crowndale at Tavistock in about 1541, Francis and his family who were Protestants had to flee from Devon when he was about eight years old and eventually lived on an old naval hulk in the Thames estuary in Kent. Francis developed

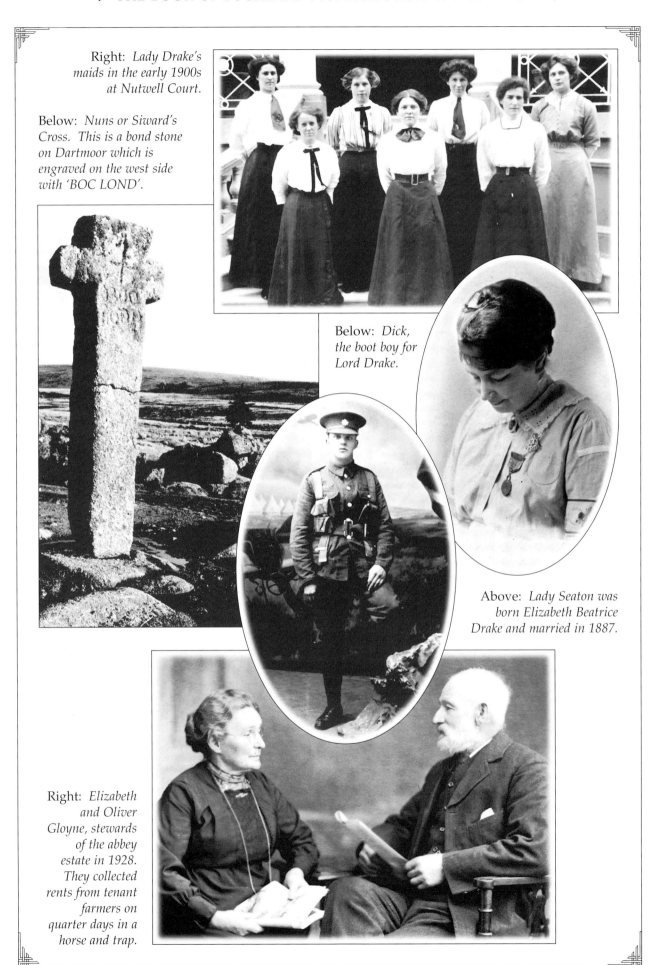

Right: *Lady Drake's maids in the early 1900s at Nutwell Court.*

Below: *Nuns or Siward's Cross. This is a bond stone on Dartmoor which is engraved on the west side with 'BOC LOND'.*

Below: *Dick, the boot boy for Lord Drake.*

Above: *Lady Seaton was born Elizabeth Beatrice Drake and married in 1887.*

Right: *Elizabeth and Oliver Gloyne, stewards of the abbey estate in 1928. They collected rents from tenant farmers on quarter days in a horse and trap.*

great skill in navigation and at about 20 years of age sailed from Plymouth on a trading expedition to Spain. Drake was a religious man and he considered the Catholics of Spain to be his enemy. His cousin, John Hawkins, took Francis as commander of one of his ten ships in his fleet to capture Spanish ships loaded with treasure. After being tricked by the Spanish at St John de Ulloa only Hawkins' and Drake's ships returned to Plymouth and Drake waged a personal war against Spain for the rest of his life. Francis married Mary Newman on 4 July 1569 at St Budeaux Church in Plymouth. She died a year after they moved to the abbey and bore him no children. Mary saw little of her husband as from 1577 until 1580 Drake was circumnavigating the world. Three years after her death he married Elizabeth Sydenham and they, too, had no children.

In 1585 Drake began to engineer the Plymouth Leat from the River Meavy below what is now Burrator Reservoir, to carry fresh water to Plymouth for the townspeople and for his ships. Three years later he was said to have been playing bowls on the afternoon of 19 July 1588 on Plymouth Hoe when news came of the approaching Spanish fleet. He is supposed to have said, 'There is time to finish the game and beat the Spaniards, too.' Sir Francis Drake knew his fleet could not move out of Plymouth Sound for three hours because of the tide. A week later the Armada was defeated and Drake wrote, 'There was never anything please me better than seeing the enemy flying with a southerly wind to the northwards.'

Drake returned to Buckland where he hunted stag, fished in the Tavy and arranged musical concerts. His leat for Plymouth, more often called Drake's Leat, flowed into Plymouth in 1591, a 17-mile channel that was to be the town's main source of water for 300 years. On the morning of 28 January 1596, sailing to Puerto Bello, Sir Francis died of dysentery on board his ship *Defiance* when he was about 55 years of age. He was buried at sea the next day in a lead coffin to the sound of trumpets, drums and cannons. The end of the life of a brave adventurer forever linked with his home of his last years, Buckland Abbey. In his will he bequeathed his property to his younger brother, Thomas, and through him the estate passed through heirs of Francis Drake until 1946. Drake's drum, displayed at the abbey, has always caused much interest mainly because of the legend that Sir Francis put upon it himself. It is a side drum that probably accompanied him on his final voyage. It was brought back to the abbey to his widow with his bible and sword after his death at sea. There is a persistent tradition that the drum will be heard as a warning if England is in trouble. Henry Newbolt's poem was printed in 1895 and romanticised the legend even further:

Drake he's in his hammock and a thousand miles away,
(Captain, art thou sleeping there below?)
Slung atween the round shot in Nombre Dios Bay,
And dreaming all the time of Plymouth Hoe.
Yonder looms the Island, yonder lie the ships,
With sailor-lads a-dancing heel-an'-toe,
And the shore-lights flashing, and the night-tide dashing,
He sees it all so plainly as he saw it long ago.
Drake he was a Devon man, an' ruled the Devon seas,
(Captain, art thou sleeping there below?)
Roving tho' his death fell, he went with heart at ease,
And dreaming all the time of Plymouth Hoe.
"Take my drum to England, hang it by the shore,
Strike it when your powder's running low;
If the Dons sight Devon, I'll quit the port o' Heaven,
And drum them up the Channel as we drummed them long ago."
Drake he's in his hammock till the great Armadas come,
(Captain, art thou sleeping there below?)
Slung atween the round shot, listening for the drum,
And dreaming all the time of Plymouth Hoe.
Call him on the deep sea, call him up the Sound,
Call him when you sail to meet the foe;
Where the old trade's plying and the old flag flying
They shall find him ware and waking, as they found him long ago!

Right: *Melody of the song 'Drake's Drum' from 'Songs of the Sea', composed in 1904 by Charles Villiers Stanford (1852–1924).*

Drake's drum.

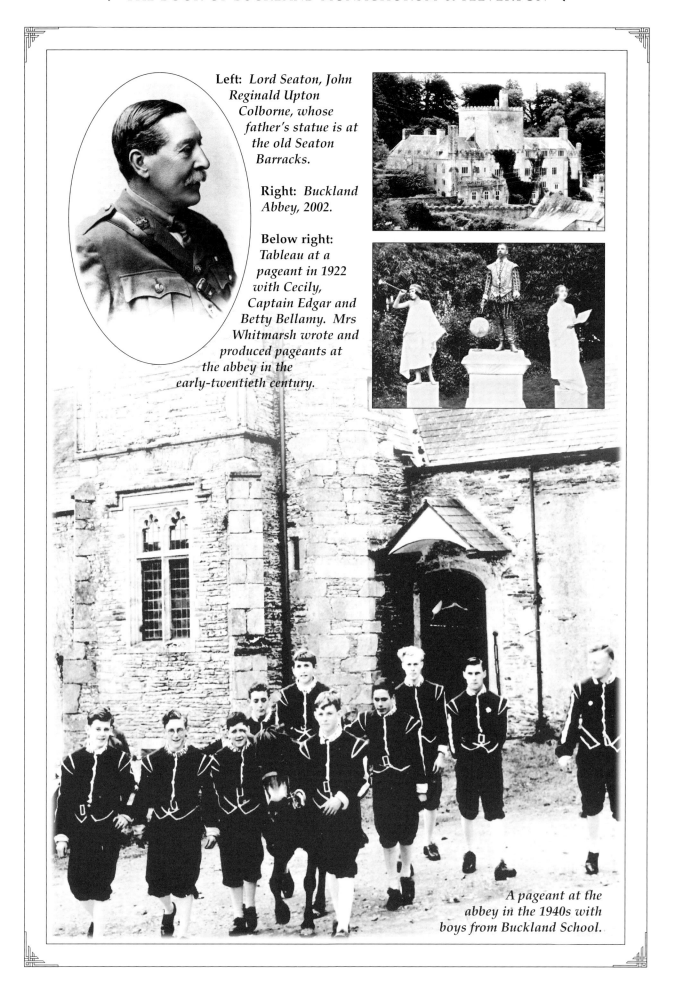

Left: *Lord Seaton, John Reginald Upton Colborne, whose father's statue is at the old Seaton Barracks.*

Right: *Buckland Abbey, 2002.*

Below right: *Tableau at a pageant in 1922 with Cecily, Captain Edgar and Betty Bellamy. Mrs Whitmarsh wrote and produced pageants at the abbey in the early-twentieth century.*

A pageant at the abbey in the 1940s with boys from Buckland School.

Many recordings have been made of men hearing the beating of a drum before a battle and the folklore is still evolving. Oliver Gloyne, steward of the abbey in the time of Lady Drake, repaired the famous drum in 1910. To obtain the correct colour varnish he used liquid from cow's dung. When the present Meavy School was built on Drake land in 1926 Lady Seaton gave a replica of Drake's drum to the school. It was placed on the roof and by means of an attached rope inside the school the drum was beaten each morning to summon the children. Understandably, it was not heard too well and a bell replaced the beater for many years. Then in 1992 Lady Kitson, a descendant of the Bayly family, opened the new position of the drum that can be seen from the road in a gable window.

The house of Buckland Abbey was the Abbey Church, converted by Grenville and altered by the Drake family through the centuries to suit the changing needs. Lord Heathfield remodelled it in the eighteenth century on the advice of William Marshall, a noted agricultural economist. Lord Heathfield was a Drake descendant through the female line. During much of the nineteenth century the abbey was rented to different tenants. In 1870 it passed to Sir Francis Fuller Eliott Drake whose wife wrote a history of the heirs of Sir Francis Drake. Lady Drake spent the summer months at the abbey travelling from their other home in Lympstone by train to Yelverton Station. Carriages to convey them to the abbey met the special train. Their daughter, Elizabeth, married Lord Seaton. She lived in the abbey until her death in 1937 and older parishioners who were invited to tea at the abbey when they were schoolchildren remember her. Lady Seaton was a great benefactor of the Roman Catholic community in the parish. Before she and Lord Seaton became members of the Catholic Church, Lady Seaton was a member of the Plymouth Brethren and the Anglican Church. Lady Seaton was received into the Catholic Church at Buckfast Abbey. She erected an altar on the site of the ancient high altar at Buckland Abbey where in 1938 Mass was said for the first time in many years. In the year following her death there was a fire at the house. Most of the west wing was destroyed but quick-thinking firemen rescued precious articles, including the famous sea captain's drum.

On Wednesday 11 March 1891 sudden blizzard conditions hit the abbey. Lives were lost throughout the country and the abbey was surrounded in 15-foot high snowdrifts. Old elm, beech, cedar and tulip trees were uprooted between the North and South Lodges and visitors to Place Barton Farm had an amazing escape. A tree fell on a horse and cart imprisoning the occupants between large branches without, it was reported, the slightest damage being done to the family. More than 60,000 trees were blown down on the Maristow estate in the storm.

Field names at Buckland Abbey were Old Orchard, New Orchard, Pound Park, Long Meadow, Middle South Field, Oxen Park, Long Park, Little Canes Hill, Great Canes Hill, Hill Ball, Little Paddock, Great Paddock, Broom Ball, Little Deer Park, Deer Park Orchard, Higher Meadow, Great Deer Park, Mill Orchard, Middle Meadow, Old Wood, Stockhill Quarry, Kiln Meadow and Higher Kiln Meadow, all to the north of Milton Combe village.

The chief interest in Buckland Abbey today is its connection with the great sailor, Sir Francis Drake. The National Trust with the City of Plymouth has administered Buckland Abbey since 1951 and the Plymouth Museum displays Drake's artefacts at the abbey. As part of the 400th anniversary celebrations commemorating the defeat of the Spanish Armada, exhibitions and facilities were refurbished in 1987. Monastery, mansion and museum, through its long history of about 730 years, is now open to the public and visitors from all over the world come to the parish of Buckland Monachorum to see the house and walk through the gardens. A little more than 50 years ago the parishioners, unless they were employees at the abbey, could not wander around the house and grounds as visitors do today. It was a grand occasion to be invited to the abbey.

As children of the village school were led to believe for generations, there had been a secret passage built by the monks from the abbey to the Parish Church. Boys and girls used to search for the entrance and invent stories about the tunnel, and an excavation in the abbey grounds at one time did reveal a tunnel entrance in the grounds, so indeed there may well have been a way between the two churches. There is much in the abbey grounds that has never been excavated so many secrets may lie beneath the soil, perhaps of settlements even before the monks arrived from the Isle of Wight. Did they come by sea and so up the Tamar and the Tavy?

Surveys and excavations were made between 1983 and 1995 and are reported in *Proceedings No. 53 1995* of the Devon Archaeological Society. A cemetery was discovered just south-west of the church where four medieval skeletons of a young man, two young women and a child were found. Their remains were reburied in the grounds during a service of burial conducted by a Brother from the abbey at Buckfast. The graves discovered on excavating in 1993, outside and south of the church, show that the parish community used the monastery. The young people perhaps sought refuge in the infirmary at the abbey when they were injured or in poor health. More research here could be illuminating as both miners and farmers in the Tavy valley probably used facilities at the abbey to trade their wares. The alterations carried out in the Grenvilles' time (1541–76), when the monastery was altered for domestic use, revealed high-quality conversions from a fourteenth-century stable block with two-storey rooms at the east end that reverted to farm use in the eighteenth

Above: *Buckland Fair, held at the abbey in 1970, with the vicar, Revd Peter Stephens, and stallholders in costume.*

Right: *The chapel at Buckland Abbey.*

Above: *The Great Barn, also called the Tithe Barn.*

Right: *The Drake coat of arms over a fireplace.*

Above: *Carriages in the Great Barn.*

century. It was probably the young Richard Grenville who chose to convert the abbey church where the abbots and monks had worshipped many times each day for 260 years into a Tudor mansion. A much-damaged thirteenth-century longhouse was found to the east of the monastic area, built over a ploughed-out double-banked circular enclosure dating from the Iron Age. To the north-west of the abbey at SX484672 a small irregular four-sided enclosure was visible as a cropmark on flat ground and seen in 1983. Measuring 40m x 60m it was listed as 'Cropmark, medieval'. At SX485668 a marshy area west of the abbey created by a former pond was probably the fishpond for the monks at the abbey.

Tenants and workers on the abbey lands paid tithes to the ecclesiastical landowners – that is a tenth part of goods or wealth. The Great Barn was probably built at the abbey in the fourteenth century and is a magnificent memorial to the Cistercian monks. It stands testimony to the vast amount of produce collected on abbey lands. The huge barn was constructed with oak beams pegged together with not a single iron nail. The barn was placed close to the abbey church under constant protection, as the value of produce stored here must have been high. Approximately 50m long and 19m wide it is believed to be one of the largest barns in Britain. In the length of the barn there are doors in opposite walls which when opened helped in the winnowing of the threshed corn, the draught separating the chaff from the wheat. It is buttressed all around, has slit windows splayed internally with rounded arches and a wooden roof of 20 bays, now slated. Until about 1920 a stream that ran between the abbey and barn here powered the abbey water-mill. The cider press at the north end dates from the eighteenth century. Recorded in the Buckland farm journals of 1795, 3,000 gallons of cider were consumed. When the Admiralty requisitioned the barn during the First World War, 1,000 tons of Manitoba wheat were stored in the building. The barn is a Grade I listed building and one of the few monastic barns in Devon. On his visit to the abbey before 1821, Samuel Rowe wrote that the Great Hall had a handsome mosaic floor and was used as a billiard room. He walked through the grounds to the salmon weir on the Tavy and up to 'Didham' Bridge.

A young apprentice, Robert Ash, was employed at the abbey from 1795 – his duties included haymaking, ploughing with oxen, picking apples, clearing stones, tending cattle and sheep, spreading dung, cutting wood, cutting weeds, collecting holly, picking and pounding apples, making cider, washing pots, pulling turnips, cleaning pigsties and making hurdles. In 1805 he received a gratuity from his Lordship for good behaviour and serving out his time. In the twentieth century Charles White, younger brother of Dick White and uncle to Richard, was banned from working at the abbey for one year. Lady Seaton, sitting unseen in a garden arbour, heard Charles swear as he worked in one of the flowerbeds. Charles used to take Lord Seaton's pony down to the river when he was fishing so that the gentleman was able to ride up Cot Lane back to the abbey. Repairing the Catholic church at Yelverton one time, Charlie White answered the priest back and found himself in front of Lady Seaton the next morning. The priest had remarked on the number of knots in the timber. Charlie responded by asking him if he had ever seen a tree without branches. Many stories are told of firm discipline by the Seatons to their employees. On the morning of Election Day the servants stood in the courtyard and, standing in her carriage in front of them, Lady Seaton always told them for which candidate they must vote. Nevertheless she was a great benefactor to the parish and the annual tea party for the local schoolchildren, including those from Meavy and Walkhampton, was a memorable event. The pupils remember long trestle-tables on the lawns laid out with bowls of strawberries and dessert gooseberries. Milton Combe residents have enjoyed the use of the Great Barn for many years. After the dedication of the Church of the Holy Spirit in 1878 the tenant, Mr Pratt, held a luncheon for all attendees in the Great Barn and village barn dances are held here still.

A building that may have been the guesthouse of the abbey stands 20m east of the Great Barn, measuring 33.4m x 7.4m. A two-storeyed building that slopes downward from east to west was excavated in 1987. Probably late-fifteenth century in origin this was not the infirmary owing to its distance from the abbey. The fifteenth-century tower may have originally formed part of the abbot's lodgings. It is small with only one room on each of its three floors. The Cider House, a Grade II listed building, was modernised by the Rodds and retains some medieval features at the southern end. Molly Rodd lived here until 1981 and it remains a private residence. The Great Hall of the abbey was originally the west end of the nave and the chapel was built over the original high altar. The National Trust and Plymouth City Museum renovated the abbey between 1949 and 1951 in preparation for the opening of the property to the public. Excavations in 1984 of the remains of the cloister north of the abbey church revealed it had been 30m square with different floor levels in medieval times.

The vicar of Buckland Monachorum, Revd Peter Stephens, conducted a pilgrimage from Quarr on the Isle of Wight to Buckland Abbey in August 1971 – the seventh centenary of the founding of the abbey. Travelling on the boat *Speedwell* eight people sailed to Weir Quay where they were met by parishioners and walked to Buckland Abbey. On Sunday 15 August Revd Peter Stephens celebrated Holy Communion in the chapel at the abbey, the congregation of Buckland Monachorum and Milton Combe taking part in the service seated in the Great Hall.

This was a unique service, an Anglican priest celebrating in the Catholic chapel. The Seatons restored the chapel after the First World War and the stained glass in the windows is reported as having been rescued from Rheims Cathedral. Four engraved glass panels to commemorate the 400th anniversary of the Spanish Armada's defeat were created by Simon Whistler in 1988. These have been set in the windows of the stairwell.

The newly-created Elizabethan garden opened on 11 July 2001 during the foot-and-mouth crisis. The herbaceous borders are a mix of flowers, herbs and vegetables of the sixteenth century. Box-topiary hedges are planted in geometric patterns. Chestnut trellis from trees on the estate support climbing plants. The reason most people visit the abbey is for the history of Sir Francis Drake, not for the almost 300 years of monastic life before he was even born. The Elizabethan theme is now within and outside the house and this new garden will mature over the years to come. Rachel Evans, walking in the vicinity of Tavistock in 1840 wrote:

The cedars at Buckland Abbey surpass in growth any I have elsewhere seen. A row of these trees bounds the garden wall. In the middle of the park is Drake's Oak so-called from tradition that Sir Francis Drake climbed into it to escape from a stag by which he was pursued.

She described the overgrown fishponds and two beautiful avenues of over-arching lime trees.

Tenants lived in Buckland Abbey when the Drake family preferred to live at Nutwell Court in Lympstone near Exeter. There are lovely walks open to the public in the abbey grounds including the orchard from where the ancient buildings and mature trees look magnificent. Nowadays thousands of visitors flock to the abbey, which is under the care of the National Trust, held in perpetuity for the nation. Around 4,000 schoolchildren visit the abbey each year and take part in projects. In 2003 the displays are to be refurbished. The abbey, of historical and architectural interest, is set in peaceful and tranquil grounds. Local residents volunteer to work in the house and gardens, maintaining a high standard of care.

Left: Holy Communion in the abbey, being officiated by the vicar of Buckland Monachorum Parish Church, Revd Peter Stephens, in 1971, celebrating 700 years since the founding of the abbey, possibly the first Anglican Mass since the Reformation.

Right: Looking to the Tavy valley from the sundial.

Below: Maypole dancing by St Andrew's School.

Chapter 5

SCHOOLS IN BUCKLAND MONACHORUM

The earliest reference to educating the poor in the parish is the deed of 1702, but there may have been a small school in the village before this time. Richard Bold, appointed schoolmaster here in 1675, signed the Deed of Foundation of the school in 1702. Dame Elizabeth Modyford, formerly Slanning, granted the church house and an adjoining property, known as David Kennard's house, to trustees for 1,000 years with £10 per annum salary to the schoolmaster. This was the schoolmaster's house where Mr and Mrs Westcott, and Ronald and Kathleen Isherwood spent so many years. The church paid for six foundation schol-ars. The building was 'in a ruinous state' in 1830 and the school was closed while the building was repaired by Sir Massey Lopes. His son, Ralph, estab-lished a fresh deed in 1844 and endowed the school for 1,000 years from that date, that is until 2844! The building had probably been a church room when Lady Modyford founded the school there. The old school and schoolhouse are Grade II listed buildings.

A National School was opened in 1859 in a field north of the church next to the established building. Boys were taught in the old building and girls were admitted to the new school up the lane close by, which had been built in Thomas Austin's garden the previous year. Thomas Austin lived in one of the cottages opposite the church. The managers, or governors, of the school decided in 1870 that a voluntary system of payment by each pupil should be adopted in the parish. The vicar and wealthy landowners started the fund. Parents had to pay 2d. a week for the eldest child and 1d. a week for other children in the family. For a labourer on low wages with many children this was a burden. Village chil-dren had to work before arriving at school, similar to those doing a paper round today but the children were much younger and the work was hard. Girls

scrubbed floors and boys worked on the farms, delivering milk and butter on their way to school. Punishment was received, a caning, from the teacher if they were late. Many teachers were cruel and took pleasure in punishing pupils they did not like, hand-ing out sweets to those they did. In the time of Revd Richard Hayne there was a Convent at Lovecombe House where the Sisters ran an orphanage for girls. The Sisters taught at the girls' school in the village. They attended the chapel built by Mr Hayne at the vicarage, the neigh-bouring house to Lovecombe.

In 1872 the upper storey of the Modyford building was taken down and the inspector wrote on his visit that the low, dark, gloomy room was now lofty, bright and cheerful. Log-book entries at this time, written by the headmaster, are fascinating:

1870 *Several girls seen playing with the boys outside school. I have sent notes to their parents. I let the boys view the sun's eclipse through smoked glass.*
1871 *Children absent on account of their relations emigrating to Canada.*
1882 *Boys warned about interrupting the old ladies in the Gift House.*
1887 *School treat in honour of the Queen's Jubilee.*
1889 *A flood arose in Buckland caused by a storm on the Down. The water was about three feet deep in the village.*
1898 *School closed for the opening of Burrator Reservoir.*

All schools and shops closed in the area for the occasion of the reservoir opening, although it was many years before water was piped to the village. At the girls' school the teacher wrote at this time, 'It seems impossible to teach these children anything.'

Mr and Mrs Bacon arrived in April 1877 and were

Old Buckland School in the early-twentieth century.

59

Left: *Younger pupils at Buckland School in 1899, with teacher Grace Symons.*

Right: *The boys' school in 1899 with Mr and Mrs William Baker.*

Below: *The boys' school in 1905.*

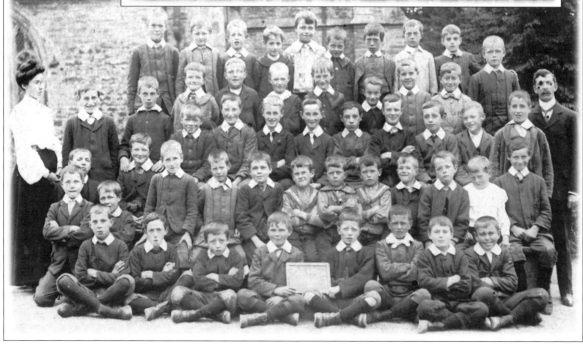

followed by another married couple, Mr and Mrs Baker, in 1892. These two teachers, although strict, were well-liked and remained at the school until 1920. The girls' building was extended in 1897 and the two schools became one school under the Local Education Authority in 1904. Buckland Monachorum C of E School had a headmaster and a headmistress. In 1914 the Bakers left the schoolhouse and moved to Paxcot in Crapstone. On their retirement the boys' and girls' schools were made into one and called Buckland School. In 1921 the lower-school pupils were taught in the Modyford building and the upper school in the old girls' school. Boys and girls were now mixed. John Swain taught the older pupils with Miss Tolly and he is remembered for holding the children's chins when he spoke to them. Mr S.L. Westcott took over as headmaster in 1926, lived in the schoolhouse in the village, and retired in 1955. He and Miss Brearley are remembered as running the school together. She left in 1950. Mrs Elizabeth Ball was cook supervisor for 16 years at the school, five years at the WI hall during the war and 11 years after her children Brian and Brenda were born.

A detached building was added to the site of the upper school in 1946 for use as a canteen but this soon became the infants' classroom and the Modyford room became the school kitchen and dining-room. The school's rocking horse lived here, a great favourite for generations of pupils, and it was taken to the new school many years later. In 1952 the school was given aided status by the Church of England. This was the year that changed the village as all children were taken from the village at the age of 11 years to continue their education in Tavistock. Pupils had entered the scholarship examination for the grammar school for years but from this time those who were not granted a scholarship attended the secondary school in Dolvin Road. This building became St Rumon's Infants School when in 1959 all pupils attended Tavistock College for comprehensive education. Prior to 1952 pupils remained at Buckland School until they reached the age of 14 years and continued by learning a trade with employers in the parish. Passing the scholarship before buses arrived to convey all children to Tavistock meant a long walk to Horrabridge Station early in the mornings and home again late in the evenings. This system of education caused tensions in families. Some members of the family went to the grammar and others stayed in Buckland where there was no school uniform. It was a burden for parents to purchase all the items for uniform, games equipment and books for certain members of the family when others felt they were left out. Buckland became a primary school, all lessons taught in the upper school and dinners eaten in the old building by the church.

Memories of schooldays are evocative and those who attended Buckland School from the 1930s to the 1960s still feel deeply about all that happened in the classroom or playground. Thomas Bromidge walked from Green Lane near the Rock at Yelverton with his older brothers, Bob and John, through Crapstone and past The Garden House. Mr Westcott was headmaster and Miss Brearley the assistant. He recalls gardening in the school garden in the war years and collecting rose-hips for rose-hip syrup from the hedges. He remembers the smell of the pasties brought by the children for dinner, warming on the old stove before the county provided school dinners. There are also memories of roaming around the village and fields at dinner-time when no one knew or cared where the children were, but punishment if late for the afternoon was a beating. The children who arrived at school early on winter mornings poured water over the playground so that it would be frozen by playtime and make a solid ice track. Children slid from the upper end, crashing into the railings at the bottom, hoping they wouldn't miss the railings and crash down the steps to the school gate. The teachers never seemed to be on duty in those days. Games of marbles, conkers and piggy-back contests, where the aim was to knock your opponent off his steed, were favourite playground pastimes as well as the huge skipping rope when the challenge was to get as many children as possible skipping at the same time. Girls at the time remember looking after the younger children, bouncing a ball against the wall and doing handstands. The boys, as in schools today, played football in their own playground. In the 1940s boys were sent to local farms in the afternoons to pick up potatoes. Tom remembers good days like Ascension Day when the school closed for a half-day holiday and dreaded days when the school dentist arrived. School dinners were brought to the WI hall in metal containers from Horrabridge during the war, before the canteen was opened at the school. A favourite pudding was jam roly-poly and custard.

Air-raid shelters were placed in the playground in 1941. They had long wooden benches down the sides where children sat out of the rain making up stories and planning the future. These shelters were never needed for a raid but practices were held in case of an attack and children crowded into them during wet playtimes. Michael Stephens was at the school in the late 1960s and remembers these shelters still in the playground but placed out of bounds to the pupils. They were by then full of old desks and unwanted furniture and the children dared each other to enter when the duty teacher was out of sight. Michael sat on the same oval raffia PE mats that had been used since 1944. The outside lavatories were near the shelters and the boys' facilities and playground were at the rear of the school. Gypsies who camped on the moor sent their children to school for a few weeks each year and evacuees arrived in 1941. Mr Ron Isherwood arrived as headmaster in 1955 and in the next year a playing-field was created out of the old

Left: *Buckland Boys' School in 1909 with boys wearing Eton collars.*

Right: *A mixed class at the school in 1904.*

Left: *Infants' class in 1900.*

Left: *The soccer team at the school in 1917.*

Right: *Pupils in 1919.*

Left: *Five- and six-year-olds in 1920.*

Right: *Buckland School, 1921. Including: W. White, R. May, G. Butland, P. Broad, J. Crocker, T. Prior, J. Curno, K. Parker, M. Prior, G. Glubb, F. Raymond, W. Glubb, L. Dawe, L. Cook, C. Northam, H. Curno, B. White, M. Beer, M. Crocker, D. Cann, L. Cross, S. Hillson, A. Head, L. Cann, W. Medland.*

Above: *Buckland School infants with Miss Metherel, 1921.* Left to right, back row: *W. Hartland, M. Warne, I. Lentle, R. Crossman, E. Kellaway, D. Northam, M. Ripley, K. Northey*; middle row: *E. Seccombe, D. Crossman, M. Beer, W. Vanstone, W. Dicker, M. Pengelly, A. Hillson, D. Parker, C. White, L. Wherry*; front row: *S. Bullen, D. Medland, A. Head, J. Guy, P. Blowey, R. Rogers.*

Above: *Group III in 1922, including Mr Swain, Miss Tolly, C. Medland, M. Beer, P. Parker, F. Hocking, W. Butland, F. Spry, B. Seccombe, G. Butland, P. Hillson.*

Left: *The school in 1924 with Miss Clarke.*

Right: *1928. Left to right, back row: W. Vanstone, R. Creber, D. Medland, W. Dicker, C. Stansbury, N. White, R. Abbot; middle row: G. Ball, W. Ball, R. Watters, M. Raymond, E. Kellaway, D. Parker, R. Crossman, E. Seccombe, M. Beer, D. Hudson, R. Haycroft, R. Cook; front row: A. Finnamore, D. Crossman, M. Pengelly, W. Raymond, A. Hillson, N. White, D. Northam, E. Smith, G. Kidger.*

Above: *The older pupils in 1932.*

Young pupils with Mrs Dove

in 1933. Left to right, back row: *Les Andrews, Ron Kite, John Northey, George Etchells, Gerald Kellaway;* middle row: *Ivy Northam, Betty Northam, Joan Etchells, Joyce King, Pat Gloyne;* front row: *Percy Crossman, Kenneth Andrews, Bert Northey, Bob Wilsmore, Norman Nankivell, Cliff Stansbury.*

Right: *Buckland School in 1950.*

Below: *Captain Charles Keys was first in the swimming pool at the old school.*

Main photograph: *An aerial view of the village, showing the new school in Chapel Meadow (centre left).*

The digger arrives in October 1975.

Revd Peter Stephens returns to the parish to cut the turf for the school which he worked hard to establish.

school gardens. He introduced the controversial ITA, the Initial Teaching Alphabet, in 1968. This was a good method for pupils in the early years but children had to relearn to read when they went to Tavistock College. A swimming pool was purchased from a school in Newton Abbot. This was placed at the old school and taken to the new school site and sunk into the ground. Work on the new school began in Chapel Meadow in October 1975, the vicar, Revd Peter Stephens, cutting the first turf. Two older pupils, Rachel Whitehead and Nicholas Stansbury, presented gifts to Mr and Mrs Peter Stephens. The school opened for pupils on 7 September 1976 after a service in St Andrew's Church. The children

processed back to school led by Ronald Isherwood, the headmaster, with head boy, Terry Northam, and head girl, Janet Redden. It was officially opened five weeks later by the Bishop of Exeter on 13 October. All the old school buildings have now been converted into private residences.

Soon after his arrival at Buckland School, Ron Isherwood took the older pupils to London in 1956. Twins Susan and Linda Bragg were amazed at the size of the crown jewels and seeing landmarks, such as Buckingham Palace, that they had only read about in books. Pupils before this time had not travelled far from the village school and television was still a novelty.

Headteachers at the Schools

1675	Richard Bold (Boys only)	1877	William Bacon (Boys)
1690	John Harris		Mary Bacon (Girls)
1711	Stephen Jutsham	1892	William Baker (Boys)
1850	Joseph Palmer		Kate Baker (Girls)
1866	Elizabeth Hext (Girls)	1921	John Swain (combined school)
1869	Nathaniel Hillman (Boys)	1926	S.L. Westcott
1869	Richard Facey (Boys)	1955	Ronald Isherwood
1873	William Wyatt (Boys)	1983	Kevin McIntosh
1874	Jessie Veal (Girls)	1986	Brian Cunningham
		1991	Bill Houldsworth

In 1963 Buckland School became St Andrew's Church of England Aided School. Assistant teacher, Mary Callen, a pupil at the school with Mr Westcott, taught the infants at the school from 1968 to 1994 under the subsequent headmasters. Mary was involved in the many changes in education at national level as well as at St Andrew's School in Buckland Monachorum.

In the summer term of 2002 there was a long waiting-list for pupils wishing to enter the school. Some pupils in the village are transported to other county primary schools as only 30 pupils are taken into each school-year group, thus making 210 pupils on roll. The school was given an excellent OFSTED report in April 2002 and nominated and short-listed for the International School Award. Headteacher, Bill Houldsworth, was one of three finalists for the Public Servant of the Year award in the education section in May 2002. Pupils at the school are given a wide range of opportunities and the Bishop of Exeter opened new facilities on 7 May 2002. The school promotes the international dimension within the school development plan. Staff travel to link countries and work in the schools, living with families and returning with good educational practices that are discussed at St Andrew's School. One motivating factor implemented was the out-of-school day

practised in Norway. Schools in that country realised that pupils had lost touch with the countryside and for one day a week all through the year, whatever the weather, pupils leave the classroom and go into the country. At Buckland the younger classes have one afternoon a week in which they are outside the school building learning about their environment, following the example of Norway. Pupils are encouraged to respect cultural, linguistic and religious diversity in the world. They welcome visitors from other countries and co-operate with partner schools to create and develop more inclusive practices and cultures within the wider community. All pupils are linked with pupils in participating schools under the direction of Mr Houldsworth, Mrs Curtis the deputy headteacher and Mrs Knight, the European co-ordinator. The British Council organises INSET courses that meet to study ways of enhancing the outlook of the school.

Julie Curtis was nominated by various people at the school for the Teacher of the Year Award in 2001 and won the south-west region. Both she and the headteacher have travelled extensively in pursuit of ways to develop the children's learning in the twenty-first century. Bill Houldsworth lived and worked with staff at a primary school in Seoul Guam, South

Left: *Teachers at St Andrew's School in 1976.*

Right: *Rt Revd Eric Mercer, Bishop of Exeter, with pupils in 1976.*

Below: *Mrs Mary Callen with her reception class in the new school.*

Left: *Bill Houldsworth, headteacher of St Andrew's School, sitting on the floor of the link school in Seoul, South Korea.*

Korea, where there are 1,300 pupils. Their technical advancement and cheapness of equipment allows classes of 40 pupils to view large screens connected to closed-circuit television, the Internet and the teacher's desk. The staff at St Andrew's, more than eight teaching members, all have links with participating schools on the Internet. The school is in an isolated community in West Devon so Bill has made a conscious effort to bring the world into his school. The theme of environmental education has developed from their links with Norway, Italy and Portugal. The weather is monitored by pupils of participating schools and e-mailed systematically to all the other schools linked togther. Saplings of ash, alder and oak were planted at the same time and the children in each country maintain a regular surveillance. With teachers and children working together in a three-year plan they have looked at cultural differences. In the first year they studied playground games, in the second they made posters on environmental issues and a school calendar and in the third year they looked at the different customs and recipes from the countries. It is not surprising that St Andrew's School has won many awards. For extra-curricular activities they achieved distinction in 'Education Extra', in sports and the arts the Gold Awards were achieved and they became first in the first round of the Eco School Award in European Standards. Other countries with which the school works are Spain, Germany and Denmark for which the British Council have formed a two-year project. With a school in Egypt they work with both Christian and Moslem communities.

Year Six pupils stay in a youth hostel in Ironbridge in the summer term to study the Industrial Revolution. Year Five pupils stay at Newquay in Cornwall to study minerals and both year groups sail in Plymouth Sound. Year Four go caving and climbing and other pupils make visits appropriate to their studies during the year. The 30 members of staff at the school, parents and governors are rightly proud of the school's achievements. Children are involved with an orchard which they have created with the help of a local resident, Celia Steven, a mile away in a corner of a field near Berrator. With the help of grants and manual work by Groundforce, all the apple trees planted are Tamar Valley varieties. Farmer David Northmore at Balstone provided the land and a stile was made into the field. Protection had to be given to the trees as deer were found to be eating the buds. The first-hand knowledge which the children experience and the enthusiasm and dedication of the staff lay good foundations for the future. There has been 300 years of schooling in Buckland Monachorum and yet only 100 years ago boys and girls were taught separately. What does the future hold for the school and its pupils in the year 2102?

Bill Houldsworth in the entrance hall of the school in 2002.

Cottages are clustered closely together in Milton Combe.

Below: *Nicholas Stansbury stands on the bridge over Milton Brook.*

Left: *The Hearn family at Milton Combe.*

Left: *Church of the Holy Spirit.*

Above: *The First and Last Inn, with Mrs Hearn in the doorway.*

Above left: *Elizabeth Clifton, teacher at Milton Combe School in 1895.*

Left: *The sixteenth-century inn has not altered much.*

Chapter 6

MILTON COMBE

Entering the village of Milton Combe is like arriving in a world of long ago. In a hollow of the hillside in a deep wooded valley, which is a coombe, the cottages cluster together with the Milton Brook flowing down the centre to Lillipit, Lopwell and beyond to the Tavy. Life here was hard 100 years ago and the people were poor. Collecting wood for fires, fetching water from a pump for drinking or from a hillside stream for other uses, throwing refuse into the brook and growing food on any available land was the way of life for the villagers. It was a village for the workers who toiled from dawn to dusk, walking for miles every day. Now it is an idyllic place to live where house prices are high and where there is an active community. The village once had a soap factory, sugar refinery, a mill and a cider press.

Occupations at the end of the nineteenth century, such as labourers, stonemasons, blacksmiths and farm workers, have been replaced at the beginning of the twenty-first century with doctors, pilots, architects and accountants. Milton Combe is keeping pace with the times. Development of buildings was restricted in 1970 when the village became a Conservation Area but the cottages have been modernised. There are about 68 dwellings and single residents live in one third of these. The names of the roads around the village give clues to some of its history – Alley Hill, Lime Road, Church Hill, Watery Lane and Abbey Road. Nearby Buckland Abbey and Maristow estate had provided much employment for villagers for centuries. Families living in the village in the fifteenth and sixteenth centuries were Balhatchet, Dunrich, Foote, Gye, Martyn, Reep, Scoble, Spry and Walter. A century later there were families named Andrew, Burgoyne, Chowen, Collum, Crossman, Goss, Lakeman, Norsworthy, Northmore, Reeve, Pearse, Stockman, Symons, Wallcraft and Westlake with occupations such as thatcher, tanner, mason, blacksmith, carpenter and labourer. In 1850 John White was the miller and owned Milton Hill, John Corber was a farmer, Goss a carpenter, Jutson a tailor and Kinsman the beerhouse keeper. William Lakeman the thatcher was a tenant at Higher Milton, which was owned by George Hunt, and John Hodges mortgaged the same property to Henry Cross in 1878.

The village name derived from 'Mile Cumbe', middle valley, and until 1890 was known as just Milton and is recorded as such in 1546 (in *Place Names of Devon*). John Walter of Milton was presented as tithingman and sworn in for duty in 1602 and in the same year John Scoble, former tenant of a tenement in Milton, died. Later the Buckland Monachorum Court Rolls listed bakers and brewers of ale whom John Walter fined for breaking regulations, and he also took millers to court for over-charging their customers. Henry of Milton and Thomas Drake of Buckland were fined for failing to attend court. Other offences, all written in Latin, were of farmers allowing their rams, ewes and wethers to stray on to Roborough Down. A century ago it boasted an infants' school, an Anglican church, a Wesleyan chapel, two inns, a Post Office and a mill. At the time of writing it has the church and an inn. Services at the church are well-attended, many of the congregation travelling some distance to attend on Sunday mornings.

The one remaining inn, the Who'd Have Thought It, attracts many visitors. Many stories have been put forward for the naming of the inn. One is that it was so named when the innkeeper was heard to exclaim the expression on finding his new home hidden in the bottom of a valley, then called the Welcome Inn. A sweeter name, I suppose, than Well I'll Be Blowed. Another possible reason for the unusual name of the existing pub is that at the end of the nineteenth century both inns were licensed only to sell beer and cider. Both landlords applied for a licence to sell wines and spirits and everyone in the village expected the more popular hostelry, the First and Last, to be given the licence. The licence was given, however, to the Welcome and the crowd of villagers rushed about and yelled in amazement – 'Who'd have thought it?' Whatever the reason, the name attracts visitors to the village and during the Second World War airmen of all nationalities came from Harrowbeer on a regular basis, and still return to their old haunts. The other inn, the First and Last, was home to the Hearn family when it closed and before that to John and Mary Spear who were listed as 'grocer and beershop keeper' in 1891. The beer seller in 1880 was James Beer and his brother, Abraham Beer, was at the Who'd Have Thought It. This inn was probably a seventeenth-century farmhouse with later extensions. In 2002 it serves a large selection of ales and a variety of meals.

Left: *Miss Clifton and her young pupils, c.1895.*

Right: *Milton Combe School with Kathleen Prowse, 1908.*

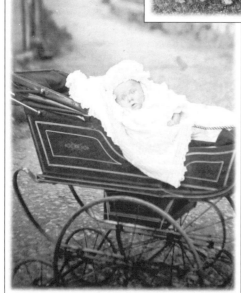

Geoffrey Waldron in 1907, before his family emigrated to Canada. They returned eight years later.

Roy Reynolds, WDCC chairman, opens the Village Hall in 1979 with Mrs Whitmarsh, Tamsyn Blaikie, Margaret Garton and Richard White.

In the census returns of 1891 there are 33 cottages listed, also a private school, Walter's farmhouse (with three generations of Whites living there), a Reading Room and the Old Mill House. The mill was worked here until 1888 when it was converted into a cottage. The mill was used to grind corn for cattle. Living in the school were Susan Arnold the schoolmistress, Emily Davey a teacher and five scholars – Cecilia Terry, Blanche Horswill, Cecilia Teague, Walter Bowers and Bertie Teague, their ages ranging from six to 16 years. There is a record of a school here as early as 1718 when a bequest of Sir Francis Drake (£3.10s.) was given to 'the Infant School at Milton lately established by Lady Drake'. The C of E Infants' School opened in 1893, continued as a church school under the LEA from 1905 and closed 30 years later. Sheepstor School closed in the same year and Milton School, as in Meavy village in 1926, was used as the Village Hall.

The Revd R.J. Hayne visited the school regularly when it first opened and examined the registers when there were 19 pupils under nine years old. The older of these children were taught in a gallery above the classroom. Some were admitted before they were three years old and Mrs Hannah Phillips of Buckland Abbey occasionally granted the children a treat of a half-day holiday. Little May Greep moved up a class in May 1894 'to be among the three-year-olds'. By 1897 the pupils numbered 47 and from 1904 the curate of the parish, Revd E. White, visited the school and saw that it was kept in good repair. The school always had excellent reports from inspectors and both teachers and pupils were highly commended.

Teachers in those 30 years were Georgina Cole (1893), Elizabeth Clifton (who was presented with a rocking-chair by the school managers when she left to marry farmer Spry at Alston Farm in Buckland Monachorum) (1895), Sarah Cobley (1899), Nora Rogers (1900), Alice Stuart-Derdan (1902), Kathleen Prowse (1905), Elsie Woodbury (1909) and Lydia Dingle (1912). Miss Dingle married in September 1915 and wrote in the log-book, 'I have begun my duties again today. My name is now Lydia Howell'. The children believed she had become Mrs Owl but still loved her! It was recorded that the school closed for a week owing to the marriage of the schoolmistress. Mrs Lydia Howell was the last teacher when there were only seven pupils on roll in 1923. She lived at Lindsay Cottage before moving to Plymouth. In her last entry as Miss Dingle she admitted Geoffrey Waldron, aged eight years – 'he has just come across from Saskatoon in Canada'. She recorded many interesting facts in the log-book:

1919 *School did not meet owing to my having a heart attack so that I was unable to come.*
1920 *There was no school this morning as I missed the first train from Plymouth, severe snowstorm.*
1923 *No school session was held this morning owing to my leaving the keys behind in Plymouth.*

The school closed at the end of the Easter term. Little children were taken to Buckland School by pony and trap, some preferring to walk. At the beginning of the next term, in the Buckland School log-book, Mr Swain, the headteacher wrote:

The infants from Milton Combe arrived in a very agitated state. The horse drawing their conveyance behaved so badly that the children got out and walked. At one point the wheels of the conveyance were driven up the bank and the cart almost overturned.

The older children had to walk to Buckland School and received punishment on being late. Alice Bere wrote in 1930 that 'the children are now driven to the top of Buckland Hill'.

Many families from Plymouth slept in the old school in the spring of 1941 when they trekked to the parish to get away from the Blitz. The villagers sought publicity 30 years later when they raised funds to purchase the old school for use as their Village Hall and worked hard to update the facilities. In 1969 the pre-school playgroup used the old building. The new Village Hall was opened in September 1979 and is used for a wide range of village activities. Indoor toilets were added in 1995 and the little stone building has become the centre of the village.

Mrs Hannah Phillips opened a men's Reading Room in 1896. The building had originally been three thatched cottages and had been converted to a chapel by the Plymouth Brethren. She sold it to Lady Drake when she left the area in 1907 for £75. Seven years later Lady Drake rebuilt the room and provided magazines and books for the working men and Mrs Phillips sent parcels for them from Oxfordshire and a clock for the room in 1921. On Lady Drake's death in 1924 she left money in trust for the upkeep of the Reading Room. Although it was demolished in 1972 the trust still provides a small income for the village. Sited as it was at the bottom of Milton Hill it was in a dangerous position. During the war years a WAAF cycling down the hill into the village lost control of her bicycle and crashed into the Reading Room. She died in the accident. A Parish Council notice-board and a memorial stone have replaced it. This granite pillar with the names of seven men who lost their lives in the Second World War inscribed on the top was placed here in 1977.

The hill is very steep and for years the villagers had to walk to the top of the hill to catch the bus. Since 1984, when the 'Dartmoor Pony' began the first regular minibus service to the village, buses have taken passengers down the hill into the village and at the time of writing there are ten buses a day. Two tithe cottages by the quarry on the hill were converted into one house in the early 1950s and called Greencliff, now Abbey Leat. Almost everyone who lives in the village has a car. A new road was built from the top of the hill and a road was closed when South West Water

Above: *The church choir of Milton Combe in 1950.*

Left: *The window of the Church of the Holy Spirit.*

Above: *The beerhouse became the Post Office.*

Far left: *Elizabeth Spurrell outside Victoria Terrace in 1920.*

Left: *Beatrice Grainger, Elizabeth's daughter, in the 1920s.*

Below, left to right: Minnie Grainger, daughter of Beatrice, with Kathleen Isherwood and Ivy Cross.

Left: Len and Fay Grainger's wedding, 5 September 1959.

proposed to build a dam and reservoir in the Milton Brook valley. Work began in 1978 – the road through the woods was constructed and the old road to Lopwell closed in 1982. The Secretary of State for the Environment ordered that the South West Water Milton Brook Reservoir Discharge should come into operation on 21 November 1980 (SX484650). The Milton Brook scheme was to be a buffer for water supplies to the Plymouth area and was designed to enable it to fill and empty very rapidly. The scheme was formulated prior to the privatisation of the water industry and before the completion of the building of strategic reservoirs at Wimbleball, Colliford and Roadford. The water could now be transferred by controlled release via river systems and ultimately into the River Tamar, whence it is pumped to Crownhill from Gunnislake. Hence the scheme was abandoned. Lopwell Dam on the River Tavy attracts many visitors and the artist, Robin Armstrong, records the wildlife here by the dam.

Mrs Hayne, wife of the vicar, laid the foundation-stone for a daughter church of St Andrew's, Buckland Monachorum, in the village in July 1877. She gave the money for the building of the church and funds to be provided for the upkeep in future years. Revd Peter Stephens still received a small amount of money in the 1970s from Mrs Hayne's fund and was amused by the enclosed notes that read, 'for the upkeep of the Holy Spirit at Milton Combe'! The *Tavistock Gazette* recorded the ceremony in 1877:

The corner stone is a fine block of Roborough Down Porphyry. The architect is Mr Ashworth of Exeter and Mr Philip Blowey of Buckland the contractor. A public tea was afterwards held in a meadow kindly lent by Mr Richard Dawe. About 160 sat down.

The building, dedicated to the Holy Spirit, was designed to hold 120 worshippers with a nave, chancel, west porch, bell turret and vestry. The stained glass in the east window depicts Christ's baptism, the coming of the Holy Spirit and two bishops who spread the gospel of Christ in Britain in the fifth century. On 11 August 1878, just a year later, the Bishop of Exeter dedicated the church during the morning service followed by a celebration of Holy Communion. A luncheon afterwards took place in the Great Barn at Buckland Abbey:

The walls were decked with evergreens and the roof with streamers, and at one end was the text in evergreens on a white ground, 'Cast thy bread upon the waters and thou shalt find it after many days'. The vicar was known as labouring at Milton long before this time and many a cottage lecture and crowded congregation had he had there.

A full account of the service and celebrations appeared in the newspaper, which recorded that Mr

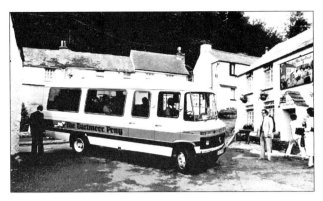

The 'Dartmoor Pony' bus arrived in the village in 1984.

Milton Combe in the 1950s.

The interior of the Church of the Holy Spirit.

Hayne was unable to attend owing to an attack of quinsy, an abscess at the back of the tonsils. The west windows were made to open in 1934 to disperse the plague of flies which 'has been so obnoxious for so many years'. This was not surprising, as the church was so near to the brook, which at that time acted as an open sewer. The centenary of the Church of the Holy Spirit was celebrated on 17 September 1978 with a special evensong. Minnie Grainger has been the organist here for 65 years. The only marriage service took place on 8 July 1995 when a special licence was granted from the Archbishop of Canterbury. A wedding was planned in September 1952 but the couple, Miss Muriel Reed and Mr Godfrey Smallbridge, had to marry in Buckland when they discovered the church was not licensed for marriages. The bride and groom returned to Milton Combe with their guests for the reception. Many gifts and donations of money have contributed to the upkeep of the church for 125 years and Christian worship continues to play an important part in village life.

The first place of worship in Milton Combe was the Wesleyan chapel, built more than 30 years before the Anglican church was founded. Alice Bere recorded that this chapel was the oldest in the parish, 'built before 1842 but inquiry has failed to ascertain the exact date when it was built.' According to the 1851 Church census it was first used in 1845. William Worthy who lived at Coombe Farm was the steward and the number of worshippers in the afternoon was 80 with 20 children attending Sunday school and in the evening there were 91 persons in the congregation. There was no service in the morning. Villagers, as those in Buckland, attended both churches on Sundays after the opening of the Anglican church in 1878 and enjoyed the social life the Methodists offered. Constructed close to the brook the chapel became a private house in 1980.

People who lived in the parish in the middle of the last century remember the socials and dances held in the villages and the music provided on these occasions by Minnie Grainger and Percy Crossman. It was a delight to watch Minnie's fingers skip over the piano keyboard and to dance to the rhythm of Percy's piano accordian. Fanny Williams at Crapstone, who was a cousin to the Brownings at 'Lindisfarne', taught the pianoforte to Minnie and the author. Minnie's maternal grandmother, Elizabeth Spurrell, played the concertina at Milton's entertainments and lived in 1 Victoria Villas. Minnie's mother, Beatrice, moved to No. 3 when she married, where Minnie was born and still lives at the time of writing. As a typist Minnie worked for the Fire Force at Briar Tor during the war and then worked in Plymouth, travelling by bus every day. Her younger brother, Len, who died in 1997, was a driving-force for improvement in the village, being a long-serving Parish Councillor and a school governor of St Andrew's. As an electrician he cared for the lighting in the village as well as the water supply and drainage. Len also oversaw the regularity of the buses. He married Fay, a young lady from Wales, on 5 September 1959.

Memories told by Barbara Beyer, who lived in one of the Drake cottages from 1957 to 1977, give a snapshot of life in the village in the years when modernisation had only just begun to reach Milton. Outside the cottages, only given the name of Drake in her time, was a standpipe that had supplied Milton

people with water from a well at Blowiscombe Farm. Barbara's husband was German and worked at Gnatts Farm. Their neighbours were George and Mabel White. Her husband's day began at 5a.m. and sometimes finished at 6.30p.m., often later. On the road from Lillipit Dick White drove his cows to be milked in the shippon in the village. She recalls the delight of looking over the stable door on the roadside when a calf was born. Fresh milk and cream were delivered daily to the doorstep. Cows made a mess in the road that attracted flies, which entered the houses in summer time. Also the cows ate the garden flowers but the animals were missed when Richard White ceased to milk his cows. Bill Yelland from one of the Lillipit cottages swept and cleaned the road through the village and passed on gossip he heard along the way.

Mr and Mrs Hodgeman ran the Post Office and stores. Barbara remembers bonfire night as being a special occasion in Milton, planned weeks ahead by both adults and children. The phrase used by most folk who lived in all the villages in the mid-twentieth century is, 'pleasures were simple and money was scarce'. Mains sewerage came to the village in 1958 and a heavy rainstorm caused flooding of the brook, especially at the Methodist church that had been built across the brook. This was not pleasant at the time when the contents of the bucket lavatories were thrown into the brook, which flowed through the village. Barbara was amazed when Maurice Harvey delivered her vegetables one year on Christmas Eve, walking from the top of the hill because of icy conditions. Doors in the village were never locked and children played outside all day long, which included catching mullet at Lopwell. Cottagers grew vegetables, some kept pigs and everyone borrowed from one another. Two district nurses lived at Sanguines, Miss Pye and Miss Evans, and the Pearce family lived in Lillipit Farm. Donald Field was running the Post Office from a converted garage in 1991 when two masked armed-raiders burst into his store demanding money. The men ran off when he called for help but were later captured and sentenced to four years' imprisonment.

In *Kelly's Directory* of 1883 Abraham Beer is the beer retailer, an appropriate name, Richard Reed Dawe a farmer, William Lakeman a thatcher, and Thomas Netten a blacksmith, with Thomas Reed at Bloiscombe and Miss Browne at The Glen. In 1902 John Hearn was running a second public house, Thomas Davey, Isaac Healey and John White were farmers and Thomas Dockett had opened a Post Office. Letters arrived at the Post Office at 7.55a.m. and 5.30p.m. Thomas Dockett was also a farmer until it is recorded that Louisa Dockett, his widow, was sub-postmistress in 1923. Joseph Creber ran the stores by this time with another shop being opened by Mary Reddicliffe in 1935. The end of the Post Office and shop came in 1992 but from October 1999 a mobile Post Office has visited the village weekly as it does in Clearbrook, where there is also neither Post Office nor shop.

The First and Last beerhouse became the shop and Post Office until 1986. The only inn – the Who'd Have Thought It – attracts many visitors with its charm and character. The village has been called one of the prettiest in Devon in recent years, which is a credit to its inhabitants. Residents commute to Plymouth daily but community spirit remains high. The roads are narrow and cottages built close together with the brook flowing in a southerly direction until its confluence with Bickham Brook when the enlarged Milton Brook turns westwards to Lopwell and the River Tavy. The Milton Brook Reservoir Scheme that never happened altered the small settlements of Lillipit and Lopwell. Bickham Brook forms the southern boundary on the west side of the parish from the lodge near the A386 and its junction with Common Lane. The brook divides the parish from the parish of Bickleigh. Maristow House is private property and lies within Bickleigh Parish.

There are now three houses in Lillipit where there was a farm and five cottages in the twentieth century. The Water Board demolished Lillipit Farm after they purchased it from the Maristow estate. Cottages in the wood were reached by crossing a wooden plank placed across the Bickham Brook; these too were knocked down for the aborted reservoir scheme. Lillipit Cottage, once tiny and primitive with no amenities, was sold by Maristow estate to owners who renovated and cared for the house and garden. Paddy and Jane Ashdown of Lib-Dem fame made their home here before he became a politician and a Dutch artist lived in the cottage until his death in the 1990s.

Lopwell, listed in 1291 as la Lobbapilla, lies at the south-western tip of the parish, within the Tamar Valley Area of Outstanding Natural Beauty. Samuel Rowe, writing in 1821, recorded that:

At Lophill the navigation of the Tavy ceases and having disembarked we shall proceed to Bickham, the seat of Sir William Elford, Bart. The grounds adjoin Roborough Down, from which there is an entrance with a pretty rustic lodge. Leaving Bickham, our route will be directed to the romantic and secluded village of Milton, completely hidden from observation in a deep valley. By the lane that follows the course of a brawling brook, we shall pursue our tour to Buckland Abbey, one of the seats of Major T.F.E. Drake.

The River Tavy is tidal up to Lopwell Dam, built in 1953 by Plymouth City Council, and joins the River Tamar not far below this point. At Lopwell there is opportunity for many leisure pursuits – bird watching, walking along the West Devon Way and cycling on the Plym Valley Cycle Way and Peninsula Cycle Route. As well as woodland birds observed above the steep slopes across the river, the kingfisher, little egret and common and green sandpipers are frequent visitors. Wild flowers, grasses, trees, insects, birds and animals are in abundance. Lopwell Dam across the River Tavy powers a hydroelectric station. A barn near the river bank has been converted for camping facilities and accommodates groups and individuals as part of a network of barns across Dartmoor, Exmoor and Tarka Country.

Two cottages had once been Lopwell Mill and the miller's cottage in the nineteenth century, the last miller being Alexander Hamlyn. The mill ceased to work in 1872 and it was made into a house. The Titball family with six sons lived in the mill house in the early-twentieth century and the boys had a long walk to Milton School when they were young and an even longer walk to Buckland Monachorum when they reached the age of eight years. It was an idyllic lifestyle for the boys, their play places being the fields and the river. Demolition of the cottages in 1979, because of the Milton Brook Reservoir Scheme which never was, ended an era that is lost forever. The toil of men, women and children creating a way of life with nature in all its seasons, below the steep woods in this once quiet valley, will never return.

Pleasure steamers once called at Lopwell and many parish outings departed from here. Steamer excursions for the churchwardens of the Church of the Holy Spirit and Buckland Monachorum Parish Church left Lopwell in the early 1900s in the *Prince Edward*. Children walked to Lopwell from Buckland for the Sunday-school outings before the First World War each summer, dressed in their best clothes and straw hats. Great fun was had all day on the steamer to Calstock or Weir Head and these excursions were the highlight of the year. The long walk home through the lanes in the dark was part of the fun. The mining of silver and lead dates from the thirteenth century and a mill ceased working in 1872 from which the millstone set in the wall of the car park was taken. H.G. Dines records that Lopwell Mine 'has an adit and two shafts on the steep western valley slope 1,000yds N by W of Maristow House.' This old silver-lead mine worked on the north to south lodes. A ferry operated at Lopwell until about 1930 and lime was brought down the Tavy before the dam was built. Maristow Quay downriver in Bickleigh Parish was first recorded in 1294. Alice Bere describes the Misses Buller driving down to Lopwell in the year 1830 at the beginning of their holiday to France in wet weather: 'They caught a boat from Bere to Saltash and had to dry their clothes in a limekiln before sailing to France.'

The South West Lakes Trust plan to use the old pump house on the banks of the Tavy for wildlife arts and an education centre. Invited guests and nearby residents were shown plans for the future development of the area in March 2002 where this independent charity is to provide opportunities for recreation, easy access and nature conservation at the upper tidal mark on the river. Built at the same time

Above: *Lillipit farmhouse before demolition.*

Below: *Robin Armstrong at his Lopwell studio.*

Above: *Milton Combe Football Club, 1955. Left to right, back row: Robin Madge, Peter Hocking, Len Grainger, Cliff Stansbury, Ernie Pike, John Stacey, Roy Northam, Tom Prior; front row: Den Crossman, Les Pike, Gordon Stansbury, Ian Bellan, George Gidley, Vic Neno.*

Left: *South West Water alter the valley of the Milton Brook.*

Below left: *Tamsyn Blaikie, the author and Mr and Mrs Leonard Hurrell at Lopwell, 2002. Leonard Hurrell gave a legacy from an aunt to assist the South West Lakes Trust plans for the area.*

Below: *Western Isle at Lopwell, 1930s.*

Right: *Lopwell.*

Above: *Jimmy Saville visits Milton Combe to present a cheque for the Village Hall after a slimming event.*

Above: *Milton Moobells, 1977.*

Left: *Easter Parade in the village on Easter Monday.*

as the dam and still containing old machinery, the building is redundant and the Trust is enhancing the site for visitors to view the river birds and animals from the windows. It is so close to the water that the Trust hopes to install a telescope and a webcam so visitors can watch otters, seals, birds and butterflies. On that March day sandpipers, swans, geese, ducks and buzzards flying overhead were observed preparing to make their homes in this beautiful spot. Fishermen were standing on the banks and in the water and walkers were crossing the river along the public highway beside the dam. This is negotiable at low tide. Stella Shaw remembers crossing the river with her children to pick primroses in the 1950s, unaware that the tide had come up making the crossing back impossible. Her husband, coming to look for them, himself an employee of the Water Board, took the boat across to fetch them only to find that the boat had sprung a leak. Ferrying one passenger at a time he was able to rescue his family. People living on the other side of the river left their vehicles at Lopwell to save the long journey to Plymouth by the only bridge at Denham, and moored their boats near the pump house.

A local artist and author, Robin Armstrong, leases a converted barn a few feet from the water's edge of the Tavy. Formerly working and exhibiting at The Garden House, Robin's studio is an amazing window on to life in and around the river. Naming it the Kingfisher Studio, the artist works here, painting and moulding the wildlife he observes. Samuel Rowe, writing in 1821, records the 'Bere Alston lead and silver mines' and the 'shelter to numerous tribes of water birds above which orchards of apples and cherries are interspersed with corn fields and pastures' as he follows the course of the Tavy.

John Stansbury, born in the village in 1902, lived in Milton all his life. He remembered milking the cow at the Rock Hotel before school and delivering bottles of whisky at 4s. a bottle to customers in large houses. Mrs Jane Brown, 80 years of age, was the midwife when John was born. She lived at the Gift House in Buckland and was the woman who attended village births at the turn of the century before nurses came to the district. John, the father of Clifford and Gordon, worked at Blowiscombe Farm, which locals pronounce Bloscombe, and carried farm butter each day to the pub in Milton or to the schoolmaster at Buckland. His father visited the First and Last where he bought beer at 2d. a pint. Sanguines was then the Post Office. The village road in the 1920s passed between fruit gardens grown on the steep hillsides all the way to Lopwell. The valley was filled with strawberries, raspberries and currants in the summer months and the women of the village picked the fruit to earn money.

Mr Stansbury bought a pony and jingle and took his wife and children every week to the Palace Theatre in Plymouth. His favourites were Harry Lauder, 'Laird of the Music Hall', a Scottish singer and comedian in his kilt carrying a crooked, knobbly stick; Will Fife, George Robey and two sisters, Elsie and Doris Walters. Lady Drake gave permission for the villagers to take wood from her woods for burning provided they were able to carry the fuel home by hand, a way to make sure people were not greedy. Working people walked great distances. In the 1920s Mr Stansbury's wife walked from Lovecombe to Stoke and back in a day to visit a relation. 'Time didn't count then. Gid 'ome. Us went to bed early, there was nought else to do.' As a boy growing up in the village he recalled pranks the boys played on the adults. Tying door latches together, ringing the doorbells and watching from a safe

Lopwell millstone in the wall of the car park.

distance as both cottagers tried to open their doors; pretending to push the baker's car up Milton Hill and being rewarded with a bag of buns. The boys were spanked by anyone in the village and if they told mother they had another beating.

The White family has lived in Milton Combe for generations. Richard James White, born in 1932, has been part of the community life for 70 years. His parents, Richard Francis (Dick) and Margaret (née Stansbury), were born in the nineteenth century and Richard is able to trace his family back seven generations to John White (1687–1772). Descendant John White, yeoman of the parish in 1856, was granted the tenement of Walters and the fields and orchard of Hams. This became Hams and Waters. Dick White was appointed as a member of the Devon Special Constabulary, as was his son, Richard. From a young age Richard helped his father who was both a farmer in the village and a local builder. He remembers Lady Seaton as an old lady tapping him on the backside with her walking stick as he stood by the side of his father, for not touching his forelock to her. Richard remembers a searchlight at the top of Milton Hill in the field over the stile, Oxen Park, in the 1940s. One dark night the sentry heard footsteps and called out three times, 'Halt, who goes there?' When no one replied and the steps grew louder the sentry fired, only to find that he had shot and killed Dick Hamley's mare from Place Barton Farm.

Dick White built Gnatts Farmhouse at the top of the hill, completed much renovation work on ancient buildings at the abbey and built the Roman Catholic church at Yelverton. His family's farm was Home Farm in the village and for years they milked the cows and delivered fresh milk to all the houses. Between 60 and 70 pints were sold each day and about 1,000 pigs were kept at Gnatts Farm. Dick White rebuilt Gate Cottage, moving it from the Cider House garden near the River Tavy to where it is at the time of writing, near the top of Winsbeer Lane. Each stone was numbered

for the rebuilding of the house. The Drake family spent most of the year at Nutwell Court near Exeter and Dick White transferred the silverware between the houses. Lady Drake's car was probably the first seen in Buckland Monachorum village in about 1912. In 1981 Richard showed potential buyers around the different lots of the abbey estate when Mrs Rodd placed it in the hands of her agent. Richard built the old millstones into the wall of his sister Doris's house, Briardene. He has been a member of the Parish Council for many years and chairman for some of those years. His performances in Buckland dramatics have been memorable and he is currently the Dame in the Milton Combe pantomimes. He married Jill Parnell from the village in the 1950s and fostered two boys and adopted a baby girl. Jill died suddenly at the age of 47 years in 1981. Richard is well known and liked throughout the parish.

Milton Combe community has organised fun get-togethers for many years and donated funds to local charities. In 1991 the Milton Combe Horse and Dog Show received 400 entries and profits were given to the Plymouth and District Leukaemia Fund as well as to local charities. Events such as the annual Easter parade, duck race, brook race, minithon (run over six miles to Maristow), barbecues, barn dances and sports events raise money for the village and various charities throughout the year. The Jill White Cup is presented annually to the villager who makes the most outstanding contribution to the community. The successful Judo Club meets in the Village Hall each week and members take part in inter-club competitions in England and France.

It may be the place to live in the twenty-first century for town folk who want to live in the country, but there are families who have always lived and worked in the area. There are those who came over 40 years ago and stayed, such as Ivy Cross at Cuckoo Cottage. I have heard that newcomers call the village Milton Com-by.

Left: *Sarah and James Warne, c.1900.*

Above: *Charles Pearce Brown lived in Challoch.*

Left: *Aerial photograph of Crapstone, 1944.*

Below: *Harvey, the butchers, in 1992.*

Above: *Mr and Mrs Brown of Challoch with their children, Lawrence, Philip and Phoebe.*

Left: *Crapstone, 1912.*

Chapter 7

CRAPSTONE

Crapstone, a settlement of houses between Buckland village and Yelverton, came into being at the end of the nineteenth century. The meaning of the name is derived from the fields on which the first building took place, belonging to Crapstone Barton. Crap in the Devonshire dialect means crop, hence a crop of stones, and when the Barton was built in the sixteenth century it could have been very stony ground as Peter Barons confirms it is still today. In the *Kelly's Directory* of 1878 the area is listed as Crapstown. The land was part of the Buckland Abbey estate granted to Richard Crymes in 1546 who set up his manor house, Crapstone Barton, on the hill above the village of Buckland Monachorum. The Crymes family sold much of their land and in the seventeenth century married into the Drake family. In 1784 Revd Amos Crymes, living in the old vicarage, sold land to the Elfords and Crapstone Barton became a farmhouse. It is surprising to discover that General Bramwell Booth, son of William Booth who founded the Salvation Army, bought a house called 'Crapstone' in Southwold, Suffolk in 1913. There may be no connection with our hamlet but the name is unusual. Young people use a coarse schoolboy slang name for this growing settlement on the edge of beautiful Dartmoor.

George Leach who married Jenny Elford had Crapstone House built for himself south of the farmhouse. Lady Seaton at Buckland Abbey bought back much of the original abbey lands in the early part of the twentieth century so that Crapstone estate became Buckland Abbey estate after nearly four centuries.

The first houses built in the 1880s were in Crapstone Terrace, as well as the house still called The Firs. Development of the area grew from that time with the building of more terraces and large detached houses. Thomas and Elizabeth Dockett, he a carpenter and she taking in lodgers, lived in Crapstone in 1873. Other family members were carpenters in Buckland Monachorum. The Warne brothers built Crapstone Villas and one of the sons, Joseph Warne, lived in No. 3 in 1902. His brother and sister-in-law, James and Sarah, lived in the Post Office with their five-year-old son, Francis. They ran the Post Office and shop but James was looking for mining work in South Africa when Sarah collapsed

and died during a miscarriage with a second baby at the shop. After her death James emigrated to South Africa and remarried. He was a mine agent like his father before him. Sarah's father had been a blacksmith at Yelverton. Sarah and James are buried together in the cemetery on the right of the path, the tombstone dated 1902 and 1918.

When the Warne family left Crapstone Post Office Mrs Jane Stone took it over, followed by John Stone in 1914 and Leonard Stone in 1919 who stayed there until the 1940s. The telephone number was Yelverton 52. Miss Crook and her brother, Lewis, took the business over in the 1950s and their sister, Mrs Prideaux helped them out. Following Miss Crook the owners of the shop and Post Office have been Blanchard, Townsend, Carrivick and, from 1986 to the present time, Mark and Jenny Bruton. It is a well-patronised shop and popular in the area.

Those listed as living in Crapstone in 1891 are Mary Foster with her family at The Firs, and in Crapstone Terrace were the families of Nicholson, Bryant, Parsons, Moor, Cumming, Evans, Steer, Miss Northmore and Miss Morrish. John Bolt lived at 1 Crapstone Villas and Richard Evans moved to The Firs in 1893. Evans' son, James, is listed as aged 21 and 'keeper of cricket ground'. Jane Stone ran the Post Office and shop from 1902 after the death of Sarah Warne. It is interesting to record those living in Crapstone in 1906:

Mrs Brewer, 1 Crapstone Villas
Oscar Browning, Lindisfarne
Alfred Collier, poultry breeder
John Cumming, 3 Crapstone Terrace
Richard Evans, The Firs
Mrs Godfrey, The Lodge
Thomas Harris, Leigh Holt
John Osborne, Myrobella
Albert Steer, Eton Cottage
Mrs Stone, shopkeeper and Post Office
Revd Edward James White BA, Victoria Villa

The terrace of houses called Woodside was probably built in the early 1900s. Access to Woodside and the green in front of the houses at one time belonged to the Maristow estate. As in Clearbrook, owners had to pay for the privilege of entering their own gates

Woodside Terrace, early 1900s.

Above: *At Crapstone cricket ground, c.1890.*

Above right: *Oscar Browning and his sister, Rhoda, at Lindisfarne, 1957.*

Above: *Mr and Mrs Oscar Browning at Lindisfarne.*

Crapstone Post Office, c.1905.

from the time the houses were built. From 1917 to 1922 Challoch and Melrose were used for the Convent of Poor Clares, with Revd Mother Abbess. Following this time John Adams Brown was living in Challoch. Miss Alice J. Bere, who wrote the book on Buckland Monachorum for the Women's Institute that was published in 1930, lived in 2 Woodside. Headteachers at Buckland School, Mr and Mrs Baker, lived in Paxcot.

In the 1920s there were about 80 houses in the hamlet with an average of two houses being built each year. Newtake Lane, the road between Crapstone and Buckland, was constructed in 1891 and the sharp corner at the junction of Pound Road became Newtake Corner, corrupted to Newdy Corner over the years. The road known as The Crescent at the time of writing was originally North Road but during much of the twentieth century it was unofficially called Harley Street because of the number of medical doctors who lived in the large houses in the road. The track known as The Glade in 2002 was originally a footpath linking the roads and the houses, and gardens built along here were the allotments belonging to Lindisfarne.

Lindisfarne was a large house with beautiful gardens, home of the Browning family. Mr and Mrs Oscar Browning had four children; Oscar, Rhoda, Elsie and Muriel. They opened their gardens to the church for fêtes and Sunday-school parties. Crapstone was the area where families lived in large houses compared with the small cottages in Buckland village. The Brownings owned shoe shops in Plymouth and travelled to Yelverton Station by horse and carriage and then by train to the town. In a stable of one of the houses in The Crescent, the timetable of the trains at Yelverton Station can still be seen, carved on a beam. Elsie Browning married William Beer from the village, which was not approved of by her parents. She played the church organ and he was in the village band. He was the school's attendance officer, known by everyone in all the villages as the kid-catcher, and Elsie was 40 years of age when she married him at St Andrew's. Billy lived in Butt Park with his deaf sister, Polly, who cleaned the church. Elsie involved the village children in dramatic productions and sewing classes in her home in Crapstone from about 1915 and was well loved by the children. She and Billy built a bungalow in Crapstone and later moved to a house in The Crescent. The new curate at Buckland Monachorum in 1904, Revd E.J. White and his wife, bought 3 Victoria Villas and their three children, Letitia, Camilla and Clement, were born there. They became great friends with the Browning family at Lindisfarne. Muriel Browning opened a small private school for young children at Lindisfarne for those whose parents did not wish their children to mix with pupils at the village school. During 1916 the Crapstone residents opened a War Savings Certificate Association, raised much money and sent parcels to prisoners of war. Families at Crapstone during this war cared for Belgian refugees.

The parish memorial stone set up to remember those who lost their lives from 1914 to 1918 was placed at the crossroads in Crapstone. Sir Henry Lopes unveiled it in 1921 and 36 names were recorded. At the ceremony he stated that 297 men from the parish served with the Forces. The vicar of Buckland, Revd E.F. Chamberlin, and chairman of the war memorial committee formally handed over the memorial to Mr S. Edgcumbe, chairman of the Parish Council, for its 'safe keeping and custody in the years to come'. The past curate, Edward White who was then vicar of Broadwoodkelly, was among the clergy of all denominations taking part in the service held on that day. The architect of the memorial was Mr Stallybrass. The inscription reads:

To the glory of God and in honour of the men of Buckland parish who died in the Great War 1914–1919. Live thou for England, we for England died.
Major R.M. Adams, Gnr J. Baggaley, Capt D.H. Bellamy, Sergt W.J. Bennett, Mech A.J. Crapper-Bovey RN, 2/Lt A. Brown, Drv A.A. Cannon, Lieut H.F. Clark, Sto 1/C1 S. Crocker RN, Sto 1/C1 C.H. Crossman RN, Cpl W.J.B. Crossman, Lieut H. Evans, Lieut H.M. Goldsmith, Pte B.W. Halls, Mid M.A. Harris RN, Lieut H.V. Hawarth, Pte M. McAssey, 2/Lt J.V. Moore, Ld Sn H.J. Palmer RN, AB A.C. Parnall RN, Pte H.A. Parnall, Mid R. Percy RN, Sto 1/C1 J.S. Prior RN, 2/Lt C.B. Rodd, Lieut L.H. Rolston, Pte W.H. Rowe, Capt W.G. Sansom, Pte C. Southcott, Capt C.N. Spooner, Pte A. Walton, Pte H. Waye, Pte F. Weeks, Pte R.G. Willcocks, Gnr J.R. Wilson, L Cpl L.J. Wyatt.
In Glory everlasting make them to be numbered with thy saints 1939–1945.
Sto S. Budge RN, Sto M. Burke RN, Dvr W.B. Chamming, Pte W.B. Cook, Pte R.J. Down, Che A.A.A. Edney RN, Capt H.S. Emerson, Lieut H.K. Epson, Pte D. Harry, Pte C.P.C. Haycroft, Sto C. Hearne RN, S/Sgt R.T. Hicks, Capt E.W.H. Blake RN, Pte R. Lowden, Sto 1/C1 S.A.J. Maben RN, RD, Adml R.A.A. Plowden RN, Civl Def H.C.R. Rendle, Sto G. Nailard RN, Comdr T.M. Napier RN, Pay Comdr D.C.R. Roe RN, Lieut R.G. Sedgwick RN, Sto J. Northy RN, Capt G.S. Pitts RN, Lieut J.R.B. Conry, Lieut J.M. Shawyer, Cpl G.R. Steer and R.J. Weeks RAF.

At the beginning of 1939 there were established businesses in the main road: Dennis Harvey, butcher; R.H. Maben, builder; Cecil Prideaux, garage repairs; Leonard Stone, Post Office and stores; and E.L. Tregeagle, motor car garage. The Ministry of Defence acquired land off Abbey Road and the NAAFI for airmen at the nearby Harrowbeer airfield was built here along with other air ministry buildings.

Left: *Revd Edward and Mrs Bertha White with Letitia at 3 Victoria Villas in 1905.*

Below: *A group in a garden at Crapstone, 1890.*

The war memorial, erected in 1921 without the present surrounding chains.

Above: *The White family outside Victoria Villas.*

Above left: *Clement White and friends with hand-bells at Lindisfarne.*

One building was used for film shows at the start of the war and if there was enough space the people of Crapstone were invited. Crapstone inhabitants often queued for an hour in the rain to see a film, sitting in their wet clothes all evening. Rita Kennedy (née Walser), now living on the Isle of Wight but used to live with her family at 2 Grimstone Terrace, recalls seeing the film 'The Song of Bernadette' with friends Pat Coaker and Ann Twining, and crying and sobbing over the film all the way home. Jennifer Jones, the star of the film, made a great impact on Rita. Another building was a gymnasium which the local residents were invited to use, and another a chapel where parishioners joined the airmen at Evensong. The late Fernley Palmer remembered that the Royal Ulster Rifles Regiment used the football field, given by Lady Seaton in 1920, when they were stationed at Harrowbeer. They were billeted at Pound and marched to Crapstone in their uniforms with yellow kilts playing music in a band of bagpipes and drums and marched up and down the football pitch before matches. Fernley also told how he collected paper and cardboard to help the war effort. Taking his trolley full of paper to the RAF collection point as a young lad, the airmen exchanged it for empty lemonade bottles that they had amassed from the many billets around the airfield. Fernley traded in these for pennies at the village shop.

Mrs Walser delivered the post in the Meavy area and daughter, Rita, delivered telegrams when they arrived in Buckland Monachorum Parish. Rita was paid 6d. to take a telegram to Buckland, 9d. to Milton Combe and 1s.6d. to Double Waters. Telephones were only installed in larger homes so an urgent message was sent by telephone to the Post Office and conveyed to the recipient by a messenger. Rita's journey to Double Waters and back on the family bicycle if it was available took her all day. She did not receive immense thanks from Mrs Oxenford at Tavy Cottage for her effort. Rita recalls the Prideaux family who lived in 2 Crapstone Terrace. Cecil Prideaux ran the garage and taxi business and Mrs Prideaux helped her sister, Miss Crook, to run the Post Office. In the 1940s they built the first house for many years in Crapstone, now called Linden Lea. The family, with four children, emigrated to New Zealand.

Robert Maben had a timber yard and sawmills and opened a shop on the road opposite the Post Office in which he sold building and household materials. He purchased a field in 1946 where the building firm stored materials disposed of by the RAF. Dartmoor Caravan Park opened in this field in 1988. Kevin Wigens opened the Yelverton Golf Driving Range in Abbey Lane in 1995. It has 20 bays, an indoor putting green and has the longest range in the area.

The road from Pound Lodge to the memorial and top of Stokehill Lane was constructed at the end of the nineteenth century and the back road of Crapstone, now The Crescent, was constructed in 1910. There were no roads to Yelverton, only paths across the moor, until the old Crapstone road was constructed around the aerodrome to avoid the runways. Crapstone men helped to build the aerodrome and it was completed in record time. In the hot summer of 1921 wells in Crapstone and on the farms went dry, but it wasn't until 1925 that water from Burrator Reservoir was brought to the village. The house Blue Haze near the war memorial, originally built in 1930, was taken down because of the airfield and was rebuilt again after the war. There is an air-raid shelter in the garden. Malcolm and Molly Spooner lived in the house next to Blue Haze, Five Oaks, for many years. They were Devon naturalists and experts in all wildlife, Malcolm reporting for the Devonshire Association. Molly, who died in 1998, painted in watercolours and her paintings of West Devon are very much valued today. The area above the war memorial and Crescent became infested with Japanese Knotweed (*Reynoutria japonica*) in 1990 and an effort has been made by the Parish Council to eradicate it, with some success.

Knighton was built by the Becklys at Newdy Corner on glebe land in 1935. A 6-acre field was attached and Edwin Beckly rented 16 acres of grassland from the Pound estate. Then came the war years and the slogan, 'Every available piece of land must be cultivated. Grow your own food, supply your own cookhouse'. The family was compelled to grow potatoes, favourites being Sharp's Express and Arran Banner, for the war effort. Edwin and Irene's daughter, Jean, young at the time, helped to plough five fields as well as caring for two ponies and a herd of cows and bullocks. The fields were called Front Field, Freezabere, Steep Field, Little Field and Marsh. Edwin Beckly ran the business store of John Yeo in Plymouth – he was a Yeo descendant and sold the store to Debenhams in 1961, as well as farming the 22 acres at Crapstone. Jean (1925–2001) enjoyed working on the land and wrote of her wartime reminiscences in *Digging for Victory*. The family were strict Methodists and much involved with the Rock Chapel at Yelverton. Being strict teetotallers they only allowed cold tea to be drunk by men from Buckland and Crapstone when they helped with the haymaking in the summer. Ginger Toop and William Friend were the main workers for the Becklys. Days were long and work was hard with very few mechanical implements. Horses for pulling machinery were borrowed from Blowey at Pound Farm and Harris at Didham. Derek Harris was helpful to Jean as she learned the intricacies of farming. A searchlight was set up and run by the airmen during the war in the field opposite Knighton. In the daytime the crew helped on the farm with the heavy jobs. Mr Solway across the road kept horses and lent them for use on the farm. People helped each other out in the war years and Jean Beckly used her John Deere tractor, the first tractor in the parish, to plough fields for

The parish memorial at Crapstone.

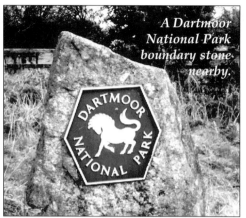

A Dartmoor National Park boundary stone nearby.

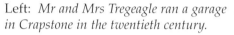

Left: *Mr and Mrs Tregeagle ran a garage in Crapstone in the twentieth century.*

Below: *Buckland Parish cricket team in the 1920s with Major Bundock (centre), Billy Beer (on left), Jim Fox, Norman Parker and Dick Seccombe.*

Bottom left: *At the cricket pavilion, early 1900s.*

Bottom right: *Miss Frances Bundock opens the cricket pavilion.*

other farmers. Jean's brother, David, was born 15 years after her and loved to be outside with her. She married David Trahair in Buckland Church in 1949. They lived in Yeoland House and had four children; Lynda, Richard, Stephen and Jonathan. Contributing much to life in the parish their service to St Andrew's was generous.

Two groups of prefabricated huts were put up in 1942 to house the families of the RAF. After the war local people and families from Plymouth lived in them for several years and were sad to leave when they were offered better housing accommodation. The huts in Stokehill Lane were put up for the Canadian, French and British Airforces. Others were in a Pound field near the end of the terraced houses. The children went to Buckland School and men and women sought work from the large householders and landowners in the parish. After the war council-houses were built on the top of Buckland Hill and many families were housed there. West Devon County Council invited tenders to demolish the huts at Pound Field and four sites at Stokehill Lane in May 1961. Employment was also found at Greenlane Nurseries where the gardens were well-kept and plants and shrubs sold to a wide area and the many farms including those in Crapstone, Stokehill, Venton, Axtown, Whistleigh, Hellingtown, Coombe, Uphill and Yeoland. Families in large houses needed help in the house and many of the houses were run as guesthouses.

Windy Ridge was originally built in 1891 and a summerhouse was added later by Norman White. Maurice Harvey bought the house and converted the summerhouse into a shop in 1957. Susan Woolacott and her husband bought the house and shop and Susan opened the hairdressing salon in 1971. She was widowed the following year and her daughter, Emma, was born soon after. The clients helped Susan to care for Emma as she kept hair appointments and the baby thrived. Emma eventually became a young assistant at the salon. Susan had a flat built over the shop in 1976.

Dennis Harvey opened his butcher's shop in the 1930s and his brother, Maurice, bought a lorry and ran a travelling greengrocery. When the Pound huts were vacated Maurice stored his fruit and vegetables in the first hut until he bought the shop. His son, Terry, helped Maurice in the 1960s and they visited all the villages in the Yelverton area until 1971 in their large van. After the death of Dennis, Maurice took over the butcher's shop where he added his green-grocery business. William, Dennis and Maurice Harvey were Roman Catholics and before the opening of Holy Cross Church at Yelverton the family walked to Tavistock to hear Mass. When nuns arrived in Crapstone in 1917 the long walks to Mass were at an end. Challoch was for the nuns and the house next door, Melrose, was the chapel, open to the small Catholic community of Yelverton. It was

known as St Anthony's Convent, Crapstone. A testimonial written for the nuns by a monk from Buckfast Abbey at their departure from Crapstone in 1922 states, 'A remarkable change of attitude towards the Catholic religion has been noticed among our non-Catholic neighbours.'

Many evacuees arrived in Crapstone from Plymouth during the war and families were housed in the huts. A Red Cross hut was erected in the lane next to the football field lane and following its closure the Goff family lived here when Mr Goff was the organist of St Andrew's Church. Next door to this hut the Brownings built Dellcote, a bungalow where Elizabeth and William Ball have lived for nearly 60 years. Their two families, Kellaway and Ball, were very involved in village and parish life from the beginning of the twentieth century. Elizabeth is the youngest child of the Kellaway family and was born in Rose Cottage. William's father was a builder. His mother, always known as Granny Ball, was a member of the Mothers' Union at Buckland for more than 50 years. Elizabeth and William attended Buckland School together and celebrated their diamond-wedding anniversary in September 1999 at Dellcote with a new-style card personally signed by Her Majesty the Queen. They were married in Buckland Church in 1939 and William joined the Royal Horse Guards for the duration of the Second World War. Elizabeth stayed in London at first but moved back to Buckland Monachorum when William was sent away. She became cook at the school until William returned and they moved to Crapstone, returning as cook after the birth of her two children.

Next to Dellcote is a bungalow, which was given to Fred and Gwen Coaker by Bishop and Mrs Daukes when they lived at Linkincorn. Their daughter, Pat Coaker, and her husband, Roy, built a bungalow in the garden where they still live at the time of writing. Fred had been both gardener and chauffeur to the Bishop of Plymouth who at the time lived in the Crapstone House opposite Woodside. Rt Revd Daukes was both bishop and archdeacon. One of the first houses to be built, The Firs, was run as a nursing home by Abbeyfield and when the elderly residents moved to Pilcher's Field in The Crescent the house was bought by the Lakeman family, who had previously lived in Buckland village as well as at Fredicott. Joy Lakeman wrote the book *Them Days* from the audio-tape recordings she made with the author's mother, Joan Bellan, in 1978 when the family lived next door to her at Rose Cottage. The book was published in 1982 and included drawings by Robin Armstrong. Joy and Geoff have three sons who are musicians. The Lakeman brothers, Sam, Sean and Seth, formed their own band after playing with Joy who played the violin and their father, Geoff, who played the concertina. The boys met up with two girls on the folk-music circuit and together they formed the band 'Equation'. They were signed up by

Jean Beckly raking in hay, 1944.

Jean Trahair with her children, Lynda and Richard, in pannier baskets on the family pony outside the Post Office.

Above: *Jean Beckly marries David Trahair at St Andrew's Church in 1949.*

Above: *Jean and David Trahair at Yeoland with Stephen, Lynda, Jonathan and Richard.*

Below: *Grimstone Terrace.*

Elizabeth Ball (née Kellaway) at Dellcote, 2002.

Left: *Children at Crapstone in 1944. Left to right, back row: David Farmer, Fernley Palmer, Rita and Kitty Walser; front row: John Prideaux, ?, Gillian Waldron, David Curno, Mavis Edgecombe.*

Below: *Houses at the junction of Abbey Lane in the twentieth century.*

Above: *Mark and Jenny Bruton in the doorway of the Post Office and Stores in 2002.*

The garden at Lark Rise at the top of the sports-field lane.

David and Jenny Miles in their garden at Lark Rise.

Warner and recorded their first album. With the money they built a sound studio in The Firs and have performed all over the world.

The author took piano lessons with Fanny Williams at Sunny Waters in The Crescent and walked home to Arranmore from there on dark winter nights after school, from the age of seven years. In later years as a musician she recalls those days in Crapstone when Fanny Williams cleaned her spectacles with her petticoat, sucked her pencil noisily and held the lid of the keyboard over her fingers to teach her to play fluently without looking at the keys. The Crescent had few houses in those days and there were fields with ponies and farm animals where now there are houses and cars.

The Ministry of Defence owned eight acres of land in Crapstone that they had used as a Naval Store Depot. The Parish Council negotiated with the MOD for five years before the purchase of half the land for sporting facilities. The remaining land was acquired by the District Council for housing development. Wimpey Homes Holding Ltd built 41 houses of mixed design in 1997 and the area is known as Stonemoor. Open land at Crapstone became part of the Dartmoor National Park in 1994.

David and Jenny Miles have opened their garden to the public at Lark Rise on the Buckland Road one day a year since 1995. Teas are served at the hairdresser's opposite the bungalow that day

for the charity. David and Jenny raise hundreds of pounds each year for the Buckland Monachorum Friends Children's Hospice South West group, organised by Linda Downing of Buckland village. David was the young boy who arrived at The Garden House with his parents in 1945 where his father worked for Lionel Fortescue. David and Jenny bought Lark Rise, built in 1927 and called Braemar, between the two lanes in Crapstone, and have transformed the garden. Returning to the parish in 1980 they moved to the bungalow with their family in 1987 and made the garden into a peaceful and colourful haven for birds and butterflies. It is surely a most beautiful garden of trees, shrubs, flowers, fruit and vegetables cultivated with love and care with a water feature and well-trimmed lawns. David and Jenny are both trained horticulturists and enjoy designing gardens and seeing their plans come to fruition. Over 500 people visit their garden on the one open day and they raise more than £1,500 for the Children's Hospice.

The Foot family lived in Crapstone for many years. John Foot was made a life peer in 1967 and he took the title of Lord Foot of Buckland Monachorum. As president of Yelverton Residents' Association he successfully fought the scheme to replace Plymouth City Airport at Roborough with a city airport at Yelverton. From the 1960s the roads to Yelverton were constructed across the aerodrome.

The Crescent.

Chapter 8

CLEARBROOK

In spring and early summer on approaching Clearbrook from the main A386 road down over Roborough Down the golden bushes of gorse welcome like sentinels lighting the way. Carpets of pink heather in the autumn and snow in the winter make the entry over the bridge of the Plymouth Leat breathtaking with the quiet hills and tors of Dartmoor beyond. This hamlet, in the south-east of the parish, has always been closely associated with the two parishes of Buckland Monachorum and Meavy. In the nineteenth and early-twentieth centuries parishioners living on the right bank of the River Meavy attended church at Buckland where they were married, their children baptised and family members buried. It was a long walk, however, across moorland before the hut

An old painting of Clearbrook, 1880s, which is now in Australia.

was built in 1901 where the vicar visited to take a service on Sundays and where children attended Sunday school. Clearbrook was incorporated into Meavy ecclesiastical parish in 1985 after being in turn part of Buckland Monachorum and Yelverton. This decision was validated at the court of Buckingham Palace and took effect from 1 March that year.

The Clear Brook rises on the east-facing slope on the southern end of Roborough Down and flows eastwards to the river. This brook flows through the gardens of the cottages and houses on the left of the road in front of Mabor and joins the river just above Hoo Meavy Bridge. From Elfordtown Farm the river forms the eastern parish boundary between the Buckland Monachorum and Meavy Parishes, the boundary not exactly following the riverbed. Not far below Hoo Meavy Bridge the boundary follows in a south-westerly direction up over the moor to the café on the hill where there was once a cattle-grid above Roborough village, now the 'Dartmoor Chef'. Mabor Farm was isolated here before 1840 where the farmer ran stock on the moor and safeguarded the land for the Drake family. There are now 51 houses in this hamlet, within the Dartmoor National Park, and a

population of mixed ages and professions. Since the magnificent millennium Village Hall replaced the old tin hut of 1901 in 1998, the community spirit has increased and many residents give much time and effort to village affairs. Visit Clearbrook on a bank holiday or when the sun shines – there is not a spare patch of moorland to picnic on across the road from the Skylark Inn. It is the first village on the moor for visitors from the City of Plymouth with large spaces clear of gorse bushes for games and dog walking.

Clearbrook houses were built on abbey lands from about 1840, before the settlements of Yelverton and Crapstone. Until recently owners of properties had to purchase the strip of land between the road and their gate from the Maristow estate. From 1872 children from the village attended the school at Meavy, which shortened the walk to school at Buckland Monachorum by a few miles. The occupations of the fathers were miner or farm labourer, and beer retailer when the Rolstone family lived at the inn from 1876. The row of cottages seen as you enter the village from the Plymouth to Yelverton road (A386) was built separately. Moorland Cottage, fifth in the row and home of Roger and Doreen Elliott, may have been the first cottage constructed parallel with the track. Mark Pearse, a mason, lived here in 1849. The first two houses in the row were the last to be built. Owner of the land, Richard Parson, sold the field as a building plot. The field was known as Parson's Field. There were springs, and wells were dug, so the supply of fresh water was no problem. Thurlow Cottage deeds record that George Frean, a miller, and Nicholas Frezzy, a miner, rented part of Parson's Field, now called Clearbrook Field, for a term of 500 years at the rent of one peppercorn yearly in 1848. E. Atwill purchased it in 1924 for £500.

James Creber lived at Mabor Farm in 1842 with the house and 44 acres of land. He rented the farm from Sir T.T.F.E. Drake at Buckland Abbey. Field names

Left: *The view to the east from Arch Bridge.*

Below: *Arch Railway Bridge in Clearbrook.*

Clearbrook before the two end houses were added to the terrace.

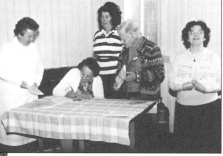

Plymouth or Drake's Leat ceased flowing in 1898.

Above: *Lilian, in the old Clearbrook Village Hall, signs a copy of her book which was printed by the Local History Society.*

Below: *Clearbrook houses, taken from the Plymouth Leat with Dartmoor tors beyond.*

were Clover Field, Barn Park, Six Acres, Bush Park, Hilly Field, Little Meadow, Great Meadow and Meadow. Other acres were of moorland where the farmer ran his stock. A total of 27 children from Clearbrook were baptised at Buckland between 1851 and 1863. The walk to church was across the moor to the Big Rock, along tracks and footpaths to the vicarage (The Garden House) and through the path-fields by the brook to St Andrew's. John and Jane Hutchings lived at Mabor Farm at the turn of the century, followed by Tom and Kathleen West until 1975. The house has since been extended and is now a private residence.

In 1860 men were employed at the farm or farms in the area, in Yeoland Consuls Mine or on the rail-way which passed through Clearbrook on its way between Plymouth and Yelverton. The arch bridge was constructed over the road between 1856–59 to carry the single track and trains became part of village life for 103 years. If you look carefully under the south side of the arch above eye-level a stone-carved lion rampant can be seen. No significance for this can be found. Clearbrook Halt opened on 29 October 1928 and, like other stations on the line, closed at the end of 1962. On the passenger journey on Saturday 29 December 1962 trains from Plymouth were prevented from reaching Launceston because of deep snowdrifts. Margaret Chapman (née West) left Plymouth at 6.20p.m. and arrived home in Clearbrook five hours later. It was two weeks before the train was able to return to Plymouth.

Family names of former days are Atwill, Bowden, Creber, Hutchings, Kelland, Lethbridge, Rolstone, Skidmore, Smale, West and Williams. The Plymouth Leat played its part in the life of the village until it ceased flowing in 1898, when water was piped to Plymouth by gravity from the new Burrator Reservoir. A mother who visited one of the cottages drowned her baby, Ann Elizabeth Trewin, in the leat. Mary Trewin had walked from Tavistock workhouse to visit Ann Hatherleigh living in Clearbrook. She drowned her baby, Ann, in the leat before walking down by the hedge to the cottages. Later in court she was found guilty of manslaughter and was sentenced to serve seven years' penal servitude. The leat was then the drinking-water supply to the city and the baby was found by a leatman. Another murder occurred on the moor in 2001 when the police called at every home asking if anything unusual had been spotted after a body was found on the moor. On 12 December 1966 the police force rushed to Clearbrook, sirens blazing, when a notorious convict by the name of Frank Mitchell escaped from a working party on the prison farm in Princetown. A call to the police that winter's night informed them that Frank Mitchell was drinking in the Skylark Inn. He was, but it was Frank from the village who had a wooden leg, not the escaped prisoner with the same name. We are not told if the policemen saw the funny side

of this practical joke. The convict, caught later by a rival gang, is reported to have been entombed in concrete under one of the motorways.

Police were in Clearbrook in August 1982 when they were called to rescue two young men and a woman from the Plymouth Polytechnic who were trapped in a mine-shaft near Margaret Worth's cottage. Margaret has lived in Chubtor Bungalow since 1950. A mine-rescue group who helped to bring them to the surface found them alive. Mine workings are overgrown but are visible each side of the river-side footpath. Sparks from the engine of the train often set fire to the woods along the railway line. Householders had to beat out the flames of the burn-ing ground and bushes. The first train must have been an amazing sight on the eastern side of the parish. Only a handful of people lived in Clearbrook in 1859 and to travel by train they had to walk to Horrabridge and back. The opening of Yelverton Station was convenient and from 1907 the train stopped at Shaugh. A fatal accident occurred on the evening of 18 November 1885, six months after the opening of Yelverton Station. The train from Waterloo had passed over Arch Bridge, became derailed at milepost 6 and toppled down the bank into the field below Hoo Meavy Bridge. The driver was killed in the upturned engine and the passengers slightly injured. People journeyed by train to the shops, to school and to entertainment in both Tavistock and Plymouth and took animals to the cattle markets from Clearbrook Halt. There was a shop next to the station that sold foodstuffs, drinks and paraffin oil. Customers at that time remember the cheese tasting of paraffin oil. At one time Mr Fred Stephens owned this shop and it is still remembered that he was so mean with his measures that he kept scissors on the counter with which he even cut currants in half to obtain the exact weight. It was taken over by Arthur Piper in 1935.

Other shops in the first half of the twentieth century consisted of a butcher, baker, two general stores and the Post Office. The Post Office was in the same house for over 100 years, now called Heathfield. Mark Moses Atwill was the sub-postmaster in 1880 when he had a bakery at the back of the Post Office where he also sold groceries. The bread was sold at Atwill's shop at Leg o' Mutton and delivered to other villages. Saffron cakes were his speciality. Mark Atwill moved to Brook Cottage, a few doors up, when he was old and his son-in-law, Alfred Halls, took over the business. A postcard sent by Halls to Jack Vanstone in 1909, the miller at Meavy, requested a sack of barley meal that was needed the following day, such was the faith in the Post Office. Emily Atwill married Walter Pepperell who built Goosey Park on the moor above a quarry, making the track to his home from the Reading Room. This room – tin hut, Mission Room, shack, church or hall – was demolished in 1998. Sir Francis Elliot Drake had

Clearbrook residents at the last coffee morning in the old hall, 1998.

Revd Richard Tebbs, rector of the United Benefice of Yelverton, Meavy, Sheepstor and Walkhampton (which includes Clearbrook), said prayers in the old hall before it was demolished.

Above: *The new millennium hall was opened in July 1998. Some committee members are in the doorway.* Left to right: *Bill Lawes, Peter Wing, Pauline Hemery, Norman Fendall, Chris Staniforth.*

Above right: *The wharf above the village on the P & DR, 1998.*

Left: *Bill Stoneman in his Clearbrook Garage, 1931.*

Below: *The Skylark Inn had two bars in 1900. Notice the monkey-puzzle tree at Clearbrook House.*

leased the land for the building of the hall to his wife and Mr Hayne, the vicar of Buckland Monachorum, so that services could be held in the village. There were strict conditions imposed on the use of the hall, both religious and educational, which were forgotten in later years when it became the centre for entertainment and whist drives. Revd Richard Tebbs, rector of the United Benefice, said private prayers on the day the hall was demolished, Friday 13 February 1998.

The villagers had worked for years to raise funds to repair the hall but with money from the Millennium Commission the construction of a new hall was made possible. Contributions from the District and Parish Councils, the National Lottery and village events totalled £150,000. The hall was awarded flagship status from 21st Century Projects, one of only 12 village halls in the country to receive this honour. In May 1998 Peter and April Wing, who live next door at Rose Hill, buried a time capsule in the foundations, containing coins and photographs. Used for monthly coffee mornings, entertainment, village events, parties and regular games evenings the hall has a fully-equipped kitchen and facilities for the disabled.

Reading rooms, as also in Buckland and Milton Combe, were given by the abbey estate for the use of villagers where books were provided and changed on a regular basis. The hall is the centre of village life. No shops remain; the Post Office closed in 1996 when Claire and Tony Rushbrooke moved to Axtown. As in Milton Combe the mobile Post Office visits once a week.

Lilian Atwill was born in the village in 1911, married in 1934 and lived in one of the cottages her parents had built until 1990, when she and her husband, Tom Lethbridge, moved to Australia to be near their son. After living in the village for nearly 80 years Lilian bravely left Clearbrook to travel across the world. Clothes put out to dry on the communal clothes line at the front of the cottages often became entangled in cows' horns as they wandered to and from the moor and the women had to chase the animals to retrieve their garments. Lilian sold soft drinks to the golfers when she was young by the leat bridge near the old tramway buildings known as Tyrwhitts Wharf. In 2002 Lilian wrote from Australia of her memories in Clearbrook during the Second World War:

Lorry loads of people would arrive every evening with blankets, food and thermos flasks and make their way to the hedge by the golf course and settle down for the night. The Reading Room was full of people and I gave shelter to two ladies I found sleeping under a gorse bush. I gave them my spare bedroom, as the younger one was pregnant. They stayed every night until the baby was born. After eight bombs dropped on the moor the number of evening visitors fell dramatically. We had a gun emplacement on the moor and the command-

ing officer visited the village to ask if the residents would allow his men to have a bath. This we did and I agreed to mend their socks provided they had been washed. Imagine my horror when I found a huge sack full on my doorstep with holes so large you could have driven a horse and cart through them. This was a weekly arrangement. There was a prisoner-of-war camp near the Moorland Links Hotel with lookout posts and barbed wire. Once or twice I saw boxes of butter and sugar etc., all the things we were short of thrown in the bushes. It was galling to see this, there may have been a black market racket going on from there. Yelverton was never the same again after all the beautiful houses on the Crapstone road were pulled down for the airfield. The people in the shops counted the planes off and would do the same on their return. When they all returned a great shout went up from every one.

The canal term, wharf, was used for the stables where ponies were rested and changed over for fresher ponies on the old tramway. The old tramway, or Plymouth and Dartmoor Railway, passed through the east of the parish. It was 25 miles long with a granite milepost at every mile. Tyrwhitt's Wharf was halfway along the track and ponies pulling the trucks of granite down to Sutton Pool must have been glad of a rest. Milepost 12 is nearby. Coal, lime and sea sand was taken back up to Princetown on the return journeys. This enterprising operation was short-lived, working from 1823 to about 1840.

The Skylark Inn was built as a beerhouse for miners in about 1850. George Rolstone was landlord in 1862 and the family lived there until the inn, as it had become, was bought by a Plymouth brewery. George named it after hearing the skylarks singing above his head over the moor as he stood in the doorway, as they still do. The original entrance on to the road had two doors leading from the porch – to the public bar and the lounge. The popularity of the Skylark grew when Mick and Midge Wilkins bought the lease and served home-made food from 1987 to 1995.

Bill Stoneman and Frank Mitchell, motor engineers, opened a garage for mechanical repairs behind Glenview in 1946. This house and several others were opened for bed and breakfast during the war where families of service men in the area stayed to be near their loved ones. Bed-and-breakfast businesses are run in the village at the time of writing and it is a popular centre for exploring the west of Dartmoor. Lou Creber from Belliver Farm across the river delivered milk and dairy products every day. Nurse Damerell delivered babies and Nurse Partridge was the health visitor. In 1980 the threat of development proposals by Plymouth City Council concerned not only Clearbrook residents but also Buckland Monachorum Parish Council, as buildings were erected ever closer to the parish.

T.E. Lawrence, Lawrence of Arabia as he was known, was a frequent visitor one summer in the

Mrs Williams' tearooms in her garden in 1950.

Above: *A walk to the top of Dewerstone from Clearbrook is a favourite route for residents, 1998.*

Right: *Norman Fendall, president of the Clearbrook and District Association.*

Ben and Bettina Lewis have lived at Cassis in the village since 1951.

early 1930s when he was in the RAF and stationed in Plymouth. He was friendly with a young man from Clearbrook Cottage and rode his motorcycle to the village and is remembered by Iris Skidmore. The Skidmore family developed the china-clay industry at Lee Moor. John Skidmore lived at Counting House at Cadover Bridge where he counted out the men's wages. He had six sons, all living in or near Clearbrook. His grandson, Adrian, enjoyed happy days in the village before his family emigrated to New Zealand in 1953. He later became the president of operations for 'Elizabeth Arden' company and now enjoys return visits to his birthplace with his wife, Darielle. A far cry from New York and London.

The Hemery family moved to Whitefriars in 1975, which had been built 20 years earlier. Eric was heavily involved in his walks and researches for *High Dartmoor*, which was published by Robert Hale in 1983. All Eric's books were written at his home here and he died on the moor near to the house in April 1986. There were few children to play with for the three children, Anna, Francesca and Gabriel, in the 1970s but transport to their schools collected them from the door. The moorland made an impact on their lives and the grandchildren love to play on the moor as they had done.

Dora and Orlando Gloyne built Sunbeam House next to the Skylark Inn and sold building plots below their house in 1941. Dora, née White, was the eldest sister of Dick and Charles White. She lived in Clearbrook until she was 93 years of age. Sunbeam House is now the home of Christine and Alan Newberry. Rosehill, next to the Village Hall, was built for the Kelland family. Nell moved from her home to live with her daughter, Mary Maddison, in Milton Combe.

The Plym Valley cycle track from Laira Bridge to Clearbrook opened in 1993 and the steep incline from the railway track to the moor was made three years later. The track follows the GWR line. Walkers, cyclists, runners and horse-riders visit or pass through the village. Dewerstone is nearby and Yelverton golf course on the moor is close to the houses. The skylark singing overhead, the heron nesting in the tall trees by the river and geese flying past add to the numerous moorland birds seen every day. The house in the woods behind Mabor is home to Bill Lawes and he was awarded four-star rating and second-best bird-feeding station in the country in 1988. In the film made by Simon King, 'The Flying Gourmet's Guide', many birds seen are from the tit family and included the marsh tit, nuthatch, jay, blackbird, crow, great spotted woodpecker, sparrowhawk and buzzard. Walks to Shaugh Prior, Goodameavy, Yelverton and Milton Combe over the moors are scenic in all seasons. Butterflies are numerous. A rare moth, *Uresiphita polygonalis*, was recorded in *TDA 97* (1965) having been found in the village. It was the first to be recorded in Devon. The lovely old oak tree below the confluence of the Clear Brook and the River Meavy is home to a variety of plant and animal life. The cuckoo arrives in April, calling its welcome notes from the trees from five o'clock in the morning in May and June. She lays her eggs in the nests of unsuspecting birds in the gardens and in the author's garden a large fluffy grey fledgling, far too big for the nest, was often seen being fed on the ground by the tiny host foster parent.

On the Buckland Monachorum Parish side of Hoo Meavy Bridge and on the lower side, the remains of a weir and sluice-gate can be seen. The line of a leat crossing the field, filled in many years ago, leads to the bottom corner of the field. This leat for the Wheal Lopes Mine, north-west of Bickleigh, was first cut in 1760 when the Lopes family mined copper, zinc and tin. The sons of the Bowden family living in Hanns Cottage near the river caught floundering brown trout in this leat when it was cleaned out once a year. The hamlet of Hoo Meavy is an ancient settlement and the bridge spanning the River Meavy was named after it, before Clearbrook was in existence.

An RAF Sea King helicopter hovered over the moor above Clearbrook in April 1981 when it lifted a two-ton piece of granite off the moor on to a lorry. This huge block of granite was transported to Tavistock where it was inscribed and taken to Yelverton aerodrome. It was used as the memorial stone for those who lost their lives in connection with the aerodrome during the Second World War.

The stone had fallen off one of the horse-drawn trucks of the Plymouth and Dartmoor Railway in about 1830 when the prepared blocks were being carried from Swell Tor near Princetown to the Plymouth Breakwater. Clearbrook is conveniently placed between Plymouth and Tavistock, with a large superstore only three miles away and Derriford Hospital only a little further. Yet the houses are in the heart of the country within the Dartmoor National Park, surrounded by moorland and fields.

Celebrations for the Queen's jubilee in June 2002 included a cricket match held on the moor above the Skylark Inn, called Clear Patch for many years because it is clear of gorse bushes. The village community purchased a skittle alley in 2001, an attraction for those who hire the hall privately and for villagers on their games evenings. In the summer months walks over Dartmoor are organised from the village that end with a meal in the Skylark. Residents can feel isolated from the parish of Buckland Monachorum in their moorland existence. Closer links are with Meavy, as Clearbrook is within the school catchment area; it is a part of Meavy ecclesiastical parish and Meavy village is only two miles distant. Clearbrook village is not far from the South Hams border and the Plymouth City boundary but entering it is like entering another world. A more detailed history of the village is found in *Clearbrook, The Story of a Dartmoor Hamlet*, written by the author in 1998.

Left: *The Dartmoor Chef café, 2002.*

Right: *Clearbrook in 1990.*

Right: *Elverton was mapped by Benjamin Donn in 1765, even before the district became a settlement.*

Below: *The channel of the Plymouth Leat in Yelverton.*

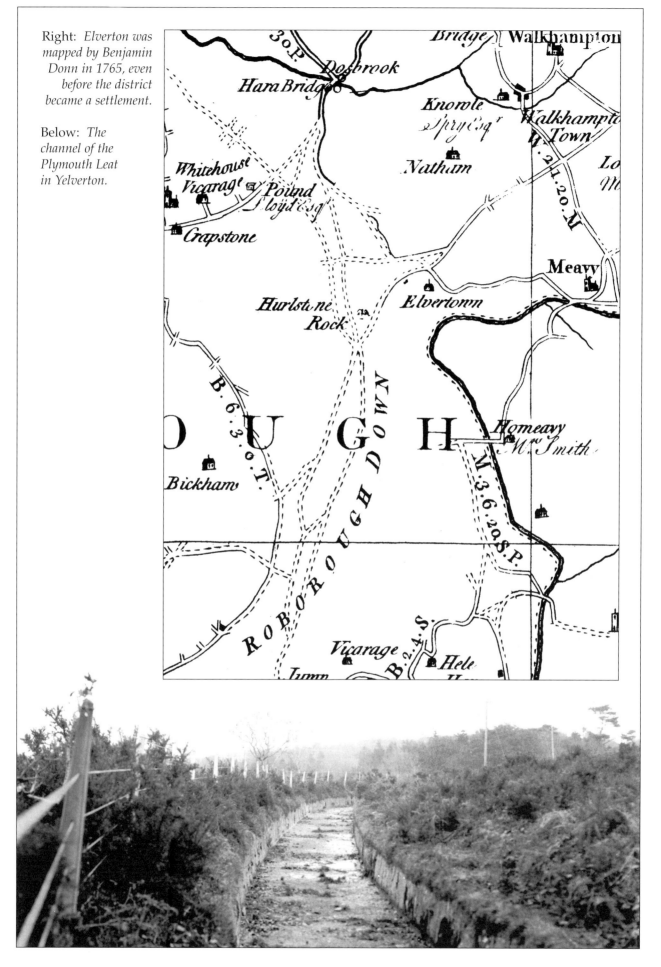

Chapter 9

YELVERTON

Residential district, village, hamlet or small town, Yelverton (600 feet above sea level) is the hub of the parish, the most populated settlement and on the main bus route where there are a variety of shops. This part of Roborough Down 150 years ago was mainly uninhabited moorland, the only houses being the Rock (Hotel), Elford Town, Axtown, the Buller's Arms at Leg o' Mutton, farms in Harrowbeer Lane and one or two cottages. It is a dormitory settlement cut in two by busy main roads.

In the second half of the nineteenth century the first new houses were built on the Horrabridge road and with the opening of the railway station at Yelverton in 1885 the development of residential houses nearby began. The views of Dartmoor when not shrouded in mist are most beautiful and spectacular in changing weather conditions. The tors above the Tavy, Walkham and Meavy valleys, from Cox Tor on the left to Sheeps Tor and Eylesbarrow on the right, form an awe-inspiring panorama.

There are three other places named Yelverton: in Norfolk, England, in Western Australia and in the North West Territory of Canada, but this settlement on Roborough Down is a corruption of Elfordtown, the farm of the Elfords. The suffix town or ton, as in Fairtown, Coppicetown, Alston and Cuxton farms elsewhere in the parish signifies a farm or settlement. The Elford family built the farmstead on the right bank of the River Meavy, within the Buckland Monachorum Parish boundary, in the fourteenth century and cultivated the fertile land. In the local dialect the letter 'y' is often slipped in front of a name beginning with a vowel. The name is recorded as both Elfordtown and Yelverton, for Elford Town House and Lower Elfordtown, listed in the tithe of 1842 as 'Elford Town or Yelverton', putting pay to the popular belief that the GWR corrupted the name when the station was opened in 1885.

George Leach married Jenny Elford and they owned Elfordtown in 1801, along with a cottage called Rock Tenement with pasture rights on Roborough Down. Leach sold the property to William Moore for £2,800 and later moved to Crapstone Barton, which he inherited from his uncle, Jonathan Elford. Moore sold Elfordtown estate in 1808 to John Brooking who sold five acres of his land, called Higher Heath at 'Yelfordtown', to Thomas

Tyrwhitt before 1823 for the Plymouth and Dartmoor Railway track. On the first-edition Ordnance Survey map of 1809 the Plymouth and Devonport Leats are clearly marked, also tracks across Roborough Down, Rock (as in Big Rock), Harrowbeer, Gratton and Elfordtown can be seen. Axtown, 'Whitley' Down and Yeoland are marked to the west of the Down. The Elfordtown estate consisted of:

Three messuages, three tenements, four cottages, four orchards, five gardens, 100 acres of land, 100 acres of meadow, 100 acres of pasture and 50 acres of woods with common pasture on Roborough Down.

Samuel Rowe observed in 1821, 'We see Yelverton, the residence of James Brooking Esq., sheltered from the Dartmoor winds by lofty trees'.

Francis Corham purchased the estate in 1832 which on his death passed to his six daughters, the last surviving one leaving it to her nephew in 1864. This he sold in the following year, an area of 75 acres, one rood and 32 perches, which was then sold off in parts to raise money during the years of local mining depression until it was bought by Louisa Bradshaw who set about purchasing all the land that had previously belonged to the farm. In a directory of 1857 a house on Elfordtown estate is called Yelverton House which was altered to Elfordtown by Louisa Bradshaw in the 1870s. Other owners of the estate listed in the deeds are William Joachim, Richard Davie, Anne Davie and John Williams. Mrs Bradshaw gave her son, Hilton, the Rock Tenement in 1868 and ten years later she sold Elfordtown to John Bayly, in whose family it still remains. Colonel Dick Spencer (1910–94) inherited the estate from his Bayly mother, Katie. It was John Bayly who gave land for the building of a wooden Anglican church in 1892. Sir T.T.F.E. Drake, along with Mabor Farm in Clearbrook, owned Lower Elfordtown and occupiers included parish farmers, Dawe and Hamlyn.

In a newspaper of August 1910 a report on the laying of the foundation-stone for the church of St Paul claimed:

The need of a new church for Yelverton to take the place of the present temporary structure has long been felt, the large number of visitors who frequent this moorland

health resort, especially during the summer months, rendering the present building totally inadequate to the growing requirements of the neighbourhood.

John Bayly's daughters who then owned the estate gave land close by for the present church. The Bayly family also owned three large houses – Inceworth and Torr in Mannamead and Seven Trees in Lipson Road, Plymouth.

Incumbents of St Paul's Church

Priests in charge
1929   Arthur Allen
1931   Herbert Harvey

Vicars
1935   Herbert Harvey
1945   Richard Welchman
1954   Thomas Grigg-Smith
1959   Thomas Watkins
1967   Thomas Owen
1974   Peter Camp
1982   Robin Ellis

Team Rectors
1987   John Ellis
1989   Graham Witts
1994   Richard Tebbs

Only small private schools have ever existed in Yelverton, held in large houses. Day schools were organised in the twentieth century by Miss Nicholls, Miss Melody, Miss Sammels, Mrs Merson, Miss Raymond and Miss Pitts. Ravenscroft School also took boarders. In the early 1900s there was great opposition to what was considered as the commercialisation of Yelverton. As early as 1914 a large number of businesses were advertised in guide books promoting Yelverton as a health resort with bracing air – doctors in Plymouth prescribing 'a dose of Yelverton' as a cure for ailments. Establishments included physicians, hotels, boarding-houses, apartments, furnished and unfurnished houses, building contractors, bakers, butchers, carriage and livery stables, dispensers, photographer, coal merchants, corn merchants, dairy, drapers, greengrocer, grocer, hairdresser, estate agents, house furnisher, library, motor garage, saddler, boot repairer and private schools. Roberts the chemist was entered by climbing up steps, the pharmacy on the left, the lending library on the right and the dark room for developing photographs upstairs. On the corner was Wherry's paper shop and above this Perraton's Café. Mrs Ford sold sweets and ice-cream. The third-class return rail fare from Yelverton to London was 37s.6d. (£1.87) in

1914. The same journey today by bus to Plymouth and train to London is £135.

The majority of these businesses were on the Down in an area between roads shaped like a leg of mutton. It is also thought that this area is so-named because men climbed a greasy pole here on fair days to reach a leg of mutton. For either reason the area became known as Leg o' Mutton but the centre of Yelverton moved from here to 'the shops' between the Rock Hotel and St Paul's Church during the latter part of the twentieth century. The row of shops were originally built as three-storey houses and matched the row of houses called Greenbank Terrace on the other side of the grass area near the roundabout. John Charles Naylor ran the Yelverton garage and above his premises was the Conservative Club, from where the results of the General Election were announced. A tennis court was added near the garage and Bidders (butchers) where residents were able to hire the courts for games and matches. The removal of the top two storeys of the row of shops leaves Greenbank Terrace looking isolated and the appearance is often likened to a row of seaside houses without the beach.

Favourite walks were through the woods to Clearbrook, walking between the River Meavy and the railway line for cream teas at Glen View. Another favourite was a walk to Double Waters, the meeting of Rivers Tavy and Walkham, over the moors passed Pound returning by Magpie (Bedford) Bridge.

Two families were significant in the area, both named Rodd and each family having three daughters – the 'brass Rodds' and the 'golden Rodds', as they became known. The former family lived at Mulfra in Hazel Grove and at Crapstone House and the other in Willowby House and at Buckland Abbey.

In 2002 Yelverton is spread out over a wide area. There are 800 houses but no centre, village green or schools, which it was proud of 90 years ago. The new Village Park near Leg o' Mutton is attracting young children and their families and a project caring for the community and older residents, YelverCare, is also drawing the community closer together. With such an attractive landscape within the Dartmoor National Park and its close proximity to the City of Plymouth and the market town of Tavistock, Yelverton is a desirable place to live in but house prices are high. A large proportion of the inhabitants are over 60 years of age.

The attractions of Yelverton listed 70 years ago have not changed. The climate, the official guide of the 1930s claimed, 'brings a sparkle to dull eyes and colour to pale cheeks'; the weather 'on the fringe of Dartmoor is favoured with a high sunshine record'; and thirdly the 'sense of space and freedom it gives to its residents'. In the same guide it stated, 'Yelverton has no attractions for the tripper class, and is well-blessed as a result'! An elderly resident recalls climbing an oak tree that grew at the top of Meavy Lane when she was a child and becoming stuck in the tree when her knickers caught on a branch. Despite the nearby shopkeepers trying to release her with awning poles she remained firmly attached until a farmer on a passing hay cart climbed the tree from the hayload and lifted her down. The Devonport Leat, passing in front of the shops nearest the lane, was a great attraction to children.

Yelverton has certainly seen extreme changes. Beginning as open moorland crossed by tracks and leats, it has seen roads constructed and altered with the addition of a roundabout. With a railway line passing beneath it there has been a busy and popular railway station, the junction for the Princetown branchline, a wartime airfield with hundreds of personnel and visitors, and the growth of population. Yelverton is where one meets friends and neighbours, old and new. It accommodates the elderly in the many homes and sheltered-housing schemes. Shops and businesses are many and varied; sporting facilities and club membership cater for a population with wide interests. Although Yelverton is comparatively new, and can be called neither town nor village, part is in Burrator Parish and most is in the parish of Buckland Monachorum, it can be considered as the main area of the parish.

The Growth of Yelverton

1291
Earliest reference is made of Ellefordlak. Elleford Lake is the stream flowing down old Station Lane to the River Meavy.

1300s
The Elford family built Elford Town.

1591
Sir Francis Drake constructed the Plymouth Leat across the moor from Burrator through the area.

1625
King Charles I reviewed troops on Roborough Down.

1626
26 April – A lease of land at Harrowbeer was made.

1701
Alice Bere found that in the burial register of this year a man called Stephens was described as being of Yelverton.

1749
William Elford MP was Mayor of Plymouth.

1763
An Act was passed to improve the road from Tavistock to Plymouth through Horrabridge and Yelverton.

1765
Recorded as Elverton on Donne's map.

1769
Parish boundstones inscribed 'Buckland Monachorum' set up on Roborough Down.

1784
Two farms at Harrowbeer shown on a map of this time.

1793
A leat crossed the moor to Devonport Docks from the West Dart River, passing through Yelverton close to the Plymouth or Drake's Leat.

1809
A map showed roads and tracks, two leats, Harrowbeer, Axtown, Yeoland and Elfordtown.

1822
The new Tavistock to Yelverton road opened. The road to Plymouth passed Leg o' Mutton and joined the old road at the Big Rock.

On 12 June the Duke of Bedford rode his horse from Yelverton Golf Club along the new road, leading a procession of 11 carriages followed by about 100 men on horseback, to celebrations in Tavistock.

You have a much better view of the country from the new road besides avoiding Horrabridge Hill and the steep but the short hills between Horrabridge and Tavistock.

1823
The horse-drawn tramway (Plymouth & Dartmoor Railway) opened. Engineered by Sir Thomas Tyrwhitt, with a wharf on the site of the present Rock Inn, it passed through Yelverton in front of the Chub Tor houses, Clearbrook and across Roborough Down. Granite cylindrical pillars were placed at the side of the track every mile from the terminus at Sutton Pool – milestone 12 is situated above Clearbrook, 13 is opposite Roughways on Chubtor track and 14 was near the roundabout.

1828
An engraving showed Rock Inn as Rock House.

1831
Mrs Bray, wife of the vicar of Tavistock, wrote that a sailor walking from Tavistock to Plymouth fell asleep by Roborough Rock. After he had resumed his walk sometime later he found that he had lost his purse. Three years later, returning to Tavistock, he passed the same spot and looked at the place he had slept and to his joy found his purse.

Right: *Devon Tors and Beech Villas, showing the old tramway crossing the green.*

Below: *Militia camping on Roborough Down in 1873.*

Right: *The Rock Hotel, run by former members of the Langton family in 1875.*

Below: *Stone was cut from the rock for road building in the nineteenth century.*

Right: *Richard Woodman's racehorses in 1919.*

Below: *Yelverton roads before 1914.*

Inset: *The Bible Christian Chapel, 1905.*

1838
Roborough Rock tin mine was advertised.

1840
Buller's Arms public house opened at Leg o' Mutton.

1840
A bronze Roman coin (AD41–54) was found at Yelverton by the great-grandfather of Mr F.E. Rossiter (*TDA* 101).

1851
Yeoland Consuls Tin Mine was working from Hoo Meavy to Yeoland Lane, west of the golf links.

1854
William Crossing first visited Yelverton with his father to see military manoeuvres. One of the regiments left soon after to fight in the Crimean War.

1856
Construction of the South Devon & Tavistock Railway, passing under Yelverton through a tunnel.

1858
8 February – Brunel's first report on the railway line to the engineer: 'At Yelverton tunnel headings have been driven through and one third of the tunnel completed'.

1859
21 June – Railway line opened, passing under Yelverton. It was to be almost 16 years before the station opened here.

1862
William Shillibeer owned the Rock Inn.

1866
The Bible Christian Chapel was built on Princetown Road. William O'Bryan founded this branch of Methodism in 1815.

1870
H. Sheere was injured in an accident whilst erecting a school at Yelverton.

The Buller's Arms at Leg o' Mutton was destroyed by fire, along with the shoe shop next door. 'There was a fire at Mutton Corner Inn where Mr Cook a shoemaker lived.'

1873
Army manoeuvres were carried out on Dartmoor with soldiers camped on Roborough Down near Pound House in hundreds of bell tents.

1874
Rock Hotel attracted visitors in horse-drawn carriages from Plymouth where they enjoyed ham and egg teas.

1875
Col W.T. Spearman built the house called Briar Tor.

1875
Land was acquired near the Tavistock turnpike road adjoining Roborough Down by R.S. Pethick. This was part of Harrowbeer estate and was bought for the building of 'Moor View Villa' in fields called Broughton's and Little Down. This was later to become the Moor House Hotel.

1878
John Bayly bought Elfordtown estate and lived in Yelverton House.

1879
Richard Woodman, horse trainer, owned Heathcott racing stables on the parish boundary (now called Woodman's Corner) and sent his horses to races from Yelverton Station.

Henry Barons and his wife, Mary, return from New Jersey in the USA with their children. Henry purchased Drake land, a field rented to Harrabeer Farm called

The Plymouth and Dartmoor Railway siding at Yelverton, 1908.

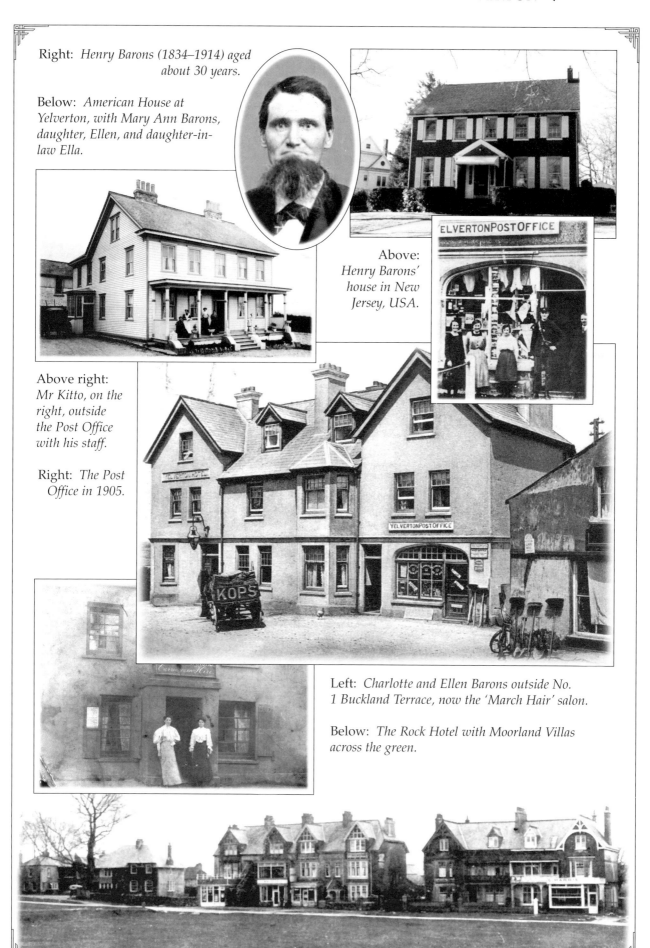

Right: *Henry Barons (1834–1914) aged about 30 years.*

Below: *American House at Yelverton, with Mary Ann Barons, daughter, Ellen, and daughter-in-law Ella.*

Above: *Henry Barons' house in New Jersey, USA.*

Above right: *Mr Kitto, on the right, outside the Post Office with his staff.*

Right: *The Post Office in 1905.*

Left: *Charlotte and Ellen Barons outside No. 1 Buckland Terrace, now the 'March Hair' salon.*

Below: *The Rock Hotel with Moorland Villas across the green.*

Long Park near the Leg o' Mutton, and built 'American House', a replica of the home they had in New Jersey. Four years later the 23-room house is advertised as 'temperance hotel, good accommodation for tourists and cyclists, public telephone call office, parties catered for.'

1883

11 August – Opening of the Princetown branch railway from Horrabridge Station. No celebrations were held. Four trains ran every weekday.

The Dartmoor Preservation Association was founded to protect the moor from exploitation.

Mark Atwill, son of Mark at Clearbrook Bakery, set up his own business at Leg o' Mutton.

1885

Friday 1 May – Opening of Yelverton Station for passengers. From this time there was rapid development of Yelverton. The station was 500 feet above sea level and the village was now 100 feet higher.

James Kitto opened the Post Office at Leg o' Mutton Corner.

1886

Two fields sold by the Drake family west of the station for building development. Ten large detached and 16 semi-detached houses with four tennis courts were planned – only two, Inglenook and Drakeleat, were built. Architect William Newby Spooner lived in Inglenook.

Maristow estate sold land for the Westella estate. William Edward Hiscock Howard named the estate and roads after villages near his hometown west of Hull; Westella, Eastella and Kirkella. Southella is a district nearby. It was not named from the stream in Station Lane nor was his wife, mother or daughter called Ella. The Yorkshire Ellas are named after the Viking King, Ella.

1887

A.J. Piper began building Moorland Villas, the shops and, from the north-east end, private houses each of three storeys. A milestone was inscribed nearby with, 'Plymouth 9 miles, Princetown 6 miles'.

Buckland Terrace at Leg o' Mutton was built. Also large houses with beautiful gardens.

1888

Rock Tea Gardens was opened by Mrs Archer. The Shillibeer sisters bought the tramway buildings after its closure and opened the Rock Hotel. The postal town of the area changed from Horrabridge to Yelverton. First postmaster was James Kitto.

1889

Kingstone, near Lower Elfordtown, was built. The Drake family leased the land to John Ward of Devonport. The porter at the station worked as a gardener at Kingstone between trains.

The Red House was built. The tennis court here was flooded in the winter months when the water froze and used for ice-skating. Owners of large Plymouth stores moved to Yelverton to live and employed many servants.

Yelverton Park Villas, off Meavy Lane, were built.

1890

A large house was built at the end of Moorland Villas, now the premises of Mansbridge & Balment and High Colton Estate Agents. Summerleaze was built, then called Larksland, later renamed by Thomas Baker of Dingles in Plymouth.

1891

Great blizzard. Plymouth Leat froze for weeks and soldiers were sent to restore the water supply for Plymouth, with no success.

July – Charles King, architect, was commissioned to design a new church for 130 people.

1892

John Bayly gave land for the building of an Anglican church.

1893

The Chrysanthemum, Fruit, Flower and Poultry Show was held each autumn from this time.

1894

A wooden structure was chosen for the new Anglican church. The cricket club played matches on the green near the tramway embankment, which is on the site of the roundabout at the time of writing. The original club began in Meavy village.

1895

3 July – The wooden church was opened and dedicated to St Paul, with chairs used for seating.

1896

St Albans was built in Meavy Lane by Henry Barons for the Rodd family. Willowby House was built by the Shillibeers. Meavy Villas were built by two brothers named Carsdale, each starting at different ends. Short of space and each man blaming the other, number four was built in front as Whisky Cottage, renamed The Nook. It had also been called Verulanium and Hopeful Lodge. Meavy Villas are numbered 1, 2, 3, 5, 6.

The Parish Council decided that Yelverton did not need a police constable as the cost was too high for the ratepayers.

A blacksmith's shop with stables and hayloft was built on Crapstone Road, now Forge Cottage near Ravenscroft.

A house was built at the top of Station Lane for the stationmaster, now 'Whistledown'.

Above: *The wooden church of St Paul in 1895.*

Above: *The interior of St Paul's wooden church. The pulpit was taken to the present building.*

Above: *Elizabeth Gloyne and five of her children in 1888. Clockwise from top: Lily, Orlando, Olive, William and Emily. Her sixth child, born in 1897, was baptised Stuart Diamond Jubilee Gloyne. Orlando married Dora White and lived in the house he built, called Sunbeam House in Clearbrook. William became a partner in the Margrett and Gloyne building firm.*

Right: *Postcard sent from the sanatorium in 1912. TB patients came here from all over the country.*

Roads near Big Rock, c.1914.

Udal Torre.

Yelverton Terrace at the top of Meavy Lane.

A car rally in Show Field, Station Lane.

Greenbank Terrace.

Across the green to the shops, early-twentieth century.

Moor House Hotel near Leg o' Mutton Corner.

Above: *Meavy Lane has not altered much in 100 years, despite heavy traffic and large lorries.*

Left: *Beechfield Avenue was built in 1907 in the field called Beech Field.*

1897

Newspaper reporters travelled in a motor car to Yelverton and returned to Plymouth. The vehicle looked spectacular to the few onlookers and was the first car in Yelverton.

Celebrations were held at Leg o' Mutton for Queen Victoria's diamond jubilee. Gratton Bridge was built over the ford on the Meavy. A bonfire was lit on Rock Hill near the golf links. A jubilee fountain, inscribed *1837 VR 1897*, was placed near Big Rock, which was also called Roborough Rock and Udal Tor. The centre of this outcrop was removed for use in road construction. From a certain angle one side of the rock resembled the profile of a prime minister and it became known as the Duke of Wellington's nose.

Water was piped to Yelverton from the Devonport Leat near Burrator. There was still no drainage system in use and cesspits overflowed, due to heavy rain, into the two leats flowing to Plymouth and Devonport.

Only three householders subscribed to receive a telephone: Mrs M. Barons at American House, telephone no. 1; Mr J. Bellamy at Hillsborough, telephone no. 2; and Dr Liddell at Penmoor, telephone no. 3.

1898

Udal Torre Sanatorium was built about this time.

1899

Sisters of Charity cared for unmarried mothers and their babies at Briar Tor, which was renamed St Vincent's.

November – The first confirmation service was held at St Paul's Church when the Bishop of Exeter confirmed 36 candidates.

Wednesday 29 November – Spooners, Yelverton and District Flower and Poultry Show's first exhibition was held in Barons' Hall. Colonel Spearman and Mrs Liddell (wife of the doctor) won many of the flower classes. Poultry classes included Indian Game, Brahma, Leghorn, Orpington, Plymouth Rock, Silver Wyandotte and Bantam classes; other poultry shown were duck, turkey and goose. T. Dockett from Milton entered the class for the best pair of plucked chickens, Mrs Ware the best pair of plucked ducks for market, J. Spry won the class for the dish of brown eggs and T. Dockett for the dish of white eggs. Advertisements in the official catalogue included Spooners house furnishers, J. Atwill of Buckland Terrace, Yelverton (baker and confectioner, established 1879), and Oscar Browning (Crapstone) as wholesale and retail boot factor.

1900

W.E.H. Howard built Moor View Terrace. Yelverton Terrace was built in Meavy Lane. Howard also built Devon Tors, then called 1–5 Beech Villas. Mr F. Sara was at Tors Hotel, telephone no. 4.

Yelverton Station had its own bookshop. The station forecourt was a scene of great activity.

A Yelverton romance between a 32 year-old temporary curate of St Paul's and an 18 year-old well-to-do young lady failed when he hired a carriage from Mr Priest's livery stables at 6 o'clock one Thursday morning to take him and the young lady to the railway station. The curate had met the young lady at an entertainment given in aid of the Yelverton Cricket Club. The agitated mother of the girl was waiting for Mr Priest on his return from the station after discovering the elopement and questioned him about the train times and destination of the couple. She immediately contacted relatives in London 'who met the couple upon their arrival and at once took charge of the errant damsel'. No information was forthcoming from the vicar, Revd R. Hayne, or the young lady's father!

1901

The plot for 6–7 Beech Villas was purchased for Rock Nonconformist Church from builder W.E.H. Howard for £360. Howard built houses in Hazel Grove behind Greenbank Terrace.

1902

W.E.H. Howard built Greenbank Terrace. 5 Hazel Grove was a Horrabridge miner's house.

A bonfire was lit near the tumulus on the moor between Crapstone and Yelverton to celebrate King Edward's recovery from illness.

A total of 60 seats were added to St Paul's Church to the original 130 and were used in the summer for holidaymakers.

Jimmy Barons, son of Henry and Mary at American House, lived in 1 Buckland Terrace, the end house opposite the Corner Shop, and advertised himself as a fly proprietor, that is a carriage driver.

John Wilson lived in Udal Torre, a house to the south of Ravenscroft, and held dances each week in the house.

1903

L.A.G. Strong, who became an author, came to live here with his parents. He described Yelverton in a book as being a four-class society at this time: service officers, professions, businessmen and trade.

1904

The telephone exchange opened in a building behind the Post Office at Leg o' Mutton.

A golf club with nine holes opened at Yeoland.

Ravenscroft was built by W.E.H. Howard.

A Devon magazine stated that: 'Yelverton is rapidly becoming a favourite health resort of the GWR'.

Joseph and Louisa Born purchased Moor View Villa and changed its name to Moor House Hotel.

1905

Algy Langton helped to run the Rock Hotel.

Willow in Meavy Lane was built and lived in by piano builders, Moons of Plymouth.

The number of communicants on Easter Day at St Paul's was 115.

1906
8 August – Foundation-stones for Rock Methodist Church were laid by Mrs Trahair, Henry Hurrell and John Yeo, principal subscribers.

A shop-front was added to 2 Moorland Villas, now Bidders the butchers. Other shop-fronts followed.

Charles Job lived at 1 Moorland Villas, William H. Gulley at No. 2, James Spry had apartments at No. 3, Bill May ran a boarding-house at No.4 and Dr Henry Liddell lived at Penmoor next door.

1907
The houses in Beechfield Avenue were built by Howard in a field formerly part of Harrabeer Farm, called Beech Field.

7 August – Rock Methodist Church was opened by Miss Lilian Yeo. It cost £2,600. Bible Christians united with Methodists in September and Revd W.H. Luxton was the minister. Architect was W. Beddoc Rees and Perkins of Plymouth built it.

1908
The Parish Council sought help from Devon County Council to widen two bridges crossing the Devonport Leat; one at the top of Station Hill and the other 200 yards to the west. Private carriages and more than ten cabs parked at the station many times each day. In the summer months about 500 passengers alighted from each train. Station Hill was filled to capacity as vehicles, horses and people made their way up to the moors. F. Blowey, Chairman of the Parish Council, wrote in the minutes on 22 September:

The village of Yelverton is growing in size, houses are being built all around that part of Roborough Down and the down is being daily visited for recreation purposes by schools and societies.

4 May – A plot of land in Kirkella Road was purchased for use by the United Methodist Church for the building of a manse.

24 August – First marriage at Rock United Methodist Church. Isabella Trathen married Robert Baker, both from the Post Office in Dousland. Robert was a railway signalman at Horrabridge. Bella Trathen was a friend of Edith Holden who stayed with her whilst writing and drawing her *Nature Notes for 1906*, published in 1977 as *The Country Diary of an Edwardian Lady*. Edith drowned in 1920 and Bella died in 1937.

F. Halls opened a boot repairs and saddlery at the Old Rock Chapel.

Harold Kitto became the postmaster.

L.A.G. Strong became firm friends with Arthur Rodd from St Albans at Hoe Prep School. He loved Arthur's mother and all the children, Dick (R.R.),

Harry, May, Fanny, Arthur, Charlie and Teddie. In later life Arthur married Mary Tetley, had three daughters and became known as the 'golden Rodds'. Dick Rodd, the eldest child, married Joan Pocock, also had three daughters and was known as the 'brass Rodds'.

1909
More than 20 children lived in an orphanage in Moor View Terrace. The girls wore navy-blue tunics and Marian Thomas played with them. They were taken to church or chapel but educated at the home.

1910
Devon Tors Hotel was opened by Charles Wilson, a strict churchman who bought the property from Mrs Frederick Sara. Mrs Sara advertised her hotel as 'seven acres of wooded and sheltered grounds, splendid situation with extensive views of Dartmoor'.

L.A.G. Strong lived in 1 Beech Villas, which his parents rented, and moved to Edgemoor near the golf links.

The telephone exchange at Yelverton had 26 subscribers. The telephones were allocated as shown below:

1 *American House*
2 *Hillsborough*
3 *Penmoor (Dr Liddell)*
4 *Devon Tors*
5 *Priest's Taxis*
6 *Haslemere (Spooner)*
7 *Later became the Electric Company*
8 *Bidder, butchers*
9 *Harris, butchers*
11 *The Retreat (Dr Revell)*
13 *W.E.H. Howard, builder*
14 *Hayesleigh (Dr Bailey)*
18 *Yelverton Golf Club*
22 *Rock Hotel*
23 *Roberts the Chemist.*

Monday 8 August – Foundation-stone laid for the stone church of St Paul by the Bishop of Exeter. The curate in charge was Revd F.W. Nutt. The site was given by the Misses Bayly who also donated £1,500. The vicar of Buckland Monachorum, Prebendary Hayne, gave £1,000. Charles Jago of Furzedown, a teacher in Plymouth and the father of Bertha, the wife of Edward White (curate of Buckland Monachorum), organised the collection of the money for the cost of building; a total cost of £5,585. 'There was a clap of thunder and rain came down in torrents after the ceremony'.

1911
Sports and a high tea were held for the coronation of King George V and a bonfire was lit in the evening near the tumulus.

Smart's painting of the interior of the Rock Chapel, 1907. He studied at Plymouth Art College in 1896 and the Royal College of Art in 1899.

Above: *Walter Hooper, a resident, was secretary of the chapel in 1907.*

Robert Borlace Smart RBA, ROI, RWS (1881–1947) painted pictures of the Rock Chapel with its red-tiled roof soon after completion.

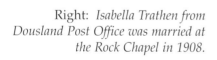

Right: *Isabella Trathen from Dousland Post Office was married at the Rock Chapel in 1908.*

Far right: *Robert Baker, who worked on the railway at Horrabridge, married Isabella Trathen. Theirs was the first marriage in the Rock Chapel.*

The golf club opened a new 18-hole course at Yeoland Farm.

November – Mr H. Kitto requested the moving of the post box in the Post Office window at Leg o' Mutton to a different position. Permission granted, 'providing the aperture is 4 feet 6 inches from the ground'. It had previously been 6 inches too high!

July – Bridge widening was carried out at the top of Station Hill and the alteration of the line of parapets over the leat was completed.

1912

10 July – St Paul's Church was dedicated by the Bishop of Crediton. The building had cost £5,689. It was completely lined with Ham Hillstone and the piers of the very tall four-bay arcades were of the same stone in perpendicular style. The church was not yet licensed for marriages. The wooden church was used as a church room.

1913

Yelverton Railway Station became the busiest station on the line when all traffic was taken into account.

Organ added in St Paul's Church, given by Miss Boger.

Gramophone put in the spire of the United Methodist Church for a recording of church bells to be played at a wedding.

Crowds attended the Yelverton Horse Show held in Show Field in Station Lane. Spectators and competitors with horses and hounds arrived by train on the day.

1914

Udal Torre Sanatorium advertised.

Leg o' Mutton was the busy shopping area of Yelverton. Buckland Terrace was the row of shops on the west side of the road where businesses open were:

R.A. Toop and Son, butchers
John Atwill, baker
M. Foster, fishmonger
Fred Lewis, Board of Trade Labour Exchange
George Shepherd, shopkeeper
George Ford, bootmaker.

On the other side of the road were Edith Andrews, newsagent; Harold Kitto, shopkeeper and Post Office; and W. Roberts, chemist. Yelverton Public Hall, part of the American House, was here. The proprietor was Albert Sidney Barons and it was used for dances.

August – A war-hospital supply depot opened in Yelverton under the presidency of Lady Harris (it closed in early 1919) and met in the church room, raising funds for the British Red Cross Society and St Dunstan's Hostel, raising over £500.

Yelverton District Development and Improvement Association purchased a fire ladder. W.E.H. Howard was secretary, Charles Wilson the chairman and

Charles Harding the treasurer.

Jimmy Barons was refused permission to join the Forces as he was born in America so he became the Yelverton postman until 1920, when the men returned from the First World War.

1915

The Misses Bayly presented the altar rail and choir stalls to St Paul's Church. The Pinwell sisters of Ermington carved the oak stalls.

1916

Sabine Baring-Gould wrote, 'Yelverton itself is a mere collection of villa residences of Plymouth men of business.'

1917

Nuns from the Franciscan House of Poor Clare opened a convent in Crapstone, St Anthony's, to serve the small RC community of Yelverton.

Udal Torre Sanatorium was presented to the Army and Navy.

Harold Kitto formed the Yelverton voluntary fire brigade and was captain for 20 years.

1918

11 November – Service held at St Paul's Church to give thanks for the cessation of hostilities of the war. A tea was provided afterwards with a concert in the evening.

American House sold, with outbuildings and a field where Grangelands houses were later built, for £1,600.

1919

A new golf course of 18 holes was laid on Roborough Down with footbridges placed across the Devonport Leat.

Discussions and arguments became heated over the proposal of Yelverton wishing to become a separate ecclesiastical parish from its mother church at Buckland Monachorum.

At the end of the war peace celebrations included tea in the Rock Chapel schoolroom and sports for children on the green. This was followed by 'dinner and a smoking concert for their elders'.

Listed in Kelly's Directory for this year as hotels or boarding-houses were:

Albert Barons   American Hotel
Leonard Coombe   Beechfield House Hotel
Beatrice Bovey   16 Beechfield Avenue
Henry Grainger   12 Beechfield Avenue
John Harris   1 Meavy Villas
Francis Hill   Carisbrooke
James Hunt   Yelverton Hotel
Algernon Langton   Rock Hotel
Emily Liddell   3 Hazelgrove
Minnie Oke   4 & 5 Greenbank Terrace
Mary Sammels   Beech Villas

Above: *Advertisement for up-to-date repairs. Fred Glanville learned his trade as a shoemaker with Mr Halls at the old chapel.*

Above middle: *L.A.G. Strong wrote about his childhood at Yelverton in* Green Memory, *published by his wife after his death.*

Sylvia Spooner with four of her horses.

Above: *R.R. Rodd in the early-twentieth century. The stained-glass window in the south aisle of St Paul's was given in his memory.*

Below: *R.R. Rodd (right) with two friends on Yelverton Golf Course in the 1920s.*

Below: *The foundation-stone of the present St Paul's Church was laid in 1910.*

Left: *St Paul's Church in the 1920s.*

Below: *The interior of St Paul's Church in its early years.*

Above: *Willowby Park.*

Right: *Ponies on the green, with the old railway embankment of the P & DR.*

Left: *Ladies musical chairs on horseback at Yelverton Horse Show, 1913, which was held in Show Field in Station Lane.*

Right: *Willowby Park terrace from White Lodge.*

Above: *The fire brigade near Devonia in 1937.
Pictured are: W. Brown (back centre); left to right,
back row: E. Wherry, G. Ellacott, W. Netherton,
W. Harvey, W. Hancock, J. Gimblett, W. Andrews,
H. Towl, J. Ellis, E. Martin; front row: L. Andrews,
S. Dawe, R. Andrews, H. Hocking, T. Jeffrey,
A. Kitto, P. Netherton.*

Above: *Yelverton Fire Brigade at Leg o' Mutton.*

Below: *Len German delivering milk in
Clearbrook, 1950.*

Programme

OF

Sheep Dog Trials

TO BE HELD ON

ROBOROUGH DOWN

ON

Saturday, Sept. 15th, 1923,

To commence at 2 p.m.

Judge
Mr. W. AKRIGG, SEDBERGH.

Timekeeper
Mr. JOHN SPOONER, YELVERTON.

Hon. Secretary
Mr. JOHN YOUNG, TAVISTOCK.

Treasurer
Mr. CLARENCE SPOONER, YELVERTON.

PRICE THREEPENCE.

Tavistock Printing Co., Ltd., "Gazette" Office, Tavistock.

*Sheepdog trials held near Leg o' Mutton
in 1923.*

*The British Legion at St Andrew's
Parish Church.*

James Spry	Greenbank
Mary Staplin	8 Beechfield Avenue
Charles Wilson	Devon Tors Hotel.

Private schools listed were at 2 Hazelgrove (Clara Merson) and 12 Willoughby Park (Mildred Raymond).

A sale by auction took place on Thursday 25 September at 4p.m. of houses and plots in Willowby Park Building estate. The vendor, Ambrose Andrews, was retiring from business. He was a builder who had been employed by Phillip Blowey of Buckland when he restored many churches in Devon and Cornwall. For sale were listed:

'The White Lodge' rented by Lady May Boothby, 'Duart' by Dr Tutton, 'Gratton' by Mr Lewin, 'Cadover' by Mr Mason, 'Oakdene' by Mrs Miles.

Also for sale were numbers 4, 8, 9, 11, 12, Woodrow and Slieve Bloom and other numbers as plots of land.

1920

Residents subscribed to the presentations to Revd and Mrs E. White after 16 years' incumbency as curate of the parish. Every contributor's name was inscribed in a presentation book.

Cars were owned by the wealthy residents who, when driving to Princetown, refilled their car radiators with water from Goadstone Pond on Peak Hill.

Charles Wilson's son, Norman, with his wife, Emily, took over the running of the Devon Tors Hotel, which was at numbers 1–3 Beech Villas.

Mr Heath started an electricity supply from a small hut near Willowby Park for residents in Meavy Lane.

1921

3 January – The Plymouth Cooperative Society purchased 3 and 4 Moorland Villas from W.H. Gulley and opened a grocery shop. William Gulley had a baker's shop here and Marian Thomas accompanied Mrs Gulley on her deliveries in Sheepstor and Dousland with her pony and trap. The roads were rough, only rolled stones, and Marian recalls the clip-clop of the pony. They made saffron cakes as well as bread. Marian was paid 3d. a week and the Gulleys moved to Tavistock and opened a laundry business. The Plymouth Cooperative Society had commenced business in Plymouth in 1860 and had opened shops in Tavistock and Princetown. Dividend was paid in the Yelverton shop twice yearly. A butchery was later added, then the pharmacy when the butchery moved into the grocery department. The telephone number was 32.

A war memorial for those parishioners who died in the First World War was erected at Crapstone crossroads.

The fire station was situated on the east side of the Devonia at Leg o' Mutton.

1922

The police station was at 4 Moor View Terrace and was manned by a sergeant and four constables.

The debut of the Yelverton Orchestral Society took place, with Kenneth Spooner as conductor.

Numbers 4 and 5 Devon Tors were turned into flats. Fairfield next door was the home of the curate of St Paul's and in turn became Len German's Dairy, Brown's Greengrocery and Stephen Thrall's Yelverton Carpets, before returning to use as a private residence.

The Army ambulance became public transport to Crapstone and Princetown.

The Poor Clare Sisters at St Anthony's left the area for Polperro.

Lord and Lady Seaton funded the building of the Roman Catholic church, Holy Cross, in Dousland Road. Mr R. White of Milton Combe built the first simple church. Lady Seaton gave the curtain posts behind the high altar, made from her four-poster bed. The little stained-glass window, high at the rear of the church, was brought from Buckland Abbey. Father Briggs refused to allow a burial-ground at the church.

Newholme in Westella Road became the home of Captain W.T. Turner, of the stricken ship *The Lusitania*, and his partner, Mabel Avery, until they were forced to leave by reporters who hounded them. He was 66 years old and had left his wife. He was made a scapegoat for the sinking of the vessel in 1915 with the loss of more than 1,200 passengers.

The local British Legion Branch opened in Yelverton.

1923

The Anglican Church bought 1 Beechfield Avenue as home for the curate of St Paul's.

The first opening and Blessing of Holy Cross took place on Easter Sunday.

15 September – Sheepdog trials were held near to the tumulus on the moor close to Leg o' Mutton. Organised by John and Clarence Spooner there was a grand exhibition by Yorkshire shepherds. Men and dogs travelled from Sheffield to Yelverton by rail. Local farmers taking part in the trials were Smale of Sheepstor, Williams of Goodameavy, Northmore of Goodameavy, Warne of Coppicetown, Pearse of Kingsett and Toop of Venton.

Norman and Emily Wilson bought the field adjoining Devon Tors from Lady Seaton and sold the land for building plots.

1924

The Bible Christian Chapel (Rock) was sold to Maristow Lodge of the Freemasons (founded 1898) for £450. The first Masonic meeting in the hall was on 23 September. Mr Hall had previously rented the chapel and opened a saddler's shop here.

9 October – Father Biggs was appointed as the first resident priest at Holy Cross, he lived in the Presbytery.

The Ladies' Section of the British Legion at Tamar View in 1930.

British Legion members.

Right: *This card was sent from Yelverton, a popular holiday resort in the 1920s.*

Far right: *Jim and Emma Thomas at 6 Yelverton Terrace, 1948.*

St Paul's Rectory in 2002 with Drake's Leat in the foreground.

Anne Rodd, eldest daughter of Arthur and Molly Rodd, on Grey Bird, 1928.

George Andrews from Leg o' Mutton flew in an Avro Biplane at Yelverton on 7 July with Berkshire Aviation tours. He ran the bicycle shop and employment exchange.

1925

The Bowling Club purchased the British Legion Bowling Club, which was on the green outside the Devon Tors Hotel. The Chairman was R.R. Rodd and the Hon. Sec. was A.C. Langton.

The golf links' new clubhouse was built.

1926

W.H. Gulley of Willowby and others signed deeds on behalf of the Methodist church for a semi-detached building in Kirkella Road for use by the minister. W.E.H. Howard sold the building plot for £62 on 10 May.

Sheepdog trials were held, making £223 profit.

10 February – Yelverton Fire Brigade's annual dinner was held at Andrews' Corner Café at Leg o' Mutton.

1927

St Paul's Church was consecrated. The altar was given by Col Johnston of Munster House in memory of David Johnston of the Royal Munster Fusiliers. He named his house Munster on the Tavistock Road.

Down Park Lodge was built and owned by Henry Hurrell.

The National Omnibus Company bought Devon Motor Transport.

The chapel at Holy Cross was licensed to hold marriages.

Elfordtown Lodge, in grounds of what is, at the time of writing, Woodcroft and home of the Rowe family, was demolished.

The first petrol pump was installed in Yelverton at Westella Garage.

Captain and Mrs Spencer Butler lived at Oakdene, 3 Willowby Park, where June was born.

Mr S.D. Margrett, manager for W.E.H. Howard, took over the building business with foreman, Mr W.G. Gloyne, as partner. William Gloyne was son of Oliver, steward at Buckland Abbey, living at Bradford Cottages in Buckland Monachorum.

A Neolithic greenstone axe was found at Yelverton and is now in Exeter City Museum (accession number 45/1927).

6 May – A British Legion Women's Section branch was founded in Yelverton.

1928

28 September – Trustees of the United Methodist Church, W.H. Gulley, Charles Harding and others, purchased the house known as The Manse on their site in Kirkella Road, built by Margrett and Gloyne.

Holy Cross Church was enlarged by Margrett and Gloyne; the entrance porch by the road, tower and steeple were added. Selected by S.D. Margrett, stone was used from Buckfast Abbey, the Roman Catholic monastery.

1929

The conventional district of Yelverton was formed.

The *Dewer Rides* novel by L.A.G. Strong was published.

W. Roberts, the chemist at Leg o' Mutton, ran a lending library. Robert Ricketts remembers that the books were mainly novels by Edgar Wallace.

1930

The *Come to Devon* official guide listed accommodation in the Yelverton district. 'Drake's country, glorious Devon'. Listed were: Mrs Prettyman, 16 Beechfield Avenue; Walter Priest, Westella Garage; A. Langton, Rock Hotel; Harold Kitto, houses to let, Devon Tors; Mr and Mrs Norman Wilson, Skylark Inn; Mrs Gidley at Clearbrook, Glenhaven; Miss Bromidge at Down Park.

Children played on the embankment of the disused tramway on the green before the roundabout was constructed. They called it the Ridge.

Marian Thomas, daughter of Jim, the porter at Yelverton Station, married Fred Hicks and bought a plot of land in Devon Tors Road for £80. Margrett and Gloyne built their bungalow, Tor Cot.

1931

Vicar of Walkhampton, Revd H.M. Harvey, was appointed as curate-in-charge of St Paul's.

The Harris family from Plymouth bought St Albans in Meavy Lane from the Rodds.

1932

The engine driver would toss his coat and bag from the cab as the train passed Harrowbeer Lane towards Horrabridge to save his carrying them back to Yelverton as he walked home.

Ladies were invited to join Yelverton Bowling Club.

1933

The Christie brothers brought a 240-volt AC electricity supply to parts of Yelverton. West Devon Electricity Company offices were in a green hut at Binkham Hill. Aubrey Maddock was telephone no. 7.

The first houses were built on the Binkham Hill estate, the development being completed in 1955. Houses were for sale at £450, with magnificent views.

The foundation-stone of St Paul's Rectory was laid south of the church.

Arguments over boundaries became heated as Yelverton pursued becoming a separate ecclesiastical parish from Buckland Monachorum. Neither parish wanted to lose the patronage of the wealthy owners of large houses.

1934

Morningside, the first house on Chub Tor road, was built.

Far left: *Bunting on St Albans for the silver jubilee of 1935.*

Left: *June Butler ready for St Cyprian's School at her home, Oakdene, in Willowby Park.*

Below: *At Kirkella Road Fire Station.*

Above: *Mounted women's patrol, 1940.*

Left: *The Electric Company at Binkham Hill.*

Left: *Ravenscroft School in 1939, with John Gelsthorpe as a pupil (4th from the left in the front row). Staff were (left to right): Matron Mrs N. Davies, Mr Beddy, Mrs Bailey, Mr Bailey, Miss Joy, Mr Disney, Mr Neale.*

Moorland Links Hotel was built with 26 bedrooms (many with their own bathroom), hot and cold water, a ballroom and outdoor swimming pool. The architects were Vanstone and Taylor of Plymouth and the builders were F.G. Williams of St Austell. Mrs A. Cockerton, wife of a director, laid the foundation-stone in August.

A fair was held annually at Leg o' Mutton. The men from the fairground would dive off Gratton Bridge into the River Meavy, the pool beneath being much deeper than at the time of writing.

1935

The employees of Spooners in Plymouth were conveyed to the sports field, now the Recreation Field, for games and sports every Wednesday afternoon when the store closed for the half-day. This field was known as Spooner's Field.

Yelverton separated from the church parish of Buckland Monachorum. The vicar of Walkhampton, Revd Harvey, became the first vicar of St Paul's. St Andrew's PCC requested that the Saxon font be returned to Buckland.

Miss Pitts advertised her school, St Cyprian's. She was keen on punctuality and correctness and was a firm disciplinarian.

George V's silver jubilee celebrations took place, with many houses decorated with bunting and flags.

1936

The first marriage service was conducted in St Paul's Church.

The font, designed by Sir Charles Nicholson and carved out of Bath stone, was given by Col Norrington in memory of his wife.

Buckland WI suggested that a bus shelter was erected at Yelverton. The Parish Council replied that, 'Commoners have this matter in hand.'

The cricket team played on the present cricket ground between St Paul's and the Big Rock, which was on loan from the Langton family, instead of on the green.

3 June – King George V and Queen Mary passed through Leg o' Mutton on their way to Tavistock.

1937

Barretts, at the southern end of the row of shops, was a high-class grocers called Moor Stores, who delivered groceries to owners of large houses. Metal railings were placed around the Devonport Leat outside the shop. The Co-operative stores also delivered to its customers in the outlying villages. Sawdust was scattered on the floor of the Co-op, swept up after closing time each day and replaced by a clean layer. Those who had sawdust on their shoes had shopped in the Co-op!

12 May – The flagstaff on St Paul's tower was erected to commemorate the coronation of King George VI.

1938

January – Yelverton fire crew, with those from Tavistock and Plymouth, rushed to extinguish the fire at Buckland Abbey.

1939

The fire station moved to Kirkella Road. Firemen and friends collected paper to raise funds for the purchase of fire-fighting equipment.

Stanley Margrett built his own house, Fairwinds, in Southella Road.

The network of old roads was destroyed. The roundabout was built and the 'Diamond Jubilee animal drinking trough' was moved across the road at the Big Rock.

Mr H.F. Bailey was the headmaster of Ravenscroft Preparatory School for Boys. The boys, who wore a brown uniform with Eton collars, walked to Meavy Lane across the moor in their tweed suits once a week for a dancing lesson with the girls at St Cyprian's School. John Gelsthorpe was a pupil at Ravenscroft and Diana Wallace and June Butler were at St Cyprian's. Fees at Ravenscroft were 40 guineas a term.

Areas of the golf course were taken over for anti-aircraft gun sites for the protection of RAF Harrowbeer.

The cricket club was forced to plant potatoes in the cricket field during the war years but they managed to keep the cricket square untouched.

A YMCA canteen was set up in St Paul's Church room.

A locomotive crashed through buffers at Yelverton on the Princetown railway line.

Gordon Palmer of Eggworthy Farm delivered milk to some areas of Yelverton.

1940

Women patrolled the moor on horseback, reporting anything suspicious to the police. They had permission to deflate the tyres of unlocked parked cars.

There were two choirs at St Paul's Church. The 10 o'clock choir sung for the Eucharist and the Matins choir for the later service. Queenie Spooner was the organist.

Rubble was brought from Plymouth after the bombing to the site of the aerodrome.

The Moor House Hotel, near Leg o' Mutton, was demolished as it was in the flight path at the end of a runway. Facing due south, it was set in more than three acres of grounds with a lawn tennis court and clock golf. The owner, Joseph Born, had died in 1927 and his widow Louisa lived until 1943.

1941

An aerodrome was built at Yelverton, called Harrowbeer, to protect Plymouth, following severe bombing of the city. The fighter airfield opened on 15 August, the first aircraft landing on 31 August. Trekkers walked to the area each evening from

Left: *Binkham Hill residents' outing to the coast.*

Below: *Kay and Arthur Wilson at St Paul's Church, 8 January 1949.*

Above: *Val Rodd married Tony Donell in January 1951. Pictured in Willowby House with them are,*

left to right: *June Butler, Mr and Mrs Donell, Mrs Arthur Rodd, Nick Bone, Eve Rodd. Arthur Rodd had recently died.*

Left: *Elizabeth Harris with her father from St Albans, 23 June 1951.*

Below: *The wedding of Winnie and Arthur Thomas, 1944.*

Above: *The Guard of Honour for Betty and Second Lieutenant Ronald Middleton as they leave St Paul's Church after their wedding, 1951.*

Plymouth to escape the devastation and returned by train in the morning. A canteen was opened at Yelverton and many slept in the Rock Chapel (the Methodist Church). A red light was placed on St Paul's tower to warn aircraft of its presence.

The spire was removed from Rock Methodist Church.

Ravenscroft School closed at the end of the Easter term. The house became the HQ for 276 Squadron. Udal Torre Sanatorium closed. The Government also commandeered the coach-house for the RAF.

1942

Number 19 Fire Force from Plymouth and district worked at St Vincent's, formerly Briar Tor. The workforce members were brought by bus from Plymouth. George Drury from Kingston-upon-Thames and Arthur Goldberg were in charge. Miss Minnie Grainger from Milton Combe was a typist with the Fire Force.

RAF Harrowbeer was a major fighter station and the skies around Yelverton resounded to the roar of Spitfires and Typhoons.

1943

One stick of four bombs fell between Elfordtown Cottage and Chub Tor during the war and another in Harrowbeer Lane.

1944

Sunday 28 May – 21-year-old Flt Sgt Jack Pringle clipped St Paul's tower with the wing of his Typhoon on take off, crashing in a field opposite Gratton where he was killed. The vicar completed the morning service that had been in progress. Thomas Bromidge, then aged nine, rushed outside with the other boys after the service where they picked up stones that were still warm. The Air Ministry paid for the repairs. A black and white board replaced the light on the tower to assist with visibility.

27 August – Maj. Glenn Miller and musicians landed at Yelverton aerodrome owing to foggy weather.

27 September – Winnie Rowe married Arthur Thomas in St Paul's Church, she a Lance Corporal and cook in the Army and he a lengthman on the railway. Winnie has always lived in Yelverton and in the same house at Binkham Hill since 1937, cooking in many large houses and residential homes.

1945

2 August – President Truman made an unexpected landing at Yelverton in his huge Skymaster, 'The Sacred Cow'. St Mawgan, his expected destination, was closed because of fog.

Revd R.N. de B. Welchman succeeded Revd Harvey as vicar of St Paul's.

A huge bonfire was lit near Leg o' Mutton to celebrate VE Day. Parish celebrations took place.

1946

April – First meeting of Yelverton Women's Institute. The President was Mrs E. Augusta Dobson.

Recreation field and hall given to the residents.

1947

Capt. Arthur Rodd of Willowby House purchased Buckland Abbey and renovated the Cider House, but died before the family moved there. His wife, Molly, lived there until 1981.

W. Roberts, remembered for his huge glass coloured bottles in his chemist shop at Leg o' Mutton, died in his own house, Devonia.

1948

Films were shown in the church hall on Friday nights. The operator came from Gunnislake and once the audience had to wait while he went home to fetch a missing reel.

Buckland Monachorum Parish Council sought permission from the Air Ministry to walk on a footpath across the aerodrome.

1949

A single bell was placed in St Paul's tower.

For several summers the Moorland Links Hotel opened the swimming pool to the parish. The author remembers cycling there as a small child and sliding down the water chute.

Arthur and Kay Wilson married in St Paul's Church on 8 January and took over the running of the Devon Tors Hotel in April.

1950

Harrowbeer Airfield closed. Sentiments expressed by residents were: 'Yelverton has changed considerably in my time here. It was lovely before we had the aerodrome spoiling the area.'

A new bowling-green was planned in the War Memorial Field.

1951

23 June – The wedding of 2nd Lieut Ronald Middleton REME and Elizabeth Augusta Dorothy Harris of St Albans took place at St Paul's Church. The reception was at the Rock Hotel. A recording of the bells of St Andrew's Church, Plymouth was broadcast from the tower. Betty Middleton is a descendant of Sir Christopher Harris who purchased Buckland Abbey for Sir Francis Drake in his absence abroad in 1581.

Dartmoor became a National Park. Yelverton and Roborough Down lie within its boundary.

Moorland Links Hotel was sold for £17,100.

The spire was removed from Holy Cross Church.

1952

Devon County Fire Service moved to the fire station next to Holy Cross Church and was manned by a volunteer brigade.

The Mothers' Union with Revd Dick Welchman.

Above: *The wedding of Pauline Palmer and Colin Northmore at the Rock Church, 17 August 1965.*

The Rock Hotel with garages.

Right: *Brownies in the church hall, 1970s.*

Below: *The Country Game Fair held at Elfordtown, July 1971. Left to right (on cart): Colin and Pauline Northmore, Mark, Glenda, Kathy Huggins. Blossom, the cart-horse, was used in the television series 'The Onedin Line'.*

Right: *A steam rally in 1972.*

The Young People's Union (YPU) was held at 6 Willowby Park, the home of the Gelthorpes.

Maria and Anthony Falkus, twin babies, were placed in the care of the Sisters at Nazareth House. Anthony died aged five months but Maria was returned to her mother. Later, Maria became a nun in an enclosed Order and is now Sister Julian.

1953
A new flagstaff was erected on the tower of St Paul's to commemorate the coronation of Queen Elizabeth II.

Edmund G. Price purchased land which was once part of the Moor House Hotel.

The bowling-green was opened in Meavy Lane.

1955
A BBC television mast and station were erected on North Hessary Tor above Princetown, changing the Dartmoor skyline.

1956
5 March – Princetown railway line was closed with great pandemonium as passengers' tempers became fraught because there were not enough seats available on the trains that day until more coaches were sent from Plymouth.

Brothers Fred and Reg Bidder, butchers in Moorland Villas, lived in Byleat and Little Forrest.

1957
24 January – St Paul's tower was struck by lightning.

7 April – Railway bridges were removed on the Princetown line over Gratton and Meavy Lanes.

1958
10 December – The Manse in Kirkella Road was sold by the trustees of the Methodist Church, as it was 'no longer required for Methodist Trust purposes'. The house was renamed Ericas.

1959
The signal-box at the railway station was closed.

August – the heyday of Yelverton Horticultural Show was held in a marquee near St Paul's Church.

1960
25 May – Harrowbeer aerodrome was inspected to determine its suitability or otherwise for development as an aerodrome to serve Plymouth and the surrounding district. This caused a heated debate between Yelverton residents and Plymouth City Council.

October – Evensong was broadcast from St Paul's on the BBC Home Service.

F.G. Trathen and Son's first European tour took place with the name of Yelverton on the coaches. The name was taken to all parts of the world until the 1980s.

The Yelverton Residents' Association was founded. Station Cottage was built for the stationmaster and the former station house became the doctors' surgery.

1961
Col T.J. Emerson was captain of the golf club.

Harrowbeer aerodrome was finally rejected by the House of Lords as the civil airport for Plymouth.

The Ladies' Group of Yelverton was formed for women who were not members of the MU. Subscription was charged at 3s.6d. per annum. The aim of the group was to give friendship and support to members, meeting once a month in the church hall.

1962
29 December – Plymouth to Launceston railway line was closed, the last train from Plymouth being delayed for hours by heavy snow. Yelverton Railway Station was closed.

Devon Tors Hotel opened a bar.

The wartime airfield was restored to common-land grazing and 'eyesores' were removed.

1963
Harold Kitto, late of the Post Office, shop and fire service, died.

Dr John and Mrs Christine Brindle purchased Willowby House and lived there until 1997.

Heavy snow and blizzards. Helicopters were used to transport nurses and doctors in the Yelverton area.

1964
Yelverton voted to keep the civil parish undivided from Buckland Monachorum. At a public meeting in the church hall a farmer warned that a division from the old parish would leave Yelverton open to the 'vulturous eye of Plymouth'.

Ron Price made the wooden cross behind the altar of St Paul's to replace curtains. At one time one side of the cross was painted red but this was disliked by the congregation and so was turned around.

Steins built Kulu in Station Lane near Elfordtown Farm, now called Little Markham. Julius Stein bought the paddock of Kingstone House for £100.

New Police station, with two houses opened in Tavistock Road.

1965
Ditches and earthbanks were built in and around Yelverton by the DNP to prevent parking of cars on the grass verges.

The cricket club joined with Plymouth Bohemians and continues to flourish.

1966
Part of the Rock Hotel was turned into flats and it became the Rock Inn.

1967
John Foot was made a life peer and took the title Lord Foot of Buckland Monachorum after his home parish.

Far left: *Maj. John Piper receives a cup from the judge at the Dog Show, with Lady Jane Roborough pictured on the right.*

Left: *Walter Alway of Willowby Park caught this enormous record-breaking brown trout of 11lb 1oz (5kg) in Burrator Reservoir in July 1967.*

Buckland Monachorum Parish Councillors.

Below: *Flt Lt Naomi Richards marries Flt Lt David Jones at the Rock Church in September 1985. The Guard of Honour consisted of members of the RAF, Army Parachute Regiment and the Royal Marines.*

Above: *A Yelverton and District Local History Society meeting in 1983.*

Mary Crane opens the bottle bank on 27 April 1987.

1968

The Paperweight Centre opened at Leg o' Mutton.

The houses at Clonway near the Red House were built.

1969

Nazareth House was for sale, which was run by the Poor Sisters of Nazareth and had been built as Briar Tor, a private house, and then used as St Vincent's, a home for unmarried mothers, followed by the home for babies.

July – A public inquiry was held in the church hall regarding the siting of a new health centre. The site at the top of Westella Road was not favoured by nearby residents.

1970

A field was sold to Wimpey for the building of the Grangelands houses.

1971

June – Devon Area Health Authority built the health centre on the chosen site which was opened by and named after Gerald Whitmarsh.

The tower at the Rock Methodist Church was removed, due to deterioration.

July – Country game fair held at Col Spencer's home at Elfordtown. Archery, fly-casting, racing pigeons and pony-club jumping were part of the show.

1972

Steam Rally held at Yelverton.

1973

20 September – Moorland Youth Club was formed for young people of the parish in the church hall.

Rock Methodist Church was restored to the Tavistock Circuit from Plymouth.

Fairfield Greengrocery was opened next to Devon Tors Hotel by Win Brown.

1974

A plan to search for a site at Yelverton for a new secondary school was revealed by the Parliamentary Education Secretary.

Arthur and Kay Wilson built Cerrito, Spanish for little tor, behind the Devon Tors.

1975

The Ladies' Open Group changed its name slightly and became unaffiliated to the Church or any organisation.

1976

Binkham Hill Pony Show was inaugurated.

1978

Lord Bishop of Plymouth opened the extension to Holy Cross Church.

St Albans was demolished and more houses built in the garden, creating St Albans Park.

16 December – modernised and larger Holy Cross Church opened.

St Paul's Church tower was repaired at a cost of £1,672.

1979

Wimpey began building houses at Grangelands.

Devonia Nursing Home was established.

1980

West Devon Highways sub-committee decided against imposing a solution to prevent problems in parking at the forecourt, the area in front of the shops.

1981

15 August – A granite block with a memorial plaque was unveiled at Leg o' Mutton in memory of airmen who served at Yelverton during the war. The Yelverton and District branch of the Royal British Legion erected the memorial stone. The block of granite had fallen from a horse-drawn P & DR wagon above Clearbrook 150 years earlier and lay beside the track. It was lifted off Clearbrook Moor by helicopter.

1982

November – First meeting of the Yelverton and District Local History Society.

Devon Tors Hotel was closed and converted into more flats.

A Garden of Remembrance, south of St Paul's, was created in memory of Audrey Camp who died in 1980. She was the wife of the rector, Revd Peter Camp.

Yelverton Ladies' Open Group meetings were held in the War Memorial Hall on alternate Thursday evenings. Speakers and outings were arranged throughout the year.

1983

The Tennis Club opened, the courts were located at the lower end of the Recreation Field.

A grand piano was given to St Paul's Church by the family and friends of Bernard and Adeline Beer in their memory.

1984

Dartmoor National Park created a mini arboretum in front of Greenbank Terrace. Trees at the old Nazareth House and Catholic Church were removed.

Yelverton War Memorial Fête was held in June in the Recreation Field. Revd Robin Ellis opened the fête that provided funds for a kitchen and toilet extension to the hall. The fête included races, dog shows, stalls and games and a farrier working on horses provided by Pauline Northmore.

1985

4–7 July – The golden jubilee of St Paul's was celebrated in July with a flower festival in the church

Left: *Thanksgiving service held at St Paul's Church for the life and service of Flt Sgt Jack Pringle in the presence of his family and the Royal British Legion with Revd Richard Tebbs.*

Stephen Thrall of Yelverton Carpets.

The shops in 2002.

Above: *Winnie Thomas has lived in Yelverton, except during her war service, all of her life.*

Above left: *Yelverton Cricket Club during a match, 2002.*

Left: *Yelverton Village Park at Leg o' Mutton is now a favourite meeting-place for families.*

and exhibitions in the hall.

Fred and Robert Moxham took over the Roundabout Garage.

Peter Brown was presented with the British Empire Medal for his meritous service with the Devon Fire Brigade.

A public notice-board was erected at the forecourt at a cost of £1,200.

Ravenscroft Nursing Home opened.

Stephen Thrall opened Yelverton Carpets at Fairfield in Beech Villas.

1986

A parish meeting was held to review the one-way traffic system through the forecourt in front of the shops. Signs appeared in February, stating 'no entry' and 'no exit'.

June – First residents moved into Briar Tor, a sheltered-housing scheme with a warden.

The Bridge Club was organised in the War Memorial Hall.

1987

Westella Works was sold for £113,000. Originally headquarters of W.E.H. Howard of Rock Vale, it was taken over by Margrett and Gloyne.

April – A bottle bank was placed at Leg o' Mutton.

A bus shelter was built opposite Grange Road on the A386.

1988

The refurbishment was carried out of public toilets near St Paul's.

The bus shelter at the forecourt was rebuilt.

8 August – High Colton Estate Agents opened.

Peter Wright opened the Caravan Park in Abbey Lane for stored caravans.

A landowner was fined for felling a line of mature trees at old Nazareth House.

1989

Planning permission for the demolition of Harrabeer House Hotel for conversion into flats was refused.

1990

Plans were made to build a new hall on the site of the War Memorial Hall in Meavy Lane, previously a timber cricket pavilion. Sue Delooze was the committee secretary.

Dartmoor National Park prepared a study of the area and reviewed development since 1977.

1991

Devon Tors, marketed as Beech Villas, was divided into seven one- and two-bedroom apartments.

Arthur Wilson died in Cawsand.

5 September – Opening of Yelverton Business Park at Crapstone, a modern office and business unit development. The units were for sale or to let on a 21-year lease.

A wooden 20-foot-high cross was taken to the top of Sheeps Tor on Good Friday by the congregation of St Paul's.

1992

Nelson Bowden opened the veterinary surgery near the Rock Inn.

Meavy Lane was closed for the laying of a gas main.

21 March – Opening of new Village Hall on the site of the War Memorial Hall by Lord Morley. The total cost was £124,000.

Tree planting was carried out by the Parish Council near Briar Tor and Leg o' Mutton. Beech, oak and birch trees were planted.

The caravan park was opened for touring caravans.

1993

Barclays Bank closed.

29 March – Royal Mail transferred the 11 delivery rounds of PL20 from the Yelverton to the Tavistock office.

1994

March – Revd Richard and Lynn Tebbs, Sarah, Andrew and Helen came to St Paul's Rectory.

3 April – The BT national code for Yelverton became 01822.

1995

Tree planting was carried out by the DNP at the top of Station Lane.

Yelverton Golf Driving Range opened in Abbey Lane.

Police station closed.

8 May – The 50th Anniversary Thanksgiving of VE Day was held on Harrowbeer aerodrome from 5.30p.m.

1996

A village appraisal was carried out to highlight the needs of the community.

Monsignor Michael Hanley retired as RC Parish Priest. Fr Terence Perkins was appointed.

1997

18 May – A Thanksgiving service was held for Jack Pringle of 263 Squadron RAF (see 28 May 1944). A new flagstaff was erected in his memory.

Binkham Farm was sold off in five lots.

A new pharmacy and Post Office opened in Moorland Villas in place of Brown's Moorland Greengrocery. The Post Office was relocated from Leg o' Mutton and the post box placed outside the Post Office from the corner by the Rock Hotel. The telephone kiosk at Leg o' Mutton was removed.

The building of Clover Park on the site of Harvey's Nurseries took place in Station Road. Will and Amy

Left: *Members of the Yelverton Fire Service, 2002.*

Below: *A plaque is unveiled at the new fire station.*

DEVON FIRE AND RESCUE SERVICE
YELVERTON FIRE STATION
THIS STATION WAS OPENED BY
COUNCILLOR B. C. J. HUGHES
CHAIRMAN OF
DEVON FIRE AUTHORITY
ON 1st JUNE 2002

P. YOUNG O.B.E. MPhil F.I.FIRE.E
CHIEF FIRE OFFICER

Above: *The Rock Inn, 2002.*

Right: *At the new fire station, with Holy Cross Church in the background, are Pauline Brown, Mary Davey, Mike Glinn, Peter and Mary Price.*

Below: *Dartmoor tors and hills look magnificent from Yelverton.*

Harvey grew flowers and vegetables here which they sold in their Rock Stores years ago. Lady Seaton of Buckland Abbey, where Amy had been in her employment, gave the land to them. Many former brides of Yelverton remember choosing flowers for their bouquets from the greenhouses. The old station lane is a private road and only provides access to the private residents of Whistledown, Station Cottage, Clover Park, Kingston, Inglenook, Little Markham and Lower Elfordtown and the fields belonging to the Langton family. This lane with a pavement was not only the entrance to the station but was once the way to the cricket pitch. Foot passengers reached the station from Meavy Lane by way of the cinder path, which followed the embankment from Hillside in Meavy Parish (see *The Book of Meavy, 1999*).

The number of households estimated by the Tavistock Rural Transport Group in Yelverton was 700.

1998

A Christmas tree was placed on the roundabout for the first time, funded by nearby businesses. This is now an annual event.

14 September – The YelverCare project was launched, the community care scheme for the benefit of residents. The volunteer helpers can be called on to assist with transport, visiting house-bound or isolated folk, walking dogs, gardening, shopping and providing domestic assistance for those in need. Each road in the area has a link volunteer and this successful scheme, with someone on the end of a telephone, always needs more helpers.

1999

St Paul's Church festival of a 'Celebration in Flowers' was held in June, coordinated by Ann Medhurst.

The Corner Shop at Leg o' Mutton reopened after several months' closure.

Nelson Bowden, of the vet surgery, was named Vet of the Year at the Horse of the Year Show at Wembley Arena.

Robin and Angela took over Leg o' Mutton Inn.

Jan Langton joined the Disabled Sports England swimming squad at the age of 12 years.

2000

1 January – commemorative seats were placed in each village by Buckland Monachorum Parish Council and dedicated by local clergy.

August Bank Holiday Monday – millennium celebrations were held at Leg o' Mutton for all ages in the parish.

Gillian Smith opened her beauty clinic near the Rock Inn. She undertakes all aspects of beauty therapy.

Sunday 10 September – opening of the Village Park at Leg o' Mutton Corner. Lord Morley cut the ribbons.

2001

A devastating year for farmers, businesses and walkers who were affected by the foot-and-mouth epidemic for most of the year.

19 November – West Devon Borough Council introduced a new 'green box' recycling scheme with weekly collections.

A scheme to demolish the old Lloyds Bank premises in Moorland Villas and replace it with a block of flats was refused. This area was once the site of Penmoor, Dr Willington's surgery in 1912.

2002

Nigel Hosking at Yelverton Garage introduced the community Internet link.

1 June – A new fire station for the Yelverton unit of the Devon County Fire Service opened with a new fire engine.

The florists, 'Heaven Scent', opened between the Co-op and Yelverton Stores.

Willowby House was renovated. The large, elegant Victorian house has an 'OnQ' home cabling system for twenty-first century communications. New houses were built in the grounds.

Wonderful stories of life in Yelverton from 1930–60 are told by so many who were children here during those years. Stories are told of the railway, children's parties in large houses, pony clubs, the British Legion, picnics at Gratton Bridge, the golf club, private schools, the shops, church services, family walks, the aerodrome and the war years. Bleak and exposed Yelverton may have been, but the friendships made in those formative years were everlasting and childhood memories from that time made an impression that developed the mind, body and spirit. Yelverton is regarded as a place to return to, as home, bringing back memories of halcyon days. The Dartmoor air was invigorating, character forming, and there was a spirit of adventure among the children who walked for miles and roamed in the countryside alone or with friends.

Charles Causley wrote a poem of seven verses titled 'Yelverton', when he spent the wartime years in the Royal Navy, which was printed in the *West Country Magazine* of 1949. One verse reads:

We've a nice little place here at Yelverton,
And although it's a bit chilly in winter
There's plenty of room on the moor for the kiddies
And we have nice little outings to Princetown.

Snow on Yelverton Green

131

Left: *Frances Buckingham at her home in Buckland Monachorum village, 2002.*

Right: *Mary Butland with Tibbles in the orchard at Cuxton Farm in 1956.*

Above: *Harold Butland, father of Mary and David, at Cuxton Farm in 1956.*

Above left: *Students and teachers of the Devon County Dairy School in the 1890s. Hilda Attwill is second on the left in the middle row. This touring dairy school encouraged modern dairy practices.*

Above: *Derek and Betty Harris at Didham in 1926.*

Left: *Derek Harris shearing sheep at Didham.*

Chapter 10

FARMS & GARDENS

Families living in the farmhouses, and men and women employed by the farmer, have farmed the acres of land within the parish boundary through the centuries. Growing crops and rearing animals from dawn to dusk was the way of life for most inhabitants of the parish. For centuries large estates, those of Buckland Abbey and Maristow, owned the land which was sold in the latter half of the twentieth century. Farms have amalgamated and the land is now farmed by a few. The farmhouses have been sold as private dwellings, not part of the farmstead. The owners of these ancient houses care for their homes and many dwellings have been restored and upgraded, the land surrounding the house being farmed by someone living some distance away.

A century ago the parish map shows all the farmsteads scattered throughout the countryside with fields and moorland surrounding the farmhouse. Land use is still mainly agricultural and in the west of the parish the River Tavy maintains a heavily-wooded character where once orchards and gardens flourished. Farms shown in the parish were at Balstone, Berrator, Fairtown, Coppicetown, Alston, Long Ash, Uppaton, Pound, Binkham (Bincombe), Lake, Elfordtown, Mabor, Yeoland, Whistleighdown, Axtown, Stoke Hill, Venton, Broom, Coombe, Uphill, Bickham, Sowton, Lower Hellingtown, Blowiscombe, Place Barton, Crapstone Barton, Didham, Cuxton and Torr. In early times the farmers met at the weekly market in Buckland but since the nineteenth century stock was taken to Tavistock and Okehampton. In the parish of Buckland Monachorum farming was the way of life. Farmhouses now lived in by the farmer and his family are few. The break-up of traditional farms is leading to larger farms and towards smaller part-time 'hobby' farms.

The oldest of these farmhouses is probably Berrator (SX477687), dating from the late-fifteenth century. It is described by English Heritage as having:

... good features from several periods and an unusual original plan of two rooms, one of which may have been a shippon. If the lower room was a shippon, the house was not a true longhouse as there was separate access for humans and animals, a reflection of a high house status.

A rare feature in West Devon is the fifteenth-century-transomed window and the building is Grade II* listed for having special architectural interest. In his notes, G.W. Copeland states that:

There is no evidence that the fifteenth-century windows of the house are not original survivors and no reason whatever for saying that they come from a medieval chapel which formerly stood at the top of Hatch Mill Lane.

Margaret Crymes lived here in 1715. The house is partly built into the hillside and is now private property. Elfordtown Farm on the banks of the River Meavy is also of this date.

Uphill farmhouse (SX502660) is also of great historic interest, having a remarkable number of old windows. This original farmhouse was built in the sixteenth century as a three-room house with a through-passage and is a Grade II listed building. It is an important house that shows an interesting development of its plan, where a shippon was added as a front wing at the higher end and a parlour wing added to the lower end. The hall was then relegated to kitchen status. A very small first-floor room behind a chimney may have been a garderobe or lavatory, which suggests a sophisticated house in the sixteenth century. William Willcock owned Uphill Farm in 1850, John Hamlyn owning Sowton Farm nearby. John Hamlyn lived at Sowton until 1925 and from 1914 he farmed Uphill fields with his own. The Beer brothers farmed Uphill from 1935. Both these farms are ancient settlements and are now private residences.

Venton, a Grade II listed farmhouse, was built in the sixteenth century and altered in 1688, the date inscribed above the granite arched doorway. South-east of the house is the ancient barn with a granary and cart shed. This has five doorways of stone arches with granite keystones. The threshing-floor was above the shippons and to the south-west of the farmhouse is another shippon with attached pigsties. Harry Hillson farmed at Venton and at the time of writing Patrick Toop farms it. Stoke Hill Farm was run by Fred Blowey in 1910 and the Hatch family later in the twentieth century. The four sisters and two brothers delivered milk, cream, butter and eggs to the Crapstone residents. At the bottom of the lane is Cumerew, a large house where the author's grandfather was employed to show special breeds of pigs

Monica Harris with her pony at Didham.

Sybil Ball helping to feed lambs when she and her husband were on holiday at Didham Farm.

Above: *Dick Barons harvesting in the 1950s.*

Right: *Phyllis Harris, 2002.*

Far right: *The shaft of a cross at Crapstone Farm in 1913.*

around the country in the early-twentieth century.

Balstone farmhouse (SX471686) was built in the seventeenth century close to the left bank of the River Tavy above Hatch Mill. This was home to Roy and Rene Creber and their sons in the 1950s after they left Fairtown Farm. This is a Grade II listed building. David Northmore who lives with his family here in a converted barn at the time of writing runs the farm. Fairtown Farm was farmed by George and Margaret Butland who then moved and became tenants of Berrator Farm. John and Frances Buckingham took over Fairtown Farm and were the last tenant farmers from 1954–75. For a time it was then run as a riding stables. Neighbouring farmers now farm the land and the house is tenanted. On the road towards the village is Orchard Hill, once the home of the Misses Chowen followed by Jim and Nellie Northam. Further along the road is Arranmore. This bungalow was lived in by Richard and Sue Northmore when they first married and before that by the Bellan family from 1938–51. Paul and Joan Bellan had lived in many houses in Yelverton, Crapstone and Buckland village before establishing a poultry farm and market garden here. In the 1940s they reared chickens, ducks and rabbits, Paul grew row upon row of vegetables and every summer harvested the field of hay at the rear that reaches Cuckoo Nest Lane.

Cuxton (Coxton in 1546) farmhouse (SX487683) dates from the sixteenth century and perhaps was formerly a mansion; it is also a Grade II* listed building. The outside of the house seen today dates from 1693. In the indenture of 29 November 1693 between Elize Crymes and Joseph Drake, Cuxton house and garden in Buckland Churchtown is described as lying west of a close of land called Butt Park and in possession of Thomas Seller, to be sold to Matthew Torr. Fields mentioned are Easter Park and Little Gratton (P&WDRO 70/119a). Living in the farmhouse in 1891 were Thomas and Mary Spry, their son, Thomas, and his wife, Mary, and their son, Thomas, with three servants, Alfred and William Beer and Annie Ball. This farmhouse is the nearest to the village of Buckland and is lived in by farmer David and Helen Butland and their family at the time of writing. Fields originally belonging to this farm were sold in the last century for housing estates in the village. David's father, Harold, farmed here before him and the previous generation of Butlands moved to Cuxton in 1908. Harold Butland married Winifred Northmore from Gratton Farm and their children, Mary and David, grew up at Cuxton. Mary married John Baker and farmed at Boynton near Whitchurch. The family has always been involved in the life of the community. David has a herd of Friesian cattle, 90 dairy cows they milk twice a day, 365 days a year, and about 130 beef cattle. Field names at Cuxton are Above the Wall, Garden Park, Hilly Park, Showland Field, Best Meadow, Five Acres, Dry Meadow, Gratton, Sewer Field and Stock Meadow. Fields at

Netherton are Lower and Higher Outer Nursery, Lower and Higher Inner Nursery, Three Corners and Bare Lane Field.

Didham Farm (SX485679) was home to Derek and Phyllis Harris during the Second World War until they retired in 1986 and bought a bungalow in Horrabridge. The farm was named from the crossing-point on the River Tavy close by, Denham Bridge, and was listed in 1281. Derek went to Didham in 1938 with his parents when he was 17 years of age. Before the Harris family arrived the Wilcocks, followed by the Rogers lived there. Mr and Mrs Harris with daughter, Monica, were tenants of Mr Endacott. Didham was about 63 acres and Derek rented more land across the Tavy. Phyllis walked 70 cattle, which included 25 milkers, along the roads to pastures new and with sheep and poultry and the upkeep of the farm days were busy. Fields, as in all other farms, had appropriate names for the farmer, First Field, Second Field, Greenlane Field and Hilda's Field. This last field was named after Hilda Waldron whose bungalow had been built in a Didham field. Phyllis and Derek supplied 70 turkeys at Christmas, giving a glass of sherry to those who collected the Christmas turkey from the farm. The largest turkey Phyllis remembers preparing for the oven weighed 39lbs or 17.7kg. Didham orchards had once reached Winsbeer at the back of the farm and a cider press was part of the farm. As a young man Derek remembered that when his family came to Didham in 1938 other farming families with the initial H came to the parish in the same year; Harris at Didham, Hamley at Place Barton, Hatch at Stoke Hill and Hillson at Coppicetown.

The farm was sold and the fields surrounding the house bought by local farmers. The development of five acres around the house and barns caused much controversy in 1989 when Buckland Monachorum Residents Association fought to stop the conversions of the buildings on the outskirts of the village. Didham is now a residential area.

Crapstone Barton (SX491679) gives its name to the hamlet of Crapstone and the Crymes family built an early-seventeenth-century farmhouse on the site of a former mansion. The windows and doorways are noteworthy and there is a large entrance porch of historic interest. One fireplace is of special architectural interest. In the principal room, over this huge fireplace which has moulded granite jambs and an oven in each side, is a plaque dated 1646 and a coat of arms of the Drake and Crymes families. Also in the Grade II* status is the garden wall and squared piers opposite the porch at the front of the house. Richard and Elizabeth Crymes bought the manor of Buckland Monachorum that included acres stretching from Milton Combe to Horrabridge (5,500 acres) in 1546. This included Crapstone Barton, but the couple never lived in the house. Their son, Ellis, moved to the house in 1567 and increased the farm acreage to about 7,000 acres by purchasing land from Sir Richard

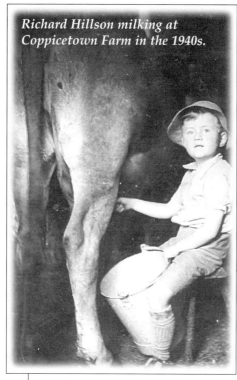

Richard Hillson milking at Coppicetown Farm in the 1940s.

Scuffling turnips at Coppicetown Farm, 1955.

Charles Horn at Blowiscombe Farm with members of the family including Blanche, Dorothy and Winifred.

Hele Cottages in 1958, scheduled for demolition, were between Coppicetown and Alston Farms.

Grenville at the abbey. The Barton was lived in by a succession of Crymes until Elize married Mary Drake. The house was refurbished so this family lived in the vicarage, or perhaps Lovecombe, for ten years during the seventeenth century. It is recorded in the hearth tax returns of 1674 that Crapstone Barton had 17 fireplaces, which suggests the house was much larger than it is today. Elize had two wives, fathered at least 24 children and was buried in the vault of St Andrew's Church.

Revd Amos Crymes sold land of the estate in 1750 retaining glebe land around the old vicarage from the present vicarage to Freezabere, and from the road down to the brook. Field names around Crapstone Barton were Bradford Meadow and Quarry Park Meadow on the right-hand side of the road to Milton from Buckland and on the opposite side of the road the fields were named Little Meadow, Great Meadow, Orchard and Barn Park. Fields around the farmhouse and along the road to Crapstone were Little Park, Edgecombes Park, The Head, Seven Acres, Three Acres and Six Acres. Land towards Abbey Lane was named Hill Park, Peterfields Park, Middle Longlands, Yonder Longlands, The Moores Platt, Conigeers Platters, Conigeers, Pease Park and Little Meadow. Where Crapstone houses now stand were two large fields called New Park and Lower New Park. Field names change over the years for many reasons and Peter Barons' names for the fields are Pathfield, Higher Nine Acres, Lower Nine Acres, Sewer Field or Pease Park, Outer Great, Inner Great, Bulwarks, Warren, Edgecombe Park, The Lawns, Bramble Park, Kiel Meadow, Kemps Hill, Hillson's Meadow, Orchard, Rookery and Barn Park. After many occupants Crapstone was sold to John Elford in 1786 who left it to George Leach. This gentleman had Crapstone House built for himself south of the Barton in 1845. Richard Hillson rented the Barton from 1892 and farmed the many fields in the centre of the parish. Lady Seaton purchased the property and once more, after 400 years, Crapstone Barton became part of the Buckland Abbey estate.

Richard Barons rented and farmed Crapstone from 1944 and from 1947, when Arthur Rodd bought the Buckland Abbey estate, his landlord was the Rodd family. An Italian prisoner of war worked on the farm from where he was billeted in Plympton. The Barons' family only knew him as Pako and allowed him to pursue his artistic ambitions to paint and draw around the farm, as he had no liking for manual labour. Dick Barons gave permission for the Buckland Flower Show to be held in his field at the top of Buckland Hill every summer when he farmed Crapstone Barton. Dick and Dorothy Barons passed over the running of the farm to their son, Peter, and his wife, Anne, in 1971 and ten years later, when Molly Rodd sold the estate, Peter and Anne purchased Crapstone Barton. At the same time, Sir John Barraclough bought Crapstone House. The farm

includes the house and 221 acres of original lush farmland, on some of which Peter grazes his beef cattle, the other land being arable. He sold his dairy herd in the summer of 2002.

Charles Horn tenanted Blowiscombe Farm (SX493661) in 1886 from Mr Gill at Bickham House. He purchased the farm in 1919 and his son, Charles, farmed here until his retirement in 1979. During the Second World War, Charles, who lives in Tavistock with his second wife, Mary, at the time of writing, employed a German farm worker, Karl Fischer, and trusted him to run the farm when the family went on holiday. Field names were Calves Platt, Poor Field, Rock Park, Cross Lane Field, First Meadow and Ten Acres. Four bombs dropped in Ten Acres in 1941, probably jettisoned as the planes left Plymouth. In 1958 a severe thunderstorm set a barn on fire out in the field.

Only four years after taking on the tenancy Charles Horn senr entered a farm prize competition. The extracts from *The Journal of the Royal Agriculture Society* of 1890 gives a fine description of his farm management and a wonderful picture of Blowiscombe, pronounced Bloscombe, Farm at that time.

In one field there was the unusual sight of the ox-eye daisy, generally so indicative of poverty, growing in the midst of most succulent clover, which is frequently taken as a proof of fertility. The daisies were significant of previous poor treatment, whilst the latter was the result of recent applications of forcing dung. A dairy herd of 20 cows is kept... 50 ewes... three horses do the work on the farm. A chestnut colt bred here was by a sire of the old packhorse breed, for which the district was at one time very celebrated and from which many a four-horse team has been taken direct from the plough to a nobleman or gentleman's stable. Hardly any corn is sold but what little is grown is mainly consumed on the farm. On this farm is the best and most convenient set of buildings met with.

The landlord, Mr Gill, was pleased with the farm prize of highly commended, it seems, and presented Mr Horn with 'manure sufficient for 12 acres of permanent grass.'

The house became a highly successful bed-and-breakfast establishment in the 1980s but is now privately-owned and the land surrounding it is farmed by Buckland Abbey estate. Lawrence and Rachel Newman, who bought property nearby from the Lopes estate in 1999, have converted barns into an elegant home and workplace, incorporating many ancient features and mechanisms discovered in the buildings. In 1851 Sarah Northmore, a widow aged 45 years, lived at 'Bloyscombe' with her children whose ages ranged from one to 23 years old. The farm consisted of 20 acres and she employed five servants. The children's names were Jacob, Martha, Jane, Emma, Maria, Joseph, Sophia, Sally, John and Mark.

Left: *Dick and Hetty Hamley, well-known farmers in the parish.*

Right: *Poultry at the back of the farmhouse at Coppicetown, 1961.*

Below: *John and Mary Dawe and their grown-up children at Yeoland in 1870.*

Above left: *John and Elizabeth Spry's children at Alston Farm. Pictured are Russell, Roy and Freda in July 1907.*

Above right: *Elizabeth Spry at Alston Farm. She was a teacher at Milton Combe School and in her last years lived in Richmond Terrace in the village.*

Coppicetown Farm (SX483689) lies in the north-west of Buckland, standing at crossroads leading to Double Waters, Hatch Mill, Alston Farm and the village. The lane leading to the moor from the farmhouse towards Double Waters is Summertown Lane. Mark and Sarah Hillson live in the farmhouse with their children, Lily and George, at the time of writing. Mark's father, Richard, moved to Coppicetown in 1938 when he was a small boy. Old granite buildings around three sides of the quadrangle in front of the house make this an attractive old farm. Richard's father moved into the farm when George Warne retired and went to live at Sunny Glen in the village. The sixteenth-century farmhouse is a Grade II listed building with a cobbled entrance. Deeds of the farm go back to 1729 and it was a mixed farm until Mark took over; he specialises in dairy farming. The farmers at Coppicetown continued making cider long after others in the parish had discontinued and up to 1954 parishioners bought the drink from the Hillsons. In the final year they sold this fermented apple juice the cost was 6d. a gallon, that is about 1p for 2 litres. Seven orchards surrounded the farm and cider-making, in the traditional method in a cider press, was carried out every year from October to the end of January. Richard and Ann Hillson lived on the farm until they moved to their new house of their own design close to the farmhouse, which they called Coppice Park. Hele Cottages at the top of Cuckoo's Nest Lane were for workers at Coppicetown Farm. The buildings were demolished in 1958, one of the last occupants being Mr Howard. Beyond Alston Farm is Down Lane leading to Alston Moor, Bucktor and Double Waters.

Lower Hellingtown Farm (SX505665) is approached from Yeoland Lane. Richard Dawe, son of John at Yeoland, lived here in 1891 with his wife, Mary. Dick Barons farmed here in the 1940s before becoming a tenant of Crapstone Barton. The charming Georgian farmhouse is a private house and at one time the farm was well known as an Arab stud. A member of the Dawe family in the nineteenth century also lived in Higher Hellingtown. In 1715 the owner was Walter Northmore.

Yeoland House or Higher Yeoland was home to the Dawe family in the nineteenth century. In 1853 John and Mary Dawe lived with their 11 children at the farm, ages ranging from one to 21 years. All the family was born in the parish including the parents. Their names were Elizabeth, John, Richard, Polly, William, Ellen, Ann, Thomas, Henry, George and Emma. Four servants lived there too; Tom Greep, Michael Pitton, Ann Jutsham and Noah Robjohn. The Dawe children married and had their own children in farms in Milton Combe, Buckland Monachorum, Yelverton, Meavy and Hoo Meavy. Many of the children married into local farming families that included Giles, Ward, Spry, Northmore, Willcocks and Hillson. John Dawe formed a group of like-minded friends to build the Baptist chapel at Hoo Meavy after he had a disagreement with the vicar of Buckland Monachorum. His wife had been Mary Andrews from Gratton Farm and members of her family are buried in the tiny graveyard at Hoo Meavy (see *The Book of Meavy*, 1999). Jean and David Trahair lived at Yeoland House with their family in the latter half of the twentieth century and Austin Northmore was the farmer at Yeoland Farm, known as Lower Yeoland in the nineteenth century when William and Mary Badcock lived in the farmhouse with their family. William Badcock was the agricultural labourer for John Dawe.

Place Barton, also called Home Farm, was built in 1851 and was home to farmer Dick Hamley and his wife, Hettie, who had been a Toop, the family before them. Part of Buckland Abbey, the tenant farmer here had supplied the inhabitants of the abbey and in 1946 the land consisted of 247 acres. Dick and Hettie retired to Crapstone Cottage and the farm was sold in 1981.

Gnatts Farm at the top of Milton Combe Hill was built in 1953 with 147 acres of land. Bill Mattacott from Lower Lake in Meavy Parish farmed here until his death in 2001 and Mrs Mattacott still lives in the farmhouse at the time of writing. Mr Beyer worked at the farm for 20 years, followed by Alida Pollard who lives at Lower Lake and ran the farm with Mr Mattacott.

The Spry family has farmed Alston Farm (SX489693) for 200 years. Elize Crymes owned it in 1687 and sold the lease to Thomas Jope. The farmhouse was built at about this time. Ward and Chowen, local auctioneers, held a successful stock sale for John Spry at Southway Barton, formerly behind the George Hotel near Roborough, on 15 August 1915 before he left the farm for Alston. In the newspaper it was reported that the stock were well shown and 'Mr Spry received many congratulations on the success of the sale'. The sale included fat ewes, Dartmoor breeding ewes, a pen of two-teeths, fat lambs, keeping lambs, a two-year-old ram, cows in calf, maiden heifers, two-year store steers, 18-month-old steers, yearlings, rearing calves, young slip pigs, sow in farrow, porkers, yearling cart colt and an unbroken three-year-old cob. Fat lambs made £2.12s.6d. each and the unbroken cob made more than 27 guineas. Alston Farm consists of about 200 acres and John and David Spry share the working of the farm at the time of writing. Their parents, John and Betty, live at Fairfield at the top of Buckland Monachorum village and bought two Didham fields. John's parents, Mary and Roy, farmed here in the 1940s and '50s. Roy's mother was Miss Elizabeth Clifton, headmistress of Milton Combe School in 1895. John and Elizabeth Spry held their golden wedding anniversary at Alston Farm in 1949. The Sprys at Alston have always rented fields near the village.

Left: *David and John Spry at Alston Farm, 2002.*

Above: *Mary Beer married Roy Spry in 1940. In the doorway of Alston Farm are her father, Ned, Russell's three children and best man, Charles Horn, who married Mary after the death of her husband.*

Left: *Richard and Sue Northmore at Torr Farm, 2002.*

Background: *Whistleigh Farm in 1952, sketched by Richard Mabey from a photograph.*

Below: *The Spry family at Alston for the golden wedding anniversary of John and Elizabeth in 1949. A visitor, the author, is third from left in the front row.*

Torr Farm (SX480684) is in the care of Richard and Sue Northmore and their son, David, and his family, who live in a converted barn at Balstone Farm. Torr Farm consists of 150 acres and the Northmores have bred a pedigree Charolais herd of cattle since 1965. Milking has ceased at the farm. A new crop on the farm in 2002 is lupins, grown for their protein content as a cattle feed. A total of 12 acres were planted with the crop in the first year. Altogether Richard and David farm 250 acres with land at Balstone, Berrator and at Lovaton in Meavy Parish. Sue runs a holiday let near the River Tavy called Wheal Bertha. The fields at Torr are known as Great Field, Higher Long Park, Lower Long Park, Middle Park, Rick Park, Wood Park, Charity Field, Eastern Park, Orchard Park and Winnamoor Meadow. Some fields at Balstone are Mine Field, Fifteen Acres, Boskenna Field and Hatch Mill Field. Richard's father, Bill, arrived at Torr as a young man in 1926. He came to Buckland Parish from Meavy where he was buried following his death at Torr in 1995. Bill Northmore will always be remembered for his dramatical skills in the Buckland Drama Group where he and Joan Bellan often played the farmer and his wife, causing much mirth with their natural Devonshire dialect. The house in the woods below Torr Farm, near the footpath to the river, is Rooksmoor, home at one time to Mr and Mrs Charles Brittan. Charles was the son and grandson of the two famous Dartmoor watercolour painters who at one time lived at Burrator House in Sheepstor.

Axtown Farm is described by G.W. Copeland as a picturesque and interesting sixteenth-century house facing west with thick walls. It once had granite doorways and had the reputation of being haunted. An old church path, once cobbled, passed the front door and a tunnel was discovered beneath the kitchen floor. Sid Bragg farmed Axtown and Bob Bragg and family were at Whistleigh. Bob and Beryl with their six children lived at Whistleigh Farm whilst Sid and Lil moved to Axtown when his parents moved. Susan Woolacott (née Bragg) grew up at Whistleigh and remembers talk of the tunnel beneath the kitchen floor at Axtown and her uncle digging a massive hole under the flagstones and being admonished by his father. There was a chapel at the farm until the 1960s. Susan and her family remember a ghost, a monk that was seen or felt on many occasions. The family delivered milk from Whistleigh Farm that had come from Axtown. Her mother, Beryl, always kept the bathroom window open during the war to prevent other windows falling out when guns were fired or an aircraft passed low over the house, while taking off and landing at Harrowbeer aerodrome. Like many other houses close to the aerodrome, occupants talk of the house shaking. Axtown Farm was sold by auction in January 1992 in nine lots. Land made £2,550 per acre. Whistleigh is now a private residence and houses were built at the top of the lane on the Crapstone Road.

Binkham Farm (SX525686) on the Walkhampton Parish border was sold in five lots on 31 July in 1997. Lot two at the rear of Heathfield is in Walkhampton Parish and the farm bungalow and about 43 acres of land is in the north-east of Buckland Monachorum Parish, west of Woodman's corner. The farm was originally Bincombe. The Peter family farmed at Binkham for many years. Binkham Hill estate is on the left of the road towards Yelverton.

Nearby in Lake Lane, close to the parish boundaries of Meavy and Walkhampton, are two Lake Farms in the parish of Buckland Monachorum. In 1891 George and Jane Palmer lived in one of the farms with son and daughter-in-law, George and Clara, and young grandchildren, Ernest, Jane and William. William Mudge, with his brother, Frederick, and sisters, Emily and Eliza, lived at the other Lake Farm. Coward's Lake Farm is probably named after John Coward who once owned the farm. Coward owned Harrowbeer Farm in 1793.

Harrowbeer Farms are no more. In the 1891 census Henry Willis and his wife, Elizabeth, were farmers at one farm and William and Mary Vigars with son and daughter, William and Mary, were at the second Harrowbeer Farm. Elias and Mark Moses were tenants here when the farm was owned by Sir Anthony Buller of Pound. William Arthur Bidder was farming at the first farm 30 years later and William Vigars the son was running the second farm. This farmhouse is now the Harrabeer Country House Hotel. Mr and Mrs Bidder and their two sons became the butchers in Yelverton, telephone number 8, still known as Bidders the butchers. Their two working horses were called Violet and Heidi. The lane and farms were part of the development of Yelverton before the coming of the railway that passed from the tunnel through the fields to Horrabridge. The Yelverton aerodrome was named after Harrowbeer from the prominence of Harrowbeer on old maps. Large houses were built near the railway line along Harrowbeer Lane, which passes between the Rock Methodist Church and the A386 above Horrabridge. Field names remembered in the twenty-first century are North Park, Lower North Park, Screechy, Lower Screechy, Council Field, Pig Platt in front of the house and Goldsmiths. Screechy fields were once one field, Higher Long Park, owned by John and Louisa Screech who purchased them from Lady Seaton in 1879. Field names of the two farms on the Tithe Map of 1842 are Round Meadow, Long Park, Broughton's Field, Homer Park, Little Three Corners, Beech Field, Barn Park, Church Park, Poor Park, Town Park, Higher Brake and Great Down Field. Beechfield House and Beechfield Avenue houses were built in the field named Beech Field. The Cann family sold fields and the paddock in the 1950s. Modern houses have been built in the lane and Grangelands estate was built in the farm fields between the lane and Leg o' Mutton Corner. The views of the Dartmoor tors provide the names for the closes in Grangelands: Cox

Above: *Lake Farm is close to the Plymouth and Devonport Leats.*

Right: *Bill, Valerie, Merrille, Susan, Linda and Helen Bragg at Whistleigh Farm, 1950s.*

Left: *Lady Kitson and the author with Lord and Lady Morley at Pound House, December 2001.*

Below: *Bunching flowers for the London market, 1949. Pictured at Greenlane Gardens are,* left to right: *Pat Coaker, Rita Walser, Jeannie Claypon, Ivy Bennett, Keith Turner, Rene Turner.*

Left: *Rita Walser picking daffodils at Greenlane Gardens, 1949.*

Tor, Vixen Tor, Ingra Tor, Great Mis Tor, Pew Tor and Leather Tor, albeit with different spellings to the Dartmoor names.

Bickham House (SX494654) is in the south-west of the parish and has been home to the Lopes family since 1919. Massey and Jeannie Lopes live here with their children at the time of writing. Bickham belonged to the Elfords in the seventeenth century until 1837 when John Hornbrook Gill purchased it. The old house was demolished in 1876 and a new one was designed by William Morris, which has a beautiful stained-glass stair window. It is a country house of fashionable design. The staircase may have been brought from Bickham farmhouse, which is 300m to the north-west and may have been the original house. The majority of fireplaces were brought from Maristow House in the latter part of the twentieth century.

Pound House, Pound Farm, Lodge and cottages are part of Pound estate. The Earl and Countess of Morley live at the house. Pound and Cumerew were sold by Mary Crymes in 1788 and later passed by marriage to Sir Herbert Sawyer, Admiral of Devonport Dockyard. He rebuilt Pound and sold it to Sir Anthony Buller in 1828. In the census of 1851 Sir Anthony Buller, aged 70 years, lived at Pound House, 'landowner and magistrate for Devon, retired pension judge of the Supreme Court of East Calcutta'. His unmarried adult children lived with him; Isabella, Louisa, Anna-Maria, Emma, William and Heriot Jacqueline. Uppaton Farm, often pronounced Tibberton Farm, was between Buckland village and Pound in Uppaton Lane. Home to Parker and Daisy Daw and their daughters in the 1930s it was farmed recently by the Vallance family and is now private dwellings.

Hatch Mill on the left bank of the Tavy was put up for sale in June 1827. It was advertised as water grist- and flour-mills with four acres of orchards.

The mills are capable of making 150 sacks of flour per week and have a never-failing supply of water; with drying-kiln, smut-machine, two bunting-mills, three pairs of stones worked by two excellent water-wheels.

It was the most important mill in the parish producing fine flour until 1906 when it then ground corn for use as cattle feed. The mills at Milton Combe and Lopwell also ground corn for cattle, Milton Combe Mill closing in 1888 and Lopwell in 1872. There were 19 acres of pasture land, arable and meadow in a high state of cultivation. Most people who frequented Hatch Mill in the 1940s and 1950s associate Hatch Mill with Miss Cann. William Cann is listed as the farmer at Hatch in 1906 and 20 years later the farmer is Mrs Mary Jane Cann. Miss Cann, their daughter served cream teas in her front garden only a few feet away from the left bank of the River Tavy and her few dairy cows wandered about on the grass verges.

Families arrived every day at Hatch Mill with picnics piled into old prams or balanced on bicycles. There were two beach areas where the river banks were sandy and everyone swam in the river, whatever the weather. Blackberries were picked from the hedgerows, damsons from the trees in the hedges and windfall apples from the fields. Those with their own teas bought milk from Miss Cann who filled the kettles with fresh water. Primus stoves or small campfires using dry driftwood were lit to boil the water. The footpath still passes the old mill and the house but the river banks are private property. All the older parishioners remember Hatch Mill with great fondness; this stretch of the Tavy is idyllic.

Greenlane Gardens (SX480681), also known as Champernowne's Wholesale Nursery, began in 1928. Mr E.B. Champernowne came from Dartington Hall. The nurseries above the Tavy valley cover 25 acres and face south. Peter Argles owns the nursery and employs seven full-time workers and five part-time staff at the time of writing. His grandfather, Lesley Wates, bought the business from E.B. Champernowne. Plants are sold to garden centres and, as with all gardeners and farmers, weather and diseases affect the business. Many local people have been employed at the gardens over the years. Rita Kennedy (née Walser) was a full-time worker for several years and in 1952 earned a wage of £3.16s. a week. Flowers, such as daffodils, tulips, iris, anemones and gladiolli were grown and sent to Covent Garden market in London. Cut early in the morning the flowers were bunched, packed into boxes and sent to the capital. From 1960 flowers were picked and transported in tight bud. After the flowering season the fields were ploughed and the thousands of bulbs collected, dried, sterilised and stored ready for planting in August. All bulbs were planted by hand, sometimes in the moonlight, making it almost impossible for the workers to stand up straight when they were allowed to go home. Anemones were cut in the frost and the fields resembled a multi-coloured carpet on those winter mornings. Rita remembers those who worked with her; Pat Coaker, Ivy and Bill Bennett, Bill and Rene Turner, Mr and Mrs Jago, Mr and Mrs Jeffreys, John Northey, Roy Northam, Les Cannon, Hilda Waldron, Maurice Howell and Sam the tractor driver. Jeannie Claypon, daughter of the owner of the nurseries, was also part of the workforce; her father had married Miss Champernowne. Hilda Waldron did the back-breaking work after delivering the post on foot to outlying farms and houses as far away as Double Waters. Always jovial, she walked into the fields calling, 'Here comes Lady', and encouraged everyone to work a little faster. She always wore a hat and gloves. The Greenlane workforce knew Hilda as Lady. The daffodil growing ceased here in the early 1990s and in 2002 the gardens concentrate on growing shrubs and herbaceous perennials in containers. E.B. Champernowne, as the gardens are called, supply the

Top left: *Buckland Monachorum Vicarage in 1912.*

Above left: *Hoeing the nursery area near Lovecombe Cottage are Tom Hooper, Maurice Northam and Bill Miles.*

Above: *The tower at The Garden House with day lilies in the 1940s.*

Left: *Jim Fox repairing the doors at The Garden House.*

Below: *View of Buckland Church tower and distant Cornish hills from the Garden House.*

wholesale market and have supplied the Eden Project in Cornwall with more than 15,000 plants. The plants are transported by Champernowne's own transport from as far as Cornwall to the north of England for sale in garden centres or in specialist nurseries.

Next to E.B. Champernowne is Buckland Cottage Nursery, owned by Colin Carver. He has his own outlet of garden plants at his garden centre at Long Ash. Situated at the top of Long Ash Lane between Pound Corner and Buckland village it is on the edge of the Down. Nearby are Uppaton and Uppaton Lodge. Down below Greenlane Gardens on the banks of the Tavy is Ludbrook, which has been the home of the Tuckett family for many years. The footpath from Ludbrook leads to Hatch Mill and on to Berrator and Coppicetown.

Farmers and landowners listed in the parish in 1938 were:

Edward Buller Champernowne	Greenlanes	Arthur Rogers	Long Ash Farm
Hon. John Parker	Pound	John Spry	Alston Farm
Rear-Admiral Richard Plowden	Shiplake	Robert Toop	Venton Farm
A. and I. Beer	Uphill Farm	John Vallence	Didham Farm
Mrs Jane Beer	Fairtown Farm	George Warne	Coppicetown Farm
Fred Blowey	Stoke Hill Farm	George Elliott	Lillipit Farm
R. Blowey	Pound Farm	Dick Barons	Lower Hellingtown
Harold Butland	Cuxton Farm		Home Farm
Mrs Mary Cann	Hatch Mill	Charles Horn	Blowiscombe Farm
Richard Hamley	Place Barton or	Thomas Luxton	Balstone Farm
	Home Farm	P.J. Peter	Binkham Farm
Richard Hillson	Crapstone Barton	John Sleeman	Hellingtown Farm
Frank Menhinnick	Berrator Farm	Mrs Henry Wonnacott	Whistleigh Farm
William Northmore	Torr Farm	Dick Hamley	Mabor Farm

'A gem of a garden' is how The Garden House (SX496682) is described. It is open to the public every day from 1 March to 31 October from 10.30a.m. to 5p.m. and is situated across the valley of the Lovecombe Brook from Lovecombe House. The ruins of the vicarage built in 1305 are surrounded with flowers, trees and shrubs of the most glorious scents and colours, a romantic terraced walled garden. The roofless stair tower is part of the first vicarage but it is not certain how this spiral staircase fitted into the house. The barn nearby was originally the kitchen with a massive fireplace almost the width of the room. With the granite archways in the garden wall the buildings are Grade II listed.

Views across the rolling lawns and flowerbeds to the nineteenth-century vicarage are uninterrupted and enclosed with graceful trees as a backdrop. The variety of plants is astonishing and the view down the Lovecombe valley to St Andrew's Church and the Cornish hills beyond is very beautiful. The Garden House is run by a charity, the Fortescue Garden Trust, which was founded in 1961. Admiral Sir Hugo White is the chairman of the trustees. With his wife, Katharine, and three daughters, Cecily, Mary and Nancy, Lionel Fortescue bought the vicarage in 1945, then known as Shiplake, and renamed it The Garden House. He had been senior language master at Eton College and brought his gardener, Bill Miles, with him to Devon. Bill and Dorothy Miles and their young son, David, lived in the Annexe. Wendy and Bernard were born later. The Miles family lived here until 1961. In those days the employees collected bracken, or ferns, off the moor and made a large rick near to Lovecombe Cottage. Men trod on the top of the bracken and watered it with a hosepipe, adding sulphate of ammonia to aid the composting process. The rick was cut with a hay knife and used in the gardens. Walking between Buckland Monachorum and Crapstone through the pathfields was always a delight. Mr Fortescue planted hardy cyclamens at the entrance gate along the borders as far as the kissing-gate that led to the footpath from the huge chestnut tree. These dainty little blossoms of pink and white created a serenity for the walker unusual among the natural wild flowers of the fields. The footpath to the church has now been sunk in the gardens to maintain the public right of way. Lionel died in 1981 and Katharine two years later.

Keith and Ros Wiley came to manage The Garden House in 1978 and extended the gardens into the surrounding fields. Lionel kept four to six Jersey cows in these fields that were milked by Cecil Northam from Lovecombe Cottage, nestling in the valley below. The Garden House was the second vicarage at the site, built in 1826, and was home to six vicars of Buckland Monachorum and their families.

Mary Northam with her father, Cecil, and goats at Lovecombe Cottage, 1938.

Bill and Dorothy Miles with David, Wendy and Bernard in 1952.

Thousands of visitors admire the gardens at The Garden House each year.

Charles Barter was the first to live in this new house after he pulled down the old vicarage. It is said that Amos Crymes who lived in the old vicarage planted the ten lime trees along the footpath to the church in memory of his ten surviving children between 1752 and 1770. In the 1940s there were nine trees and now there are eight. The field is always known as Ten Trees. Children remember climbing on the chestnut tree with its huge low-slung branches where the clergy made a swing for their children. Keith Wiley has interpreted the landscapes of many countries he has visited into acres of the garden. More than 20 different areas of plants make the whole garden a vision that has materialised into a colourful dream garden. Ideas from South Africa, Crete, Switzerland, the Alps and the British countryside form the oval garden, a bulb meadow and quarry garden. Cottage gardens form the sunken garden, the prairie garden and the walled garden. Keith is inspired by natural landscapes and believes that The Garden House is at the forefront of a revolution in the gardening world. He has moved away from the traditional garden and is passionate about the future, the site, the soil and the coming together at the right time of a balanced garden with plants, birds and butterflies.

'I know,' he declares, 'that it will be the best garden of the twenty-first century in this country.'

The tennis-court lawn was the site of the older vicarage and the tower's granite spiral stairway links the different levels of gardens. One of the villagers, Tom Hooper, began working for Lionel Fortescue in 1946 and worked in the gardens until he died in February 2000. The steps near the 'bowling-green' were placed in his memory. The scent of bluebells in the month of May, the marvellous colours of the trees with blackbirds singing from the hedges are enhanced with flowering shrubs and local stonework. It is a romantic garden; there is a special atmosphere. There is a restaurant in the house where paintings by Ros Wiley are displayed. She paints in the Annexe, which was the old chapel built by Revd Richard Hayne when he was the vicar of the parish. Robin Armstrong, the artist who has a studio at Lopwell, once used the Annexe and many of his paintings date from the time he spent in the tranquil settings of the garden. The Garden House employs about 20 local part-time staff and the target number of visitors each year is 28,000.

Lovecombe House (SX496684) is of sixteenth-century origins with modern additions. In a beautiful situation the house retains late-sixteenth and early-seventeenth-century remains with a plain late-eighteenth-century addition at the west end with thinner walls. The granite doorways and windows in the house are very old and the present owners have discovered further huge granite fireplaces. It is home at the time of writing to Admiral Sir Hugo and Lady White who care for the beautiful gardens. Captain Charles Keys, former owner of Lovecombe, planted many of the trees. Elize Crymes married Mary Drake in April 1636, joining two prominent families of the parish. They supposedly lived at Lovecombe while their home, Crapstone Barton, was rebuilt. Mary wrote to her brother who was on military service: 'From Lourcombe, this Thursday 1640. Sweet brother, I shall intreat you to bye me a fan and six thousand of pinns.' The little cottage below, Lovecombe Cottage, is the birthplace of the author.

I remember, I remember,
The house where I was born,
The little window where the sun
Came peeping in at morn.

Thomas Hood (1799–1845)

The winding road leading down to the cottage from Crapstone and the footpath through the fields to Buckland Monachorum village made this a halfway-house where the teapot was always warm. Built in the seventeenth century it had two rooms down and two rooms up, although today it has the addition of a bathroom and a conservatory. The little cottage was a welcome retreat for so many callers when it was the home of Barbara and Cecil

Lovecombe Cottage.

Northam. Their two daughters, Mary and Rachel, were born here and it was their home for 50 years. Surrounded by gardens, orchards and the brook flowing past the front door, the cottage was built into the hillside below Lovecombe House. Wild flowers filled the Dell and the Platt, a weeping-willow tree overhung the brook and vegetables filled the cottage garden. An idyllic childhood playground in a sylvan glade.

The two arches of Denham Bridge, 1912.

Maristow House in 1921, which is on the border of the parish at Lopwell.

Grenofen Bridge, 2001.

Above: *The Rock Hotel, 1913.*

Left: *Copper was mined here at Virtuous Lady, near Double Waters.*

Chapter 11

LOCAL INDUSTRIES

In the past landowners in the parish provided employment in tin and copper mines as well as in agriculture and horticulture. Businesses provide work in the twenty-first century in the leisure industry, attracting visitors from all over the world to country-style accommodation and entertainment. Mining minerals out of the ground was once of great importance, providing work for labourers and their families. Mostly found in the river banks and the nearby hillsides, mines were opened along the borders of the parish mainly in the nineteenth century. Workers walked for miles to the mines and laboured hard for 12 hours before the long walk home, six days out of seven. Mines were worked hard from 1830 for about 50 years. Stone tracks were created over the moors down to the valleys, still used as footpaths, and many hundreds of men from the parish were employed in the mines. Tin had been streamed on Dartmoor from the rivers for centuries before this and the tin ingots taken to the stannary towns on the edge of the moor to be sold. Tavistock was one of these four towns and the first great court was held at Crockern Tor in 1494. Nineteenth-century tin and copper production was carried out by digging and blasting it from under the ground.

In the Tavy valley about six mines were worked near Double Waters where the Walkham flows into the Tavy. There were the Devon Consuls, Lady Bertha, Virtuous Lady, William and Mary, Walkham United and Wheal Crebor. The ore was taken from the mines to Morwellham by pack-pony and from there it was sent to South Wales for smelting. It was usual for a miner and his family to work in a mine although children under 12 years of age were not allowed underground. The boys took the ore by pony up the hill-

*Ruins of a mine building
at Double Waters, 2002.*

sides of the Tavy for collection at Orestock. Virtuous Lady (SX474698) was a copper mine and in 1871 the amounts recorded were 244 tons of copper ore to the value of £1,455 and 2 tons of black tin valued at £156. This mine is probably named after Queen Elizabeth I. Henrik Kahlmeter visited this mine in 1724 and noted that it was 10 feet wide. He estimated the quantity of fine copper in the ore was 16 per cent. The mine captain's house was 100 feet above the River Tavy on the left bank and the foreman's cottage was later the home of Mary Oxenford, who owned the mine at the end of the twenti-eth century. This is now Tavy Cottage and is lived in by her nephew. She stipulated in her will that the nephew who inherited the house must live in it. Mrs Oxenford had lived at the site for 40 years and took visitors down into the mines. Her adopted daughter, Maureen, drowned in the river near her home. The Virtuous Lady was profession-ally examined in 1920 and it was found that the lode had been exploited to a depth of about 220m at a location 200m from the confluence of the two rivers. By 1937 only a few adits and ruined build-ings remained. Below Double Waters near to the River Tavy there was Bertha Consuls (SX471689), Bertha Consuls East (SX478690), Lady Bertha (SX471689, 300m north of Balstone Farm) and South Lady Bertha north of Denham Bridge – all producing copper and arsenic in the nineteenth century. Some records were kept on the production at these mines but if rocks could divulge their secrets the silence of these hills would come to an end. Miners returning to the site of their workplace of silent abandonment after the mines closed found it difficult to recognise features they once knew so well.

THE BOOK OF BUCKLAND MONACHORUM & YELVERTON

H.G. Dines states that: 'Copper was one of the earliest metals known to man and has always been an important commodity. Next to iron it is the most valuable of the base metals.' Recorded outputs of the Lady Bertha are 8,200 tons of copper ore from 1855–94, including 530 tons of pyrite, 6 tons of black tin, 1,715 tons of arsenic and 5,300 tons of mispickel. The Bertha mines were small mines. South Lady Bertha was also known as Ludbrook Mine. Ponies were not used underground in the Tavy valley but two blacksmiths' shops were near Double Waters where ponies were shod and tools made and sharp-ened. Pumping and crushing mecha-nisms were worked by wheels, driven by the water carried by leats which was taken from the river to the mine, and leat channels can be traced. Leats were granted by a licence, issued by landown-ers. Sir Massey Lopes gave permis-sion to the mine captains for a head-weir or dam to be placed on the River Walkham in 1856, the rent being £50 a year for one such leat to the Tavy valley. In one of many accidents a boy was killed here in the engine house. In Calstock churchyard his tombstone reads:

The Devon Tors, a thriving hotel, with Dartmoor ponies on the village green, 1960s.

Sacred to the memory of Isaac Sleep who was killed in the Virtuous Lady Mine by the crank of the water-wheel, 18 August 1831. Age 14 years.

Houses and buildings at the site were pulled down when the mine closed but wheel pits and low-arch bridges can be found covered in moss, bracken and trees. There is a circle pit lined with stones that con-tained the capstan where a pony walked around pulling the chain which brought large buckets of ore and men out of the shafts. These iron buckets were called kibbles. Near the wooden bridge over the Walkham before its confluence with Tavy was where the women, or bell maidens, broke the ore, washed it and stacked it on the cobbles for collection for Morwellham. Women wore hessian aprons and bonnets with a stiffened peak in an attempt to protect their eyes from flying stones. Men wore sacks around their waists and shoulders, leather boots and felt hats. Scant protection for their safety. Many bridges on the Tavy below here were washed away in floods, especially after the thaw of the 1891 blizzard.

Mines closed when prices for the ore collapsed and mounds and shafts, covered in vegetation, are all that is left from a thriving nineteenth-century industry

which made money for the owners and hard labour for the workers. Farmers whose animals have fallen into old shafts have called out firemen to rescue them. In 1978 the Yelverton crew rescued a heifer stranded part way down a 180-foot-deep shaft in the Walkham valley. The owners of mines were often a group of men who put money into the project but took no interest in the conditions of the people who went underground. The Plymouth and Dartmoor Mining Company was formed in 1835. The joint owners were listed as William Evans, William Prance, William Walker, William Burnell a grocer, Joseph Lindon a merchant, William Paley a chinaman, William Eales and William Pitts a malt-ster, all of Plymouth, and John Paull of Tavistock.

These people being desirous of undertak-ing the mining of tin, copper and other metals in Devon and Cornwall agreed to raise the sum of £100,000 in 2000 50-pound shares and to form themselves into a company partnership society.

This company sold the mines in 1844 and they changed hands again in 1855. In the Walkham valley on the parish border there were mines where villagers worked, usually sleeping roughly at Horrabridge during the working week. Wheal Franco, named after Ralph Franco who changed his name to Lopes, stretched under the River Walkham. This was drained in 1870 after nearly 40 years of output producing more than 10,000 tons of copper ore. Miners walking from the village of Buckland Monachorum walked the paths that led in a direct line to Horrabridge through fields and over West Down. There were clay pits near to Bedford Bridge in the nineteenth century and the West Devon Brick Works occupied a site where red bricks were manufactured bearing the name Horrabridge. Near Grenofen Farm is the site of an old ferro-ceramic mine. Many farmers are sure that iron was mined there but no record of output has been found. The ore extracted was of such poor quality that it was used for brick making. Within the parish and away from the valleys a small copper mine opened near Stokehill Farm in 1851 and again in 1861. It was named after Sir Anthony Buller who lived in the mansion at Pound. Known also as South Roborough Down Mine it extended to Roborough Rock and produced 1,514 tons of 6.5 per cent copper ore.

In 1938 new workings were begun at a mine on Roborough Down that had been only worked for one year in 1864. Trial shafts were sunk half a mile south of Clearbrook Halt from which small quantities of rich wolfram were obtained. About 20 men were employed to the west of the railway line and machinery put in place. Bad weather caused flooding and a subsidence blocked the mouth of the workings. Little work was done and the machinery was removed in 1940.

There were grist- and flour-mills at Hatch on the left bank of the River Tavy below Balstone and a sale notice of the mills in 1827 describes the buildings and 19 acres of fields. Situated four miles from Tavistock and two miles from Lopwell quay, from where the flour was shipped, the mill was advertised as producing 150 sacks of flour a week, 'for a person desirous of carrying on an extensive and spirited trade'.

Lower down the Tavy valley near Maristow two mines were worked on north-to-south lodes. Lopwell Mine was in the parish of Bere Alston but provided employment for people living across the river in Buckland Monachorum Parish. In the valley of the River Meavy on the east of the parish Yeoland Mine was first worked in Elizabethan times, all shafts driven east to west. The main lode of Yeoland Consuls crosses Roborough Down three-quarters of a mile south of the old Yelverton Station. The workings of the mine were east of Yelverton Golf Club and it was worked from about 1851 to 1858. The buildings and machinery of the tin mine at Yeoland Consuls were removed in 1935. Walking from Yelverton to Hoo Meavy through the woods on the right bank of the Meavy, Yeoland House is seen on the left. It was the mine captain's house. A leat carrying water from the River Plym near Legis Tor was used to power the water-wheel, a good distance away on Dartmoor beyond Cadover Bridge. The leat crossed the River Meavy by launder. The mine was open by 1851 and the captain was Joel Manley until 1884. J. Beare was captain in 1887 and the last one was called Pote. In one week in 1887 Beare sold 6 tons 11 cwt of black tin at £59 a ton making a profit of £100. East Yeoland was worked from 1882–88. Miners collected their wages by climbing an outside staircase on Yeoland House, then known as Counting House, and receiving cash from a first-floor window. Mine workings crossed Roborough Down to Yeoland Mine and ravines on the golf course between the 13th and 16th holes, as well as at the 2nd and 18th, are still visible and create hazards for golfers. Yeoland Tin Mine consisted of Yeoland, South Yeoland, East Yeoland and Yeoland Consuls.

Roborough Down stone, used from an early period in Devonshire churches, is found near Tavistock and is a hard porphyritic elvan, taking a fine polish. Many quarries were opened in hillsides in the parish for stones used in building materials.

Forestry is another important industry in the Tavy valley where trees are grown for timber and fuel.

Softwood trees are being replaced by hardwoods. At Lopwell limestone was brought up the river in a raw state by barges and farmers collected lime from the kilns, travelling along Lime Road above Milton Combe. The cartloads of lime were spread on the land to adjust the pH, neutralising the soil.

Tourism is still an important local industry, bringing visitors to the parish to stay in hotels and guesthouses and to visit the many attractions the parish offers. Some parishioners open their homes for bed and breakfast, a list of which can be found on the Internet at www.drakesdartmoor.co.uk which gives contact addresses. Phrases describing the accommodation include:

Peaceful setting in lovely gardens with stunning views; ideally suited for Dartmoor and the coast; unspoilt countryside with superb country and river views; ideal for walks and cycling.

Guesthouses and hotels are advertised and there are cottages let for self-catering in the villages and on the farms. The parish has always attracted visitors for the healthy air and panoramic views of Dartmoor, and none more so than Yelverton. This settlement has an elderly population and consequently four residential homes have opened in large Victorian houses.

The Devonia Nursing Home was built as American House or the Temperance Hotel by Henry Barons, known as Yankee Barons in Yelverton when he returned from the USA. He and his wife, Mary, both born in Devon in the 1830s, had lived in New Jersey where two of their children were born, James in 1872 and Ellen in 1875. Another son, Albert Sidney, was born in Yelverton in 1880. A young country postman, Edward Worth, was staying at the hotel in 1891 as was 24-year-old Eliza Gilbert. Jimmy Barons married Eliza and four years after her death married Charlotte Holliday. He is listed as living in 1 Buckland Terrace in 1902 as a fly proprietor, or a one-horse taximan. Mrs Mary Ann Barons was running the Temperance Hotel in 1906 and her son, Albert Sydney, ran it in 1914. Jimmy and Charlotte Barons' family tree passes down to Rose Muriel Hockey, Audrey Doidge, Sara Ferry and Paula Hunter and their children – many generations of one family in Yelverton since it first began to be built upon.

Ravenscroft, a nursing home since 1985, was built as a private house, became a school, officers' headquarters in the Second World War and a private house again. In 1989 Sheila Cassidy, director of St Luke's Hospice, opened a new wing in the home. It provides for a wide range of nursing care and special needs for the elderly inhabitants. Yelverton Nursing Home in Greenbank Terrace occupies two Victorian terraced houses and was formerly Glen Maye. The Red House, on the Tavistock Road, was one of the largest houses in Yelverton when it was built at the beginning of the twentieth century. The views from the house are magnificent, looking out onto northern Dartmoor. Dr Henry Warren Crowe owned the house in 1901 when he bought Yennadon House and the 81 acres of land in Dousland. Beechfield Nursing Home, recently closed, began as a hotel when it was built in Beech Field belonging to Harrowbeer Farm.

There were two inns at Leg o' Mutton Corner in the nineteenth century. The first inn was the Buller's Arms, named after Sir Anthony Buller in Buckland Terrace, and on the opposite side of the road was the Leg o' Mutton Inn. The first inn was recorded here in 1840 and publicans named before it was burnt down in 1870 are Clark, Pomeroy, Lock, Small, Sloman and Smith. The Leg o' Mutton Inn has been called the Yelverton Inn as well as the Foxhunter Inn during the twentieth century. Devon Tors was a thriving hotel in the first half of the twentieth century under the ownership of the Wilson family following Mr and Mrs Frederick Sara. The row of terraced houses was built as Beech Villas on

The longest-runner-bean competition in one of the bars at the Rock Inn.

the land of Harrowbeer Farm called Beech Field. There are bars open at the Devon Tors, and the remaining villas and a house called Fairfield have been converted into flats and sold privately. Other inns in the parish at Milton Combe, Buckland Monachorum and Clearbrook are described in the relevant chapters. Knightstone tearoom, a house on the southern end of the aerodrome near the Big Rock, is on Crapstone Road opposite Ravenscroft. The building, where morning coffee, lunches and cream teas are served, had a small part to play in the Second World War.

The Moorland Links Hotel also has a bar where it serves meals in peaceful surroundings. This, the largest hotel in the parish, was built near the golf course in Sowton Road in 1934.

Harrabeer Country House Hotel in Harrowbeer Lane uses the spelling of the seventeenth-century farmhouse that was extended in the nineteenth century. There were two farms in the lane, once surrounded by fields, which have been developed by builders of the railway and private houses. Harry Cann purchased the property in 1949 and ran it as riding stables, selling it in 1971 to Frank Callicott. Michael and Amanda Willatts bought the licensed property in July 2001, the licence having been granted in 1973. Amanda was among 20 finalists in the

AA Landlady of the Year Award in 2002.

The Rock Inn holds a prime position in Yelverton, close to the shops and near the junction of the roads from Plymouth, Tavistock and Princetown. Originally a farmhouse on Roborough Down it was one of the first buildings in what is now Yelverton. William Shillibeer is listed as living here in 1862 and in 1873 his daughter, Elizabeth, was running the Rock family hotel. Elizabeth was 35 years old and officers from manoeuvres on Dartmoor stayed at the hotel. In the 1891 census returns the family living at the hotel were Elizabeth, Edmund, Annie and John Shillibeer. Maggie Langton, 18, and Nellie Blackler, 17, were daughters of married sisters and living at the hotel. John Shillibeer, aged 32 years, died later that year and Edmund died three years later. Algy Langton was running the hotel in 1914 when he was 36 years of age. In 1919 the hotel was enlarged and Algy inherited the hotel in 1924, with the telephone number of 22. In the 1930s Algy hired out motor cars and it was a thriving hotel. In 1953 it had a lift to 30 bedrooms and 16 garages were in use. After the closure of Yelverton Railway Station, Algy closed the Rock Hotel and converted the building into flats in 1966. Two years later his son, George, took over the running of the business now called the Rock Inn. The inn is often referred to as the 'wet rock' as opposed to the much older rock to the south called Big Rock, Roborough Rock or Udal Tor, and locally the 'dry rock'! The former stables and garages were converted into a shopping precinct and George Langton's son, Paul, and daughter, Sue Callow, carry on the tradition of running the family business at the time of writing. The inn is open all day and meals are served at the bar and in the restaurant. Fields behind the hotel, where there was once a tennis court used by the residents of Yelverton and where vegetables were grown for the hotel menus, were sold in 1974. Grenville Park houses were built on the land.

Employment in the parish is found in shops, businesses, leisure industries, on farms and the land, but most of the inhabitants of the parish work in larger towns and cities. This rural parish in the Devon countryside on the edge of Dartmoor will always attract visitors. Families are eager to live in the villages and those families who have lived in it for generations feel greatly honoured to call it home.

Chapter 12
THE GREAT WESTERN RAILWAY

Travellers who used the railway for work or pleasure enjoyed the journey in and out of the parish from 1859 to 1962. From Plymouth, the engines puffed through Bickleigh Vale, through the tunnel near Shaugh Prior, up the Meavy valley close to the river, through the tunnel at Yelverton and fields and farmland to Horrabridge. The trees on each side of the track gave delight in all seasons. Entering the parish on Roborough Down from Plymouth the track kept close to the River Meavy whilst the Wheal Lopes leat from Hoo Meavy Bridge to Bickleigh meandered underneath the track in a series of culverts. Huge pipes carrying water from Burrator Reservoir to Plymouth by gravity were passed beneath the track in 1897 and from the following year to the present day water to the city passes this way and pipes are checked regularly by South West Water. Workmanship was always of a high standard and every stone bridge and

A busy station.

archway is beautifully finished. The sounds and smells of the steam railway through the parish are now sadly lost forever. Farmers and workers on the land once set the time by the trains and transported animals to markets on them. Engine drivers and firemen brought goods such as animal foodstuffs, from the town for those who lived near the track, and threw the sacks from the passing cab to the waving recipient. Tom West at Mabor Farm at Clearbrook was one such farmer. Until the coming of motor transport, trains were used by hundreds of people walking over moorland tracks to the stations to visit towns or the docks from where ships took parishioners to another land where it was hoped they would make their fortune.

Hundreds were there to greet the first train when it arrived in Horrabridge in June 1859, the only station at that time in the parish. Many must have stood near the track to watch the engine and carriages pass along through the countryside. Rates for the railway through the parish were fixed at £400 each mile but

reduced to £100 a mile when the Parish Council threatened to take court proceedings. Emerging from Shaugh Tunnel the train approached Clearbrook. The Halt here opened on 29 October 1928 and remained in use until the line closed at the end of 1962. It is now in the garden of the house called Whittle Down. It had a corrugated-iron waiting-room and a bench seat. It was lit at night by lamps on posts that used paraffin oil. In the early evening the guard from Plymouth lit these lamps and on the last train back to Plymouth he collected the lamps off the posts and took them back to the depot where the wicks were trimmed and lamps refuelled ready for the next evening. The platform was very long and the name-board was wooden with CLEARBROOK HALT spelt out in cast-iron letters. The entry to the station from the Clearbrook Road was by a flight of steps through the hedge opposite Mabor Farm. A shop at the station provided drinks to passengers and a variety of goods were purchased here by the villagers of Clearbrook. Passengers came in great numbers by train to picnic down by the river where they could buy teas from Mrs Williams' tearooms at Glen View. Today the Plym Valley Cycle Track uses this disused track from Plymouth as far as this private garden, from where it passes up a very steep incline leading to the moor and along a track to the Village Hall. People in the community used this railway halt as well as those living in Meavy and Brisworthy, as it was much nearer to them than Yelverton. Schoolchildren caught the trains to schools in Tavistock and Plymouth and many farmers in the area took their wives and families to the Halt by horse and cart, collecting them after a day's shopping by the same mode of transport.

On the evening of 18 November 1885 a train that had travelled from Waterloo, its destination Plymouth, came off the rails 500 yards beyond Clearbrook at milepost 6. The driver was killed in the upturned engine but the fireman, guard and

Right: *A train at the station, 1910.*

Below: *A watercolour painting of the old Yelverton Railway Station by Jan Marks of Whinacre near Chub Tor, 2002.*

Right: *The Rodd family with railwaymen.*

Below: *Footbridge across the tracks.*

Above: *Looking towards the tunnel at Yelverton.*

Left: *The train accident on 18 November 1885 at milepost 6 near Clearbrook.*

Cinder path at Yelverton, 1955.

Station Lane with snow, 1967.

passengers were only slightly injured. The cause of the accident was thought to be a broken coupling but:

The Board of Trade inquiry attributed blame to the engine's long 16ft 6in wheelbase and faulty elevation of the curved track. The No. 442 engine struck a rock face, rebounded across the track and fell down an embankment together with the leading brake van, which became uncoupled. (Maggs 1995)

The engine, once repaired, continued to be used in the Exeter area for another 72 years.

Leaving Clearbrook the train for Tavistock and Launceston passed over Arch Bridge and through the woods along the Meavy valley. Householders living on each side of Arch Bridge kept beaters nearby to extinguish the flames caused by sparks from the engine setting alight the dry sticks in the woods during the summer months. The track is now private property but the Railway Company opened a lovely walk between the river and railway that is now kept in good condition by the Dartmoor National Park Authority. From the right bank of the river above Hoo Meavy Bridge the footpath passes upstream, through two pedestrian gates and leads towards Yelverton Station, which is also private property, but the footpath leads up to the Chub Tor track and so to Yelverton. The journey from Clearbrook to Yelverton by train took four minutes. The passenger station at Yelverton opened on 1 May 1885. It was destroyed by fire 20 years later and rebuilt. Local inhabitants had petitioned for a station in the early days but the proposal was turned down in the belief that there would not be enough traffic from the station to pay for even one porter. How the years ahead proved this to be wrong. From early in the twentieth century it became the busiest passenger station on the line from Plymouth to Launceston. The hill from the station in Yelverton was crowded with people walking both to and from the trains. A cinder path was made along the Princetown railway embankment from below the bridge over Gratton Lane leading to the platforms for Plymouth and Princetown. People living in the Meavy Lane area walked to the station that way. An iron railway gate was placed beside the road south of

the arch bridge. Before 1859, when the Railway Company acquired the land for the track from the Baylys at Elfordtown House, they built a carriage bridge from the garden over Station Lane to the fields opposite, which led directly to the main Plymouth to Tavistock road. This bridge is still in good repair at the time of writing.

Station Lane was entered at the top by crossing the Devonport Leat. The bridge over the leat was widened soon after the station opened to take the amount of traffic going down the steep hill. Carts and wagons drawn by horses were left at the bottom, on the wide grass verge opposite the station gates, waiting to transport the owners back home from their railway journey. From its opening came the growth of Yelverton. Large store owners in Plymouth wished to live in the country away from the towns and campaigned for it to be built. It was a special station, as it became the junction for the famous moorland railway, the Princetown branch line. This line had opened two years earlier in 1883 and operated from Horrabridge.

The three platforms at Yelverton Station were built, one each side of the straight line for the Plymouth to Tavistock trains and the other curving north from the down platform away to Gratton Lane, Meavy Lane and towards Dousland. The platform surface was of diamond-etched blue Staffordshire bricks to prevent slipping. The canopied wooden buildings, with Staffordshire ridge-tiles, housed the waiting-rooms and ticket office. The wooden name-boards had iron letters that read YELVERTON – CHANGE FOR THE PRINCETOWN BRANCH. Other signs instructed passengers not to cross the lines but three walk-ways were supplied for the porters. Normal crossing was over a standard GWR iron and wooden bridge. At the turn of the century the station had its own book stall. A brick-built signal-box was constructed at the southern end of the platform. It had sliding windows on three sides to give good vision. Below this was a small siding. Here horses from Woodman's stables and carts from Veales of Walkhampton were loaded into wagons. The Princetown branch platform sported a very unusual building that was polygonal in shape with a

The turntable for the snow plough.

Interior view of the signal-box.

Above: *The houses in Beechfield Avenue shook every time a train passed underneath through the tunnel!*

Above: *Grenofen Viaduct was demolished when the railway closed in the 1960s.*

Right: *Signalman Percy Wilmot hands a staff to fireman Crocker in the 1950s. Percy built his house, Hillside, at the end of the cinder path in Meavy Lane.*

Below: *Yelverton Station with autotrain in the early morning, 1934.*

central three-potted chimney. Here were the toilets, ticket office and waiting-room. Part of this platform was shortened in 1933. The Princetown line leaves Buckland Monachorum Parish almost at once, enters Meavy Parish but returns to Buckland near Meavybourne, passing out of the parish again east of Woodman's Corner. The branch line closed, unfortunately, in 1956, ending one of the most scenic railway routes in Britain.

At the station was a turntable, over 26 feet (8m) in diameter, and an inspection pit. The turntable was normally only used to turn the snowplough when it was needed on the Princetown line. The branch-line engines did not usually turn round but went into a spur siding so that the empty carriages could be run into the station by gravity and the engine then reconnected ready for the run back. It was after such a manoeuvre in 1939 that a locomotive fell down the embankment onto the cinder path. After the uphill journey from Plymouth these steam locomotives were in need of a refill from one of the two water cranes. The water was supplied from a well in the field above the tunnel entrance. Also above the well was the second stationmaster's house. With a clear view down to the station it was built in the 1930s. The first, on the other side at the top of Station Lane, was not on GWR property and had been rented. The busy station supported a full-time stationmaster, complete with frock-coat and gold-braided hat.

In 1959, three years after the Princetown line had closed, the 35-lever signal-box was no longer required so the signals were disconnected and the line to Plymouth converted to a single track, the station becoming partially staffed. On 7 April 1957 the two stone arch bridges crossing Gratton Lane and Meavy Lane were demolished. This station was the pride and joy of all who worked there and a delight to all the passengers. Rhododendrons and rose bushes, birds and butterflies were all in profusion and the tree-lined Station Lane from the church, with the small stream running down the hill, was a great contrast to the town stations. The road was so busy with traffic that a pavement was added on the opposite side to the stream. Many inhabitants still remember struggling up the steep lane to their homes and the shops. In later years buses waited at the station and coincided with the arrival of the trains. Even after the station closed the buses continued to wait outside the station for non-existent passengers for a further nine months. The drivers kept quiet about this, perhaps to have a rest amidst the silence of the trees!

The Drake estate sold land near the station for the development of 26 houses in 1886 but only two houses were built, Inglenook and Drake Leat. These large houses with gardens, including four tennis courts, were to be built in fields near the existing footpath. Leaving the station for Horrabridge the train passed under Yelverton through a tunnel 641

yards (586m) long, emerging in Harrowbeer Lane. The tunnel is absolutely straight and the light at the end of the tunnel is a diminutive shape from the entrance near the station. Much rock cutting took place in the 1850s for both the tunnel and Station Lane. Only about ten years after the large houses development plan was abandoned prematurely, terrace houses were built over the tunnel. These were at the Harrowbeer end, 100 feet higher above sea level than the station. The home of Elsie Grainger in the 1920s was at 12 Beechfield Avenue and her niece, Minnie, remembers the noise and rumble of the trains that shook the house as they travelled beneath them. Travelling to Horrabridge Station the railtrack crossed the A386 below the turning to Buckland Monachorum near the old toll-house over a bowstring-girder bridge.

Waiting on Horrabridge platform for the train to school, or running down over the moor from Pound, the train could be seen curving into the platform. The two platforms were constructed on a gentle curve with waiting-rooms and a ticket office. It was from here at the beginning of the twentieth century that so many parishioners left their native Devon, the only land they knew, to venture into the unknown. To cross the sea and to emigrate to America, Canada, Australia, New Zealand or South Africa, villagers entered the station by using the level-crossing from the moor. Passing over Grenofen Viaduct towards Tavistock the railway leaves the parish boundary. This beautiful viaduct, spanning the River Walkham, was designed by I.K. Brunel and was built of wood until it was replaced in 1910. This girder bridge was taken down soon after the railway closed. Stations from Horrabridge to Launceston were Whitchurch, Tavistock South, Mary Tavy and Blackdown Halt, Lydford, Liddaton Halt, Coryton and Lifton.

The twisty branch line from Yelverton passed through Dousland, Burrator and Sheepstor Halt, Ingra Tor Halt, King Tor Halt and the terminus was Princetown. Tim Emerson remembers catching the train at Tavistock when he was a boy with a group from Mount House School, changing trains at Yelverton, leaving the train at Ingra Tor and running across the col of the moor to catch the train again at King Tor. This was good fun for many young passengers. The rail track followed the contours of the moor and climbed around the tors. Tim also remembers being allowed to ride on the footplate of the customary 2-6-2 tank locomotive to Tavistock. A wistful memory of an earlier time! A yearning that the steam trains could run again from Yelverton is a sentiment felt throughout the community. John Alway, who was born in Beechfield Nursing Home and lived in Willowby Park as a boy, recalls his father, Walter, taking him to watch the trains at Yelverton Station and pushing him up the hill on the cross-bar of his bicycle. The railway embankment passing

An engine waiting on the track of the Princetown line.

Passengers waiting on the platform. Note the polygonal waiting-rooms on the Princetown line. At weekends the fare to Plymouth was 6d. return from Yelverton and became known as the Woolworths train because items at that store cost 6d.

Right: *A photograph from 1900 looking towards Plymouth and showing the original track layout and unusual signal in the foreground. Ponies and traps wait in the lane.*

Above: *Long-service awards were presented to Eric and George Thomas.*

Right: *Jim Thomas, porter at Yelverton Station.*

Far right: *Eric Thomas, on engine 4568, was born at 4 Yelverton Terrace.*

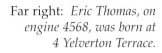

alongside the gardens of the Meavybourne houses was a play area for children and the houses shook every time a train went past, like those in Harrowbeer Lane. Travelling to schools in Tavistock and Plymouth by train is a memory for many boys and girls from the parish. There was a long walk at the other end of the journey from the stations.

The trains to Princetown passed close to the houses at Binkham Hill and Mary Davey recalls standing near the track with her sisters, waving to the driver and passengers like the characters in *The Railway Children*. There was an unscheduled halt near here where the engine driver stopped the train for the children to travel to and from their Uncle Hedley Maddock's house, the crossing-keeper at Dousland. Passengers remember that when convicts were being escorted on the train a dining-car was added. There was an outcry from the public when they were informed by British Railways that the branch line was to close in 1955. It was doubtful that the line had ever made a profit, but with the closure of the quarries and dwindling passenger traffic the writing was on the wall. Great protest followed, especially from the inhabitants of Princetown. Throughout the year hundreds of people made the journey and the last day was eventually Saturday, 3 March 1956. Yelverton was crowded with cars and hundreds of people filled the platform to make the journey for the very last time. Policemen controlled the queues. Normally the train was of one engine and one carriage but on that day it consisted of two engines and six carriages. Around 200 people were on the last train. For some it was the first time, only realising that what had been taken for granted was to cease forever. The final train left Princetown for Yelverton at 10.20p.m. In September 1956 Lydford Parish Council considered purchasing the line but the idea did not get very far. Today some of the trackbed has been built on but much of the moorland track has become a very popular cycle route.

The station at Yelverton remained open for nearly another seven years for the Plymouth to Launceston line. Yelverton finally came to an end as part of the Beeching plan. The last day of operation was Saturday, 29 December 1962. The train left Plymouth at 6.20p.m. but did not reach Yelverton until nearly midnight. It was snowing heavily and deep snow-drifts covered the line. The train did not reach Launceston and was unable to return to Plymouth until two weeks later. Tracks and buildings were removed from the station in the spring of 1964. The bare station and land surrounding it, including Station Lane, was returned in 1969 to the former owners at Elfordtown, descendants of the Bayly family. Col Dick Spencer and his wife, Millicent, spent many years following the closure of the station in developing the site as a nature reserve. Now, 40 years on, the station and trackbed are overgrown and

there is no admittance to the station. Station Lane is a private road, not a public right of way. The railway footpath from near Lower Elfordtown to Clearbrook and Hoo Meavy may be reached from St Paul's car park. Following the footpath along by the Plymouth Leat, parallel with the A386 as far as Elfordtown Cottage, descend and turn right on to the West Devon Way. This public footpath passes under the stone arch railway bridge and through the iron kissing-gate close by.

Jim Thomas worked as a porter at Yelverton Station for 46 years (1902–48) out of its 77 years of existence. His three sons, Eric, George and Arthur, all worked on the railway. They lived at 4 Yelverton Terrace before moving to number 6 where Jim died in 1958. Jim worked under eight stationmasters at Yelverton: J. Laskey, F. Wyatt, W. Roberts, J. Wingate, N. Roberts, W. Thomas, C. Badcock and L. Cullum. Jim Thomas remembered well the Lady Drake Special that pulled into the station each summer during his early years. There were horse boxes, vans for luggage and coaches for the staff, and coaches for Lady Drake and her guests who were joining her for the summer. It used to cause quite a commotion. He also remembered soldiers standing guard above the tunnel when King George V and Queen Mary passed through the station on their way to a siding at Horrabridge to spend the night. Jim should have retired at the beginning of the war but stayed on to help cope with the large increase in traffic due to the number of service camps in the neighbourhood. In 1948 he finally retired, aged 69, and was presented by the railway with an electric cooker and kettle. Percy Willmot, who built Hillside, a short distance from the station, was senior signalman for many years. Journeys made on the Princetown line were haz-ardous in winter months. In 1946 14 passengers were stranded on the 7.45p.m. train from Yelverton until the following morning. The train did not reach Princetown because of heavy snow. Another engine was sent to rescue the passengers and on reaching Yelverton they were given refreshments in the station waiting-room.

The station is laid to rest beneath trees and flowering shrubs where birds, butterflies and a variety of wildlife enjoy the protection of a private sanctuary. T.W. Roche's poem of six verses, 'Yelverton 1967', describes this station of three platforms that has passed into history but was the cause of bringing families to settle in Yelverton in the late-nineteenth century. Indeed, the existence of an ever-growing popular residential area today is due to the opening of this station more than 117 years ago.

The branch lines of Devon are dying and only
Prodigious embankments still show where they led
Their former trim stations stand silent and lonely
While Yelverton lies like a tomb of the dead.

Right: *Aerial photograph of the aerodrome, 1943.*

Below: *Squadron Leader Ronnie Hamlyn of 276 Squadron, January 1943.*

Above: *Margaret Simms preparing for Spooner's paper-chase in 1939.*

Below: *Edmund Kaminski married Doris Littlejohns. Rosemary Piper and Rita Walser were bridesmaids.*

Anson at RAF Harrowbeer.

193 Squadron at Harrowbeer.

Chapter 13
HARROWBEER AERODROME

'We will remember them' is a phrase repeated annually on Remembrance Sunday. The anxieties and skills of the men and women who served on the aerodrome at Yelverton during the 1940s can only be imagined by those who were not involved in flying in and out of the area to protect our country from the enemy in those wartime years. All were very young men of 17 to 20 years of age. Sleeping in their flying suits and boots, dancing in their suits and boots, all in readiness to run to their aircraft after being 'scrambled' or called to duty, was the way of life for the airmen prepared to fly into the unknown. Many hazards were part of the routine in Yelverton. Weather conditions, the low cloud and mists of Dartmoor were a constant problem. The weather the airmen recall at Yelverton is rain, rain and still more rain. Two hazards to be avoided were St Paul's Church tower on take-off and the Big Rock on landing.

In December 1940, before Harrowbeer was developed, a decoy aerodrome was planned to the right of the main A386 road from Plymouth at the turning down to Clearbrook and marked 'most secret'. Buildings were erected each side of the Clearbrook Road. Whether this ever fooled the enemy into believing this was Plymouth Airport is not known. Early in 1941 the construction of Harrowbeer airfield began by a local building firm and a local workforce. The name Harrowbeer was chosen as, looking at a map of the area at the time from headquarters, the name Harrowbeer is printed nearest to the moorland area where the airfield was to be built and to avoid confusion, as Yelverton sounded too much like Yeovilton in Somerset. The hardcore used for the airfield was the waste rock from the mines. Rubble from the buildings and houses bombed in the Blitz in Plymouth were used for the three runways and the perimeter roads, which were completed in record time. This rubble was brought by train, unloaded at Yelverton Station and transported up Station Lane by lorry. Aircraft pens, or bays, inside the perimeter fence were constructed and three Bellman and eight Blister hangars were built. It was a busy fighter station and Second-World-War base and in the four years of operation was controlled by 10 Group Fighter Command. The official opening was on 15 August 1941 and enemy action was seen nearby only two days later. The first aircraft to land on the

aerodrome was a Blenheim bomber on 31 August. The three runways and their lengths were:

Runway 11/29 South Plantation to the Roundabout, 3,840 feet long.
Runway 17/35 Roborough Rock to Pound Track, 3,345 feet long.
Runway 05/23 The Roundabout to Roborough Rock, 2,736 feet long.

Known locally as the aerodrome it was planned as a fighter airfield and the code was QB, painted in large letters to be seen from the air in front of the control tower. Hurricanes, Spitfires and Blenheims were the first aircraft to arrive, followed by Typhoons, Whirlwinds and Swordfish. Two Lysanders operated from here in sea-rescue missions. The control tower, the foundations of which can be seen in the grass north of Whistleigh Down, was situated between runways 11 and 17 at the west of the aerodrome. To the east of the control tower was the compass platform, the concrete base of which is still visible on the grass and a little further on is a brass base with engraved lettering that held the mast for the wind-sock. Behind the control tower were the Bellman hangars. Runway 11/29 was in line with St Paul's Church and the airmen had to veer to the left on take-off, flying over the railway tunnel and the roundabout to the north-east. The row of shops, which before the war began was a row of three-storey houses, was reduced in height to one storey in order to allow a safer take-off. A black and white board was placed on the church tower to warn the pilots of its height.

Polish airmen arrived on 1 November 1941 – a Spitfire Squadron. One night in November an enemy aircraft was shot down and four enemy airmen baled out and were taken prisoner. One was found on the cricket pitch, in a field to the east of the aerodrome, looking for his lost boot! Another Spitfire Squadron manned by pilots from Czechoslovakia followed in May 1942. Some of these Polish and Czech airmen married local girls after the war was over and remained in the area, such as Edmund Kaminski from Poland who became a successful businessman and lives in Tavistock at the time of writing.

Local workmen were still building the accommodation and aircraft dispersal bays when the aerodrome

No. 19 Fire Force outside St Vincents.

Above: Fire Force officers and typists. Minnie Grainger is second from the right in the back row.

Above: Fire Force officers from Plymouth at Yelverton, 1945.

A Westland Lysander.

was first in use. WAAF members arrived in May 1942 after the women's quarters were opened near the aerodrome north of Pound House. At this time there were 1,253 personnel stationed at the airfield, which altered the population of Yelverton completely. Boarding-houses and hotels, as well as Yelverton Railway Station, were kept busy with the many relatives who visited their loved ones stationed at the aerodrome. Yelverton was changed forever.

Site plans of Harrowbeer, dated 1944, position the aircraft dispersal bays and the buildings. Near the WAAF site was the officers' mess and quarters, sick quarters, water tank, dining-room and institute, bath house, barrack huts, fuel compound and picket post. Buildings listed are the watch office, fire-tender shelter, tractor shed, squadron office, Bellman hangars, agricultural implement shed, technical latrines, gas clothing and respirator store, gas defence centre, lubricant and inflammable store, main store, armoury, cine-camera gun shop, main workshop, parachute store, gas chamber, squadron ops block, station HQ offices, link trainer building, MT shed and office, camouflage paint store, fire-tender house, guard house and fire party, battle headquarters, bulk petrol installation, bulk oil, compass platform 60 feet in diameter, petrol tanker standings, small arms ammunition store, compressor house, water tower, destructor house, hurricane type pens, Blenheim pens, defence units, barrack huts and latrines. Defence officers' quarters and latrines, WAAF ablution and latrines, sleeve streamer mast, fuel store, blast shelters, static water tank, barrack huts, bomb stores, cannon test butt, emergency signals cabin, US Navy huts and a telephone exchange were also shown.

In the Crapstone area there were sick quarters, ambulance garage and mortuary. This was on the site where the Yelverton Business Park has been built. In Stoke Hill Lane there were officers' quarters and latrines, showers, sergeants' quarters and barrack huts. The main site in Crapstone was in Abbey Lane near the village where there was a gymnasium, officers' mess and bath house, squash court, sergeants' mess and showers, fuel oil tanks, stores, institute, destructor house, decontamination centre, ration store, local produce and grocery store, barbers, tailors, shoemaker's shop and a dining-room.

The main Plymouth Fire Service Headquarters were at Briar Tor, then called Nazareth House, and the workforce were brought to Yelverton by bus. Miss Minnie Grainger from Milton Combe worked in the typing pool for the duration of the war under Betty Easton from Plymouth who later became the mayor of the city. Tom Lethbridge from Clearbrook, in the fire service during the war, was stationed in Plymouth and was in charge of all water installations in Devon and Cornwall. These men and women were the unsung heroes of the war, extinguishing fires in the city during the Blitz and saving lives and property where at all possible. Tom's wife, Lilian, at

home in Clearbrook, mended servicemen's socks by the sackful, week after week, and other residents in the village offered bathing facilities and a free home-cooked meal. Bombs rained down on Plymouth and men, women and children sought refuge away from the fires and devastation. Night after night people from the city trekked away from their burning streets in all directions, hundreds passing through Roborough, Clearbrook and on to Yelverton. After the building of the aerodrome folk did not feel so safe in the Yelverton area and caught the train to Horrabridge or Tavistock, returning to the town to work the next morning. The glow of Plymouth burning was visible in the night sky from the parish and a sight never to be forgotten.

Frank Mares (pronounced Marish) was a Spitfire pilot in 312 Squadron during the summer of 1942. Arriving in Yelverton after an exciting escape from Czechoslovakia, Frank flew many daring exploits. The Czech pilots became feared and admired. They were fighting for the freedom of their own country and were glad to assist Britain in their battle with the enemy. Frank settled in Brook, not many miles from the airfield from where he flew many dangerous missions in 1942 as a young man. Locals remember ducking their heads when a 312 Squadron Spitfire took off and the shopkeepers counted all the planes going out and coming back again. When they all came back the Yelverton folk at the shops clapped but if any were missing they were in sombre mood. Flt Sgt Mares reported for flying duties at Harrowbeer on 16 June 1942. Frank wrote in his book *Mission Accomplished* that they were in a constant state of readiness, capable of being scrambled within seconds. 'Speed was of the essence, above everything else, to take off, intercept, give chase and if possible destroy.' Frank's book has been published in Czech and he holds the manuscript written in English. Pilots in Spitfires searched the sea for survivors and dropped smoke bombs to mark the spot for their rescue by sea-plane or motor launch.

Until 11 September 1942 the Squadron's operational sorties from Harrowbeer were of convoy protection patrols or searching for ship movements along the enemy coast. Frank received an award from King George VI on 2 September 1942 when a telegram marked 'most secret' arrived at Harrowbeer. It read:

To: Harrowbeer – 312 Squadron – Exeter – 310 Squadron From: 10 Group
2/9 HM the King has been graciously pleased to award the DFC to S/Ldr F Dolezal 310 Sqdn the DFM to F Sgt Mares F. 312 Sqdn. These awards are not, repeat not, to be published. AOC extends his heartiest congratulations – 1055.

Air Marshal A. Orlebar arrived at Harrowbeer to present some decorations, including Frank's Distinguished Flying Medal. Frank said:

Sammy Samuels of 193 Squadron at Harrowbeer.

Frank Mares in his plane.

Canadian Rod Davidge in 1943.

Above left: *Flt Sgt Frank Mares receives the Distinguished Flying Medal from Air Marshal Orlebar at Harrowbeer.*

Left: *On 15-minutes readiness for combat.*

A Typhoon at Harrowbeer. Out of 27 pilots of 263 Squadron in January 1944 at Harrowbeer only 11 survived the war.

We got the works that day. The Czech band gave a concert in the Sergeants' Mess and then another later in the afternoon in the Station gymnasium. In the evening we held a dance in the airmen's Mess, which was a great success. In all a great day to remember.

These buildings were at Crapstone in Abbey Lane.

Typhoon fighters arrived in December 1942. They were hidden away as far in the blast shelters as was possible in the north-west of the aerodrome, in 'Tiffy Corner' as it was known, not far from Pound Lodge. Tiffy was an affectionate nickname for Typhoon aircraft. These aircraft flew from Yelverton for the next two years and Harrowbeer was dubbed a 'Typhoon Station'. Many Spitfire squadrons arrived for 6 June 1944, D-Day. On one day in July 1944 at midday, 48 Spitfires took off from Yelverton to attack enemy targets in France.

Harrowbeer operations ended in July 1945 but for a few years it became a station for the care and maintenance of aircraft. President Harry Truman landed at Harrowbeer in his huge DC4 aircraft, called the 'Sacred Cow', as fog had closed RAF St Mawgan. No one was at Yelverton to greet him officially and it was recorded that he looked like 'an ordinary little man in a felt hat'. Valerie and Merrille Bragg, two of the children at Whistleigh Farm, remember waving to President Truman as he passed them in a car. From here the president travelled to Plymouth to have lunch with HM King George VI on board HMS *Renown*, which was at anchor in the Sound. There were other famous visitors to Harrowbeer. HRH the Duke of Gloucester visited the aerodrome on his way to the Middle East on 7 April 1942. He had lunch in the officers' mess, that was Ravenscroft, where he talked to the pilots. The Duke came again to Harrowbeer on 12 July in the same year. Glenn Miller and his orchestra landed on Monday 28 September 1944 on their way to perform at the US Navy hospital at Manadon. Maj. Glenn Miller and the 40 orchestral members landed because of foggy conditions. Two days later Glenn Miller and the orchestra were driven in Navy trucks to Yelverton and flew to Bedford. In December Glenn Miller disappeared in mysterious circumstances when his plane was lost on a flight from Bedford to Paris.

A number of accidents occurred at or near Harrowbeer. On 24 October 1942 residents rushed to see three captured German aircraft land on the runway at Harrowbeer. A week later a pilot leaving Harrowbeer was unable to gain sufficient height because of adverse weather conditions and crashed his Hurricane north of Yelverton. Two pilot officers were killed, including RAF pilot officer Gavin Sellar,

R.A.F. STATION
HARROWBEER.

1943   CHRISTMAS DAY   1943

Menu.

BREAKFAST.

Porridge *or* Cornflakes *or* Shredded Wheat
Fried Bacon & Egg   Sauté Potatoes
Tea *or* Coffee   Marmalade

CHRISTMAS DINNER.

Tomato Soup
Roast Turkey Stuffed & Roast Pork
Forcemeat Balls   Game Chips   Brussell Sprouts
Boiled & Baked Potatoes   Onion Sauce
Home-made Bread Rolls
Home-made Christmas Pudding & Rhum Sauce
Cheese & Biscuits
Beer   Minerals   Cigarettes   Oranges

TEA.

Home-made Christmas Cake (Iced)   Mince Pies
Cold Ham   Pickles & Beetroot
Lemon Curd   Sweet Biscuits   Bread & Butter

SUPPER.

Brown Windsor Soup
Home-made Sausage Rolls   Cornish Pasties
Sandwiches (variès)
Dundee Cake
Coffee

"A Happy Christmas to you all."

Form 250 (Inset).   15 A.
(In books of 50)

ROYAL AIR FORCE.

CIVILIAN'S PASS.

No. of Pass *39* .... Holder of Pass *Mr. G. V. Echello.*
Address *Yelverton Cottage, Yelverton.*
Occupation *House Decorator.*
Employer's name *R. W. Mayber.*
Address *Builders, Crapstone.*

Permission is hereby granted to the Holder of this pass, whose signature appears below, to enter and leave *RAF Stn. Harrowbeer* between the hours of *0830* and *1800* during the period *27. 2. 42* to *31. 3. 42*, for the purpose of conducting the above business.

The Holder of this pass has access to the following :—
RAF. Harrowbeer.

Whether deposit of 2s. 6d. has been paid ....
Station *R.A.F. STATION, HARROWBEER, DEVON.* *D. Swain*
Date *26- 2- 1942.* Commanding ....
                                    R.A.F.
Signature of Holder *G. V. Echell*

CONDITIONS ON WHICH PASS IS GRANTED.

1.   This pass is issuable only to British subjects.
2.   It is not to be issued to those for whom a special permit is required, vide A.M.C.O. A 17/40.
3.   It is not transferable and is to be produced on demand.
4.   It does not entitle the holder to enter any part of the establishment unconnected with his business or to remain in the establishment after the expiration of his business. If issued for trading purposes it is available only for the residential portion of the establishment and nowhere else.
5.   It is tenable only for the period mentioned, on the expiration of which it is to be surrendered and application made for renewal.
6.   The Holder of this pass is forbidden to take photographs or to communicate with the press on service matters.
7.   The deposit, if any, of 2s. 6d. on this pass will be forfeited unless the pass is delivered up when required. Application or return of deposit must be accompanied by the receipt.
8.   In the event of its loss the Commanding Officer is to be notified immediately.

[P.T.O.

Above: *Civilian pass, 1942.*

Left: *The Christmas Day menu at the Harrowbeer RAF Station, 1943.*

Below: *276 Squadron on the steps of Ravenscroft celebrating their 100th rescue on 27 May 1943.*

Below: *Aircraftsman Yeo and pilot.*

Below: *President Truman at Yelverton, 2 August 1945.*

Above: *The Duke of Kent with the Czech Squadron at Harrowbeer.*

Right: *Lifting the huge stone for the RAF memorial on Clearbrook moor.*

Below: *The RAF band playing for entertainment at the station.*

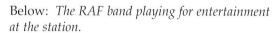

when their Liberator crash-landed at Harrowbeer on 31 October 1942. This large bomber, with a wingspan of 33.5m, was not based at Harrowbeer. Another fatal accident occurred when an engine cut out over the aerodrome and the aircraft dived into the ground at Leg o' Mutton near the shops. Both crew members were killed and customers in the café had a narrow escape when part of the plane crashed through a window. A Lancaster crossed the A386 one morning in November 1942 after skidding into a pile of stones on landing and tipped onto its nose. A Mosquito aircraft crashed near Ravenscroft and several visiting aircraft crashed on landing. Many airmen requested that their ashes should be buried at Denham Bridge, a place where they spent happy hours swimming and diving into the River Tavy when not on duty.

In May 1943 an aircraft hit a lorry belonging to the Searchlight Regiment whilst taking off, injuring the pilot and six men on the lorry and killing another three Army soldiers. A Typhoon pilot was hit on a shipping reconnaissance mission but managed to land safely back at Harrowbeer. His cigarette lighter, which had been dented by a bullet head, had saved his life. He was married a few days later. The menu for Christmas Day 1943, for the hundreds based at Harrowbeer, went a small way towards alleviating homesickness among the personnel and created employment for local people. Christmas Day was commemorated in the time-honoured RAF tradition with officers waiting upon the WAAFs and airmen and challenging the NCOs in a game of soccer.

On 22 April 1944, 838 Squadron of the Fleet Air Arm planned operations to find and attack U-boats in the Channel. This was formed at Knightstone, now a restaurant, on the corner of the aerodrome. On their first practice the Squadron lost three aircraft in crashes on Dartmoor. A further Swordfish exploded at 1,500 feet in July; the crew, unusually including a husband and wife, all lost their lives. A Mosquito crashed and blew up near Ravenscroft and the crews who failed to return to Harrowbeer during these years are remembered on the memorial stone at Leg o' Mutton. It is surprising that no plane ever crashed into Roborough or Big Rock. Civilians working at the aerodrome needed a pass to enter the gate of the airfield. Employees of Maben's at Crapstone were granted personal passes for carrying out repairs at the RAF station which was surrounded by a high wire fence.

A young Typhoon pilot, Jack 'Paddy' Pringle, following his fellow officers in take-off from Harrowbeer on a practice flight in 1944, clipped his wing on St Paul's Church tower. EK211 of 263 Squadron managed to avoid the houses in Meavy Lane but crashed in a field opposite Gratton Farm. Morning service was in progress at the time but the vicar, reading the Second Collect at Matins, continued even after the sound of falling masonry. The Typhoon caught fire and Flt Sgt Pringle died in the crash. A service of thanksgiving was held in St Paul's 55 years

later and Paddy's sister, Pat Purser, unveiled a plaque on the north door, celebrating the gift of the flagstaff from his family in Paddy's memory.

In January 1945 No. 275, an Air-sea Rescue Squadron, moved into Whistley, a large house in Axtown Lane where it was so cold that rum was authorised to the airmen. RAF Harrowbeer was to close on 31 July 1945. It had played a great part in Fighter Command especially in the air-sea rescues that had saved so many lives and raised morale in the squadrons. The aerodrome closed as an operational airfield in 1949.

RAF Harrowbeer Memorial Committee organised the setting up of a memorial stone in 1981 to all those from the aerodrome at Yelverton who lost their lives. The granite boulder used was found at Clearbrook near the old Plymouth and Dartmoor Railway track. It had fallen from a truck on the way from Princetown to Plymouth in the early-nineteenth century. Lifted off the moor onto a lorry by helicopter it was taken to Tavistock for the lettering to be added. Lt Col Ron Middleton was the chairman of the committee. The inscription reads:

RAF Harrowbeer Operational 1941–1949

From this Station flew pilots of many Commonwealth and Allied Countries including Britain, Canada, Czechoslovakia, France, Poland, Rhodesia, and the United States of America with the support of their ground crews and Airfield Defence units.

This stone is in memory of all who served here and especially of those who gave their lives. Many local residents helped build and maintain this airfield. Unveiled by the first Station Commander, Group Captain the Honourable E.F. Ward, on the 15th August 1981, the fortieth anniversary of the opening of the Station.

The first Station Commander, Group Captain the Hon. E.F. Ward, returned to unveil the granite stone commemorating all who had worked at the aerodrome. At the ceremony he spoke of the many squadrons based at Harrowbeer in the war years. A Nimrod and three Royal Marine helicopters flew over the scene at Leg o' Mutton that day.

Ravenscroft was the officers' mess at the station throughout the war. For a time after the war it was believed that the Polish airmen had buried gold and silver objects from their churches on British airfields. Polish gold hunters, as they became known, damaged the grounds of Ravenscroft in their search for Polish treasure. Blue Haze, a large house near the war memorial, was pulled down at the beginning of action on the aerodrome and was built again after the war. It still has the air-raid shelter in the garden. Many people opened their houses to the airmen and tried to bring some normality to their lives. Mr and Mrs Walser at 2 Grimstone Terrace in Crapstone made their front room into the airmen's room and provided books

Below: *Repairs to an aircraft.*

Left: *Rescued by a Walrus and returned to Yelverton.*

Right: *Members of the Home Guard at Axtown Farm in 1942. The picture includes Sgt Willcox, Sid Bragg and Bill Kendall.*

Repairing a Spitfire.

The Home Guard, 1940. Many of the men were farmers and others worked on the land. The group is pictured outside the Devon Tors Hotel, with the author's father in the middle of the front row.

and made them feel at home. Others cared for those who left the hospital but needed convalescence. Large huts were erected on the right of Abbey Lane and were used to house the corporals', sergeants' and officers' messes, the NAAFI, a cinema, billiard room, squash court, church, gymnasium, cookhouse and dining-rooms. These buildings were taken over by Devonport Dockyard after the war and until 1963 more than 100 workers were brought out to Crapstone by Royal Navy coaches each morning and collected again in the evenings. The drivers would give lifts to schoolchildren walking home from the railway station or bus stop from Yelverton to Crapstone. Later the Royal Navy built homes for naval families on this site but relinquished the land in the 1980s. One of the large hangars on the aerodrome was taken to Plymouth Hoe and set up on the grass where it became a café and remained so until the late 1970s. Waitresses served tea while a band played jolly music on summer afternoons by the sea under the canopy that had housed large aircraft in wartime at Yelverton.

Rita Kennedy recalls the huts that were put up on the perimeter of the runways along the road from Stoke Hill Lane to Pound. Towards Longash from Pound on the grass area opposite the football pitch was a German POW camp and some of the men were taken to work at Maben's sawmills. The wooden huts arrived at Horrabridge Station to be erected in the vicinity of the aerodrome. Rita remembers walking past the camp on the way to Buckland with her sisters and father when the men would call out asking for cigarettes. The prisoners tossed coins over the hedge and Harry Walser chatted to the men whilst the girls ran back to Crapstone to purchase the cigarettes from the Post Office. The camp was for displaced persons and Polish and Czech men were also housed there.

Men of the parish who were excused from joining the Forces because of ill health or because they worked on the land became part of the Home Guard. These men met in garden sheds and private houses. A group photograph was taken in front of the Devon Tors Hotel in the early 1940s (see opposite page).

In 1950 Buckland Monachorum Parish Council sought permission to have a road made across the aerodrome. This was eventually granted. Ten years later Plymouth Corporation applied for permission to develop Harrowbeer into a civilian airport. Opposition to the plan came from Dartmoor preservationists and residents of Yelverton and Crapstone. Letters appeared daily in the Western Morning News for and against the proposal and the arguments became heated. On 5 January 1961 Plymouth City Council tried to win support for the city's airport to be built at Harrowbeer. 'Harrowbeer must be secured now or never.' 'Roborough is too small, it is an airfield not an airport.' 'Harrowbeer site can be extended to 5,000 feet. Harrowbeer is cheapest.' They recommended that Yelverton aerodrome was acquired and redeveloped for the Plymouth airport. On 17 May

after a nine-day hearing the select committee decided that the Bill should proceed no further.

Harrowbeer is used as a public highway from Yelverton to Crapstone and to Pound, and animals graze on the grass. Picnickers set up tables and chairs, play games and fly kites, and vendors sell ice-cream from their vans parked near the Big Rock. The aerodrome had played a great part in fighter command during the war and in air-sea rescues. Many lives had been saved by aircraft pilots and their crews based at Harrowbeer. In 1948 for about two years the aerodrome was used as a gliding school providing tuition to cadets until August 1950. In 1949 it came into use as accommodation for RAF Sharpitor on Peak Hill but both units closed in 1950. Items were auctioned and at least one RAF lorry was used in a local garage. Scottish country dancing was in fashion in Yelverton in the 1960s and at times groups of people danced the reels on the aerodrome with car headlights illuminating the scene. Boys in the 1950s remember building land yachts using old tricycle wheels and racing on the old runways after RAF Harrowbeer closed. It is always breezy on the aerodrome. The site has been suggested for a school as the population in the parish grows, saving problems of transport and the over-crowding of the existing schools. Harrowbeer, once grassy moorland, is now the playground for the city dwellers of Plymouth, where people walk their dogs and children enjoy the play equipment in the Village Park near Leg o' Mutton.

Residents of Yelverton in the war years all have stories to tell. In 1939 a YMCA canteen was set up in St Paul's Church Hall. After the Blitz in Plymouth in 1941 Frank Harris of St Albans was in charge of the canteens in the area. When the trekkers arrived from Plymouth they queued up outside the church hall where they were allowed entry at 9p.m. Yelverton residents made corned-beef sandwiches and served mugs of tea before the trekkers settled down for the night. A mobile canteen was sent to RAF Sharpitor on Peak Hill where men swarmed around the van for tea and sandwiches. This air station had an air navigation system that covered a large area of England and the Western Approaches. When bombs were dropped from enemy planes near Chub Tor the only casualties were a pony and a rabbit. Soldiers from the Devonshire Regiment were stationed at Yelverton and held band concerts on the green. Residents gave these men hospitality as well as to the other regiments stationed at Yelverton: The Cheshires, Royal Northumberland Fusiliers and a Warwick Regiment. Americans camped with tanks in the woods at Gratton. Many of these soldiers visited the Royal Oak Inn at Meavy and the Who'd Have Thought It at Milton Combe. Joy Pike remembers being given a ride in an American jeep with her friends through the lanes of Milton Combe. The servicemen, away from home, missed their own families.

Women riders on horseback patrolled the moor

around Yelverton from dawn to dusk, riding in pairs from 1940. Mary Simms, joint section leader of the group, rode on the moor from 5.30a.m. in four-hourly shifts. The women did not carry firearms but wore white armlets on their left arms marked 'Mounted Patrol LDV'. Most had their own horses but George Langton at the Rock Hotel lent his mounts free of charge when necessary. Anything suspicious was reported to the police or to the head of the Home Guard and the women were given the authority to deflate the tyres of an empty unlocked car parked on the moor. In the summer of 1940 spies were discovered in Yelverton. Betty Harris at St Albans played in her own garden with children from The Nook but was not allowed to visit them. Late one night her father, Frank, heard the tapping of Morse-code signals and realized that messages were being sent from The Nook. Frank Harris fetched Sergeant Jewell and, listening together under the window, they heard the transmissions being relayed in German. The policeman arrested the family and they were never seen in Yelverton again. In this same year a sentry was posted at the top of the tower of St Paul's Church to watch for enemy parachutists and to shoot at enemy planes.

St Albans House was full of lodgers from the onset of the war. The first two were Harry Barnes, senior civil engineer for the RAF station at Harrowbeer, and his assistant, Ray Paddock. A barrage balloon, used as a defence against low-flying aircraft, landed in the trees at the entrance to Elford Park on a dark winter's night in January 1944. Mrs Harris from St Albans called the fire brigade as huge flames shot in the air and trees caught fire. No damage was done to the nearby houses but the gate at St Albans had to be replaced by the Air Ministry. In this same year a close combat between fighter aircraft caused the bus driver taking pupils to Tavistock Grammar School to stop the vehicle, as the aircraft screamed overhead, and order the children to get out of the bus and lie on the ground. Whilst the dogfight roared above them the pupils lay face down on the road. Arriving late and dishevelled at school the pupils were made to wash and iron their school uniform and little work was achieved that day!

Marian Hicks (née Thomas) was born in 1912 and was married to Fred at Buckland Monachorum Church on 1 February 1930. They bought a plot of land behind the Devon Tors Hotel and built Tor Cot in what is now Devon Tors Road. She clearly remembers aircraft flying low over her house on the perimeter of the aerodrome, the gunsight at the top of her road and another one near to Hinnies, next to Devonia. Over her garden hedge was a field, in which more than 200 coloured American soldiers were camped in tents in the 1940s. Marian's husband was in Burma and she and her two children were kept awake by the loud snoring of the men. Arthur Thomas who worked on the railway regularly called to see his sister and the Americans were grateful to him for occasionally buying them bottles of beer for which they paid him. It was not safe for these men to visit a bar in Yelverton because of their colour. Marian thinks fondly of a sergeant at this camp who gave her family chocolate and oranges, rare in the parish near the end of the war. She even corresponded with his mother in the USA until he was killed at Slapton Sands. One morning close to VE Day the Hicks family awoke to find that the men, tents and equipment had disappeared from the field but they had left huge packs of cheese, meat, sides of bacon, sugar, apples, oranges and khaki army blankets sealed as new. Marian and her neighbours hurriedly collected the goods and hid them in their houses. Food and clothing was rationed and the Americans knew what joy this would give the families nearby. Other people talk of the vast amounts of food available to the Forces when only a small percentage of these goods were obtainable with coupons from ration books, even if money was available. The Second World War and the building of the aerodrome altered Yelverton. The way of life was changed forever.

Below: Post-war Yelverton showing bunkers on the deserted aerodrome.

Above: *The mounted patrol is inspected by Mrs Simms and Mrs Goss, 1940.*

BIBLIOGRAPHY

ANTHONY G.H., *The Launceston and Princetown Railways*, 1971 (reprinted 1983). The Oakwood Press, Lingfield.

BARBER Chips, *Around & About Roborough Down*, 1998. Obelisk Publications, Pinhoe.

BERE Alice, *Buckland Monachorum*, 1930. Buckland Monachorum Women's Institute.

BILLING M., *Directory and Gazetteer of Devonshire for 1857*, 1857.

BLAIKIE Tamsyn, *Milton Combe*, 2001. Yelverton & District Local History Society.

BOVETT Robert, *Historical Notes on Devon Schools*, 1989. Devon County Council, Exeter.

BRAY Mrs Anna Elizabeth, *The Borders of Tamar and Tavy* (2 Vols), 1879 (3rd ed.). W. Kent, London.

BREWER Jerry, *Airfield Focus 27: Harrowbeer, Peterborough*, 1996. GMS Enterprises.

BROWN Cynthia Gaskell, *Buckland Abbey, Devon: Survey and Excavations 1983–95*, 1995. Trans Devonshire Association, 53, 25–82.

BROWN Mike, *Buckland Monachorum Graveyard Survey*. Dartmoor Press, Plymouth.

BROWN Mike, *An Exploration of Buckland Graveyard*. Dartmoor Press, Plymouth.

BROWN Mike, *An Episode in the History of the Crapstone Estate, Buckland*, 1784. Dartmoor Press, Plymouth.

BUCKLAND ABBEY, *Buckland Abbey Guide*, 1991. The National Trust.

BUCKLAND MONACHORUM, *The Parish Church of St Andrew*, 1927. Buckland Monachorum PCC.

BUCKLAND MONACHORUM, *A Guide to St Andrew's*, 1979. Buckland Monachorum PCC.

BURT Roger, WHITE Peter and BURNLEY Ray, *Devon and Somerset Mines – Metalliferous and Associated Minerals 1845–1913*, 1984. University of Exeter in association with Northern Mines Research Society.

CARDWELL Jean, *Living With History, Dousland*, 1991. Celtic Cross Publications 72–96.

CARTER Clive, *The Blizzard of '91*, 1971. David & Charles, Newton Abbot.

CHANTER Revd J.F., *16th Report on Church Plate*, 1927. Trans Devonshire Assoc, 59, 87–125.

CITY OF PLYMOUTH MUSEUMS, *Buckland Abbey*, 1991. The National Trust.

COOKE G.A., *Topographical & Statistical Description of the County of Devon*, c.1815. London.

COPELAND G.W., *Buckland Abbey – An Architectural Survey*, 1953. The National Trust.

CRIMES Philip A., *C(h)rymes or C(h)rimes*, 1985. Privately published by author, London.

CROSSING William, *Guide to Dartmoor*, 1909. *Western Morning News*, Plymouth.

CUMMING Alex, *Buckland Abbey*, 1972 and 1981. Jarrold & Sons, Norwich.

DARTMOOR NATIONAL PARK, *Yelverton, Horrabridge and South West Dartmoor – Draft Planning Study*, 1990. Bovey Tracy.

DARTMOOR NATIONAL PARK, *Informal Local Plan for the Yelverton, Horrabridge, Buckland Monachorum*. Bovey Tracy.

DAVIES Margaret, *A Cruce Salus – A Brief History of the Church and Parish of Holy Cross, Yelverton*, 1983 (2nd ed. 1996). Privately published for the church.

DINES H.G., *The Metalliferous Mining Regions of South-West England*, 1956 (reprinted with addenda 1988). HMSO, London.

DITMAS E.M.R., *The Legend of Drake's Drum*, 1973. The Toucan Press, St Peter Port.

DRAKE Elizabeth, *The Family and Heirs of Sir Francis Drake* (2 Vols), 1911. Smith, Elder & Co., London.

EMERSON John, *The First Eighty Years*, 1985. Yelverton Golf Club.

EVANS Rachael, *Home Scenes of Tavistock and its Vicinity*, 1846 (2nd ed. 1875). Simpkin Marshall, London.

FRANCIS Edward and THOMAS Bernard, *The Official Guide to Yelverton: Devon with its Surroundings*, c.1911. Homeland Handy Guide No. 26, London. [Red colour. 6th ed. c.1916]

FRANCIS Edward and THOMAS Bernard, *Yelverton (Devon) with its Surroundings*, c.1920. Homeland Handbooks No. 89, London. [Yellow colour 2nd ed. c.1922]

GELSTHORPE John, *St Paul's Church, Yelverton*, 1987. Yelverton PCC.

GILL Crispin, *Buckland Abbey*, 1st ed. 1951; 3rd ed. 1968. Plymouth.

GILL Crispin, *How to Look at Buckland Abbey*, c.1953. The National Trust.

GILL Crispin, *The Brief History of Yelverton*, 1984 (2nd ed. 1988). The Grey House Press, Torpoint.

GOVER J.E.B., MAWER A. and STENTON F.M., *The Place-names of Devon* (Vols 8 and 9 of the English Place-names Society), 1930–31. CUP, Cambridge.

GRAY Vera, *A Leat on Roborough Down and an Early Seventeenth Century Tinners' Dispute*, 1990. Trans Devonshire Association, 122, 71–82.

HAMILTON-LEGGETT Peter, *The Dartmoor Bibliography 1534–1991*, 1991. Devon Books, Exeter.

HARRISON Bill, *Dartmoor Stone Crosses*, 2001. Devon Books (in assoc. with Halsgrove), Tiverton.

HEMERY Pauline, *Clearbrook: The Story of a Dartmoor Parish*, 1998. Devon Books, Tiverton.

HEMERY Pauline, *The Book of Meavy: Dartmoor Parish, Village & River*, 1999. Halsgrove, Tiverton.

HEMERY Pauline, *Emma and the White Rajahs of Dartmoor*, 2000. Halsgrove, Tiverton.

HOSKINS W.G., *Devon*, 1954. Collins, London.

ISHERWOOD Ronald, *The Story of a School 1675–1976: St Andrew's Buckland Monachorum*, 1976. Appeal Committee St Andrew's School, Buckland Monachorum.

ISHERWOOD Ronald, *A Guide to St Andrew's Church*, c.1985. Privately printed.

JENKIN A.K. Hamilton, *Mines of Devon Volume I: The Southern Area*, 1974. David & Charles, Newton Abbot.

KELLY'S Directories of Devonshire, 1856, 1866, 1873, 1883, 1889, 1893, 1902, 1906, 1910, 1914, 1923, 1926, 1930, 1937, and 1939.

KENDELL H.G., *The Plymouth & Dartmoor Railway*, 1968. The Oakwood Press, Lingfield.

KINGDOM Anthony R., *The Princetown Branch*, 1979. Oxford Publishing Co., Oxford. (Reprinted in 1991 by Forest Publishing, Newton Abbot.)

KINGDOM Anthony R., *The Plymouth, Tavistock and Launceston Railway*, 1990. ARK Publications, Newton Ferrers.

LAKEMAN Joy, *Them Days – From the Memories of Joan Bellan*, 1982. Tabb House, Padstow.

LETHBRIDGE Lilian, *Clearbrook in Those Days*, 1990. Yelverton & District Local History Society, Yelverton.

LYSONS Revds Daniel & Samuel, *Magna Britannia – Vol 6, Devonshire*, 1822. Thomas Cadell, London.

MARSHALL William, *Rural Economy of the West of England*, 1796 (reprinted 1970). David & Charles, Newton Abbot.

MARTIN Brian P., *Tales of the Old Villages*, 1997. David & Charles, Newton Abbot.

MEGGY O.D., *RAF Harrowbeer, Yelverton 1941–1949*, 1981. Privately published by author.

MILLS Bernard, *The Branch – Plymouth – Tavistock – Launceston*, 1983. Plym Valley Railway, Plymouth.

MURRAY, *Murray's Handbook for Devon and Cornwall* (4th ed.), 1859 (reprinted 1971). David & Charles, Newton Abbot.

OKASHA Elisabeth, *Corpus of Early Christian Inscribed Stones of South-West Britain*, 1993. Leicester University Press, London.

PUPILS of St Andrew's School, *Buckland Monachorum Through the Eyes of the Pupils of St Andrew's School*, 1998. Buckland Monachorum School.

REICHEL Oswald J., *The Origin and Growth of the English Parish*, 1921. The Society of SS Peter & Paul, London.

RICHARDSON P.H.G., *Mines of Dartmoor and the Tamar Valley after 1913*, 1992. Northern Mines Research Society, Sheffield.

RICHARDSON R. (Compiler), *Through War to Peace 1914–1918*, 1919. Jolliffe and Son, Tavistock. [A short account of the part played by Tavistock and neighbourhood in the First World War.]

ROWE Alan, *Buckland Monachorum – A West Down History*, 1999. Privately published by author.

ROWE Samuel, *The Panorama of Plymouth or Tourist Guide*, 1821. Rowes, Plymouth.

ROWETT Helen, *Roundabout Family Rambling*, 1995. Plymouth.

SAUNDERS E. Symes, *Roborough Earthworks, S. Devon*, 1934. Trans Devonshire Assoc, 66, 325–326.

SHEPHERD Eric R., *The Plymouth & Dartmoor Railway and Lee Moor Tramway*, 1997. ARK Publications, Newton Abbot.

STOATE T.L., *Devon Muster Rolls 1569*, 1977. Privately printed by author, Bristol.

STOATE T.L., *Devon Subsidy Rolls 1524–7*, 1979. Privately printed by author, Bristol.

STOATE T.L., *Devon Hearth Tax 1674*, 1983. Privately printed by author, Bristol.

STOATE T.L., *Devon Subsidy Rolls 1543–5*, 1976. Privately printed by author, Bristol.

STREET R.C., *Buckland Monachorum*, 1934. Trans Devonshire Assoc, 60, 201–209.

STRONG L.A.G., *Green Memory*, 1961. Methuen & Co Ltd, London.

STRUTT & PARKER, 'Buckland Abbey Estate' Auction Sale Particulars, 1981. Exeter.

TEAGUE Dennis C., *A History of RAF Station Harrowbeer*, 1989. PDS Printers, Plymouth.

THORN Caroline and Frank (Eds), *Domesday Book* (2 Vols), 1985. Phillimore, Chichester.

TREVELYAN Robert E., *A Winter Remembered*, 1998. ARK Publications, Newton Abbot. [Events recalling the winter of 1962 and its effect on the railways of Dartmoor.]

WHITE William, *History, Gazetteer and Directory of Devonshire*, 1850.

WICKES Michael J.L., *Devon in the Religious Census of 1851*, 1990. Privately published by author.

WILEY Keith and FRASER Stuart, *The Garden House, Buckland Monachorum*, 2000. The Fortescue Garden Trust, Buckland Monachorum.

WOOD John D. & Co., 'Buckland Abbey Estate, Devonshire' Auction Sale Particulars, 1946. London.

WOODHEAD Sally, *Illustrated Guide to the Catholic Church in the Diocese of Plymouth*, 1992. Privately published by author, Plymouth.

WORTHY Charles, *Devonshire Parishes* (2 Vols), 1887–9. Pollards, Exeter. [Vol 1 includes Buckland, 77–120.]

YELVERTON, *Farm Prize Competition, 1890 Class II Highly Commended Farm, occupied by Mr Charles Horn, Blowiscombe, Yelverton*, 1890. J. Royal Agri. Soc., 3rd ser, 1.

YELVERTON, *Yelverton and District Official Guide*, c.1930. Vickery, Kyrle & Co., London.

YELVERTON GOLF CLUB, *Official Handbook*. Temple Publicity, Bournemouth.

YOUINGS Joyce, *Drake, Grenville and Buckland Abbey*, 1980. Trans Devonshire Assoc, 112, 92–99.

OTHER RESOURCES

Numerous articles and cuttings from:

Dartmoor Magazine; Dartmoor, The Country Magazine; Devon Life; Devon Today; Monachorum Miscellany; Outreach: The Magazine of the Parish of St Andrew [includes numerous notes by Tamsyn Blaikie]; *Plymouth Evening Herald; Plymouth Mineral and Mining Journal; Roundabout: The Magazine of the United Benefice of Yelverton, Meavy, Sheepstor and Walkhampton; Tavistock Times; Yelverton and District Local History Newsletter; Western Morning News.*

INDEX

SUBSCRIBERS

The Allen family, Buckland Monachorum, Devon

Pam and Richard Allgood, Buckland Monachorum, Devon

Paul Ames, Buckland Monachorum, Devon

Les Andrews

Mary Baker (née Butland), Whitchurch, Tavistock, Devon

Brian W. Ball, Frampton Cotterell, Bristol

W.S. Ball, Crapstone

Mrs Sybil M. Ball

Keith and Rosemrey Bancroft, Yelverton, Devon

Peter and Anne Barons, Crapstone Barton, Buckland Monachorum, Devon

Mrs D.D. Barons, Tavistock, Devon

Professor and Mrs K.L. Barratt, Yelverton, Devon

Jade Imogen Baxter-Smith, Buckland Monachorum, Devon

Julie A. Beesley, Buckland Monachorum, Devon

Mr A.J. Berry, Horrabridge, Devon

John and Christine Berry, Yelverton, Devon

Frances Mary Billing, Plymouth

Tamsyn Blaikie, Lopwell, Roborough, Devon

E.J. Blott, Yelverton, Devon

Ewart and Margaret Blowey, Mount Tavy, Tavistock, Devon

Mr Blowey, Stokehill and Torr

Norah C. Boniface, Buckland Monachorum, Devon

Mr and Mrs R. Booth, Hook

John, Julia and Harriet Boston, Yelverton, Devon

David F. Bowden (Buster), Meavy Village, Devon

Carol and John Branch, Crapstone, Devon

Christine and John Brindle, Hoo Meavy, Devon

S.J. Brocklebank, Yelverton, Devon

Jane Brown, Crapstone, Devon

Canon J. Philip Brown, Teignmouth, Devon

Miss Phoebe E. Brown, Tavistock, Devon

Joanna Brown, Crapstone, Devon

Michael Brown, Crapstone, Devon

Julie Brown, Crapstone, Devon

K.J. Burrow, Bucks Cross, Devon

The Butlands, Cuxton Farm, Buckland Monachorum, Devon

Joan Charleston, Buckland Monachorum, Devon

The Christmas family, Uppaton House, Buckland Monachorum, Devon

Mrs A.M. Churchill, South Brewham, Somerset

Dr Jeremy Clark, Milton Combe, Devon

John and Susan Cole, Meadow Barn, Didham Farm, Buckland Monachorum, Devon

Elizabeth Cole, Sampford Spiney, Devon

Kate, Murray and Reuben Coleman, Crapstone, Devon

Ronald C. Collier, Dousland, Devon

Pamela M. Colton, Yelverton, Devon

Mr and Mrs K.H. Cook, Tavistock, Devon

Anthea, David, Jennifer and Sophie Cox, Buckland Monachorum, Devon

A. Craig-Mooney, Uphill, Buckland Monachorum, Devon

The Creber family, Buckland Monachorum, Devon

Diana Croft (née Rendle), Yelverton, Devon

Martin and Jan Cropper, Buckland Monachorum, Devon

Dr David Dance, Buckland Monachorum, Devon

Dartmoor National Park Authority

Mary Davey (née Maddock), Yelverton, Devon

J.W. and P. Davies, Buckland Monachorum, Devon

Alice S. Daw (née Hillson), Tavistock, Devon

John Dawe, London

Philip and Cathryn Dawes, Crapstone, Devon

Derek E. Diggins

Mr Noel Dilnot and Mrs Brenda Dilnot (formerly Hannaford), Yelverton

Dolly, Hatty's House, Horrabridge, Devon

Linda Downing

Mr David J. Eggins, Yelverton, Devon

Darren, Tania, Louise, Chase, Taylor and Anja Elsworth, Buckland Monachorum, Devon

Elizabeth Emberson

Colonel John Emerson, Yelverton, Devon

Shirley and Dennis Fairchild, Buckland Monachorum, Devon

Sara A. Ferry, Yelverton, Devon

Richard, Rosiland and Oliver Field, Plymouth, Devon

Paul Finegan, Birmingham

Mrs A.P.M. Finegan (Pat)

Peter Ford, Yelverton, Devon

Rachel Glanville, Buckland Monachorum, Devon

Sarah Glanville, Buckland Monachorum, Devon

Ann and Alan Glanville, Buckland Monachorum, Devon

Susan Golding-Cook, Horrabridge, Devon

Alan J. Gray, Roborough, Devon

Dr Tom and Elisabeth Greeves, Tavistock, Devon

Mr A. and Mrs L. Griffiths, Crapstone, Devon

Yvonne Hanns (née Lashbrook)

P.M. Harris, Tavistock, Devon

Lin and Terry Harvey, Buckland Monachorum, Devon

Patricia Harwood, Buckland Monachorum, Devon

Michael and Carol Harwood, Buckland Monachorum, Devon

Mr and Mrs David Hawkins, Buckland Monachorum, Devon

Michael and Lucy Hayes, Knightstone Tearooms, Yelverton, Devon

Martin and Hilary Head, Crapstone, Devon

Edna and Fred Herring, Bexhill-on-Sea, East Sussex

Richard and Ann Hillson, Buckland Monachorum, Devon

Sally Hillson, Horrabridge, Devon

Dr Bob Hodgson, Yelverton, Devon

Charles Horn

Mary Horn, Tavistock, Devon

Roger and Kathy Howard

Stephen and Yvonne Hughes, Yelverton, Devon

Paula R. Hunter, Yelverton, Devon

Colin Jaszczuk, Buckland Monachorum, Devon

Edna and John Jaszczuk, Buckland Monachorum, Devon

Jenny and Rebecca, Meavy, Devon

Mr G.L. Johnson

Briony C. Jones, Yelverton, Devon

Elise D. Jones, Yelverton, Devon

Len Jones, Glenholt, Plymouth

The Jones family, Beechfield Avenue, Yelverton, Devon

Elizabeth Jordan (née Harris), Devon

Diane Lang Kelly, Wilmette, IL, USA

Mrs H.M. Keys

Colin C. Kilvington, Stoke, Plymouth, Devon

Christopher Kirwin, Yelverton, Devon

Tony and Fiona Lamb, Crapstone, Devon

Mr John Lane, Buckland Monachorum, Devon

Dr C.K. Langley, Hitchin, Hertfordshire

Muriel Lashbrook, Moorshop, Tavistock, Devon

Margaret and David Latham, Yelverton, Devon

The Lawrences, Dousland, Devon

Sonja C. Lawson, Estover, Plymouth

Dave Leach, Buckland Monachorum, Devon

Barbara Lockyer, Ferndale, Yelverton, Devon

Pat Lovell, Tavistock, Devon

Louise and Patrick Lyons, Yelverton, Devon

Mr Iain and Mrs Sheila Macfarlane, Lonnachsloy, Crapstone, Devon

Pete and Julie Matthews

Marion and Colin Maxwell, Buckland Monachorum, Devon

Mr Algy Mayne, previously of Buckland Monachorum

Patricia Medlen (née Edwards), Hoo Meavy, Devon

Dr and Mrs R. Middleton, University of Bristol

Lt Col. And Mrs R.A. Middleton, Yelverton, Devon

David and Jenny Miles, Crapstone

Anthony and Barbara Miller, Yelverton, Devon

Bernard and Audrey Mills, Buckland Monachorum, Devon

Alastair and Barbara Monteath, Heathfield Park, Yelverton, Devon

Steven J. Moore, Crapstone, Yelverton, Devon

The Earl and Countess of Morle

Dr and Mrs P.M. Murphy, Crapstone, Devon

Mr and Mrs T. Murrin, Bere Alston, Devon

National Trust, Killerton

Mrs Bernice Northam, Crapstone, Devon

Nigel J. Northam, Horrabridge, Devon

Barry J. Northcott, North Beer, Launceston, Cornwall

John and Janet Northey, Horrabridge

Mr and Mrs John Vincent Northey

Bert Northey, Buckland Monachorum, Devon. Born 1929

Pauline Northmore, Gratton Farm

Tom Orchard, Yelverton, Devon

Mary Osborn, Yelverton, Devon

Mr and Mrs K.G. Owen, Tavistock, Devon

Mrs Mavis Palmer

Mr and Mrs. A. Parker, Elfordtown

David and Terri Parnall, Dousland, Devon

Robert and Phyllis Parriss, late of Yelverton

Brenda Partridge, Yelverton, Devon

Mr and Mrs P.M. Perry, Plymouth, Devon

J.O. Piper, Buckland Monachorum, Devon

Major and Mrs John Piper, Yelverton, Devon

Misses L.K. and A.E. Pollard, Crapstone, Devon

The Pollock family, Crapstone, Devon

Ron Price, Yelverton's adopted son

Audrey Prizeman, Plymouth, Devon

Mr and Mrs D.W. Puttick, Eastbourne, East Sussex

Mr B. and Mrs G. Raeke, Yelverton, Devon

P. Read (née Greenhalgh), Lancashire

Mrs Gwen Redden, Axtown, Yelverton, Devon

Garth Redgrave, Buckland Monachorum, Devon

Michael Rendle, Yelverton, Devon

Nigel W. Rendle, Buckland Monachorum, Devon

Jean Richards, Yelverton, Devon

David and Joy Richards, Yelverton, Devon

Rolande Richards, Crapstone, Devon

Ken Rickard, Lydford, Devon

Martha Elizabeth Roberts, 1a, Rock Hotel, Yelverton, Devon

Mandy Robinson - Licensee, Drake Manor Inn, Buckland Monachorum, Devon

Sarah Roche, Crapstone, Devon

Liz Roe, Yelverton, Devon

Margaret Rogers, Buckland Monachorum, Devon

Marg Rogers (née Finney)

Mr and Mrs Rolfe, Tamerton Foliot, Plymouth, Devon

Mr and Mrs Rolfe, Lower Dimson, Cornwall

Tony Rushbrooke, Yelverton, Devon

Tony Shafto, Crapstone, Devon

Margaret Simms, Yelverton, Devon

Norman and Elspeth Sitters, Edgemoor, Yelverton, Devon

June Smalley, Sampford Spiney, Devon

Mrs Hazel M. Smith, Buckland Monachorum, Devon

Doctor J.C. Speller, Tavistock, Devon

Wendy A. Stead, Crapstone, Devon

Mrs Alexis Steele, St Peter Port

Prebendary Peter and Mrs Joyce Stephens, Thurlestone

Michael Stephens, Upper Norwood, London

Timothy Stephens, Godalming, Surrey

Celia Steven, Buckland Monachorum, Devon

Michael and Sarah Stone, Buckland Abbey

Mrs P.A. Symington, Oporto, Portugal

Mr Bob Taylor, Buckland Monachorum, Devon

Terry and Mary Thompson (née Fitzmaurice), Links Lodge, Yelverton, Devon

Graham Thorne, Maldon, Essex

Rene Thurston, Buckland Monachorum, Devon

Anne and Paul Tilden, Yelverton, Devon

Mr Robert H. Toop, Yelverton, Devon

Alex Topham, Whistly Down,Yelverton, Devon

Vivienne A. Trathen, Buckland Monachorum, Devon

Tony Tremlett, Plymouth, Devon

F.L. Tuffin, Buckland Monachorum, Devon

Ronald E. Tyrrell, Buckland Monachorum, Devon

Charles H. Upton, Crapstone, Devon

Margaret Maria Vere, Yelverton, Devon

Gordon C. Vickery, Leatgarth, Yelverton, Devon

Mr G. Waldron, Plymouth, Devon

Dr Martin Walker, Buckland Monachorum, Devon

John F.W. Walling, Newton Abbot, Devon

Mr and Mrs J.C.C. Warren

Rita (née Mayne) and Humphrey Warren, Buckland Monachorum, Devon

A. Warren-Green, Horrabridge, Devon

Anthony Wates MBE, Winsbeer, Buckland Monachorum, Devon

Mr Charles Westlake, Okehampton

Mr P.D. Whitcomb, Salisbury, Wiltshire

Ruth and Graham White, Buckland Monachorum, Devon

Jo and Hugo White, Lovecombe, Buckland Monachorum, Devon

The White family, Milton Coombe, Devon

Ted Whitehead, Yelverton, Devon

Eileen Willcocks, Crapstone, Devon

Gwen E. Williams, Crapstone, Yelverton, Devon

Rosamond Wixon (née Stevens), Yelverton, Devon

Mr R.C. (Peter) Yelland, Milton Combe

Zenta, Ray, Hana and Fern Zubka-Hill, Yelverton, Devon